G000017491

Patricia Gogay was born in 1942. Her working life began as a nurse in training before a restless spirit led her to several other careers: a lab technician, croupier and two years as a social worker before choosing the probation service.

She met Ken, her complimentary half, in 1980. During 1981-88 they built a boat together and spent the next 15 years sailing around the world.

In 2003, Ken suffered a catastrophic stroke – thus beginning a different, though no less rewarding adventure.

For:
Sarah Spray
Carole Cumbers
Sharon Arnold
Ann Scott

Our 'sisterhood' of carers who with compassion and grace have also 'carried Ken in their arms', so to speak.

Patricia Gogay

THE WIND HAS WEIGHT: NEITHER WIND NOR FATE BEARS MALICE

AUSTIN MACAULEY
PUBLISHERS LTD.

Copyright © Patricia Gogay (2017)

The right of Patricia Gogay to be identified as author of this work has been asserted by him in accordance with section 77 and 78 of the Copyright, Designs and Patents Act 1988.

All rights reserved. No part of this publication may be reproduced, stored in a retrieval system, or transmitted in any form or by any means, electronic, mechanical, photocopying, recording, or otherwise, without the prior permission of the publishers.

Any person who commits any unauthorized act in relation to this publication may be liable to criminal prosecution and civil claims for damages.

A CIP catalogue record for this title is available from the British Library.

ISBN 9781786933867 (Paperback)
ISBN 9781786933874 (Hardback)
ISBN 9781786933881 (eBook)
www.austinmacauley.com

First Published (2017)
Austin Macauley Publishers Ltd.
25 Canada Square
Canary Wharf
London
E14 5LQ

Acknowledgments

To whoever it was who first showed me a *male* stickleback in breeding colours, a stag beetle, a giant puff ball, a grass snake basking in the sun.

Offering wonder and curiosity to a child brings them a lifetime of gifts.

PROLOGUE

The wind has weight and many moods. Both on land and over the oceans, all living things dance and sing to its tune. Each spring it flirts with the emerging leaves. Each autumn, like an act of infidelity, it then strips them petulantly from the branches. Its vocal range is operatic: the whisper of a catspaw, a howl, a roar, screaming, soughing, and whistling. Sometimes it feels like a lover's caress, an affectionate stroke to your cheek, then in a fit of pique, bows you down until you surrender.

Invisible. Unpredictable. Irascible. And every sailor learns to both love and fear it.

The history of the world owes as much to ships and sailors as to armies, rulers, architects, and Saints. Centuries before the birth of Christ, single-mast rowing boats carrying one square sail set out in search of 'Terra Incognito' only to discover a world beyond their imagining. Carried along by the whims of current, wind, and tempest, their discoveries were no less momentous for being a matter of chance.

Other than to maritime historians, the names of these bravest of our forebears are largely forgotten: Coleus of Samos, Pytheas the Carthaginian, Ottar the Viking. As early as the 7th century BC through to the 9th century AD, they traversed the Mediterranean, sighted the Atlantic Ocean from Gibraltar, circumnavigated the British Isles, and travelled much of the East Coast of Africa.

Accounts of their exploits, written by contemporary chroniclers or preserved in ship's logs, gather dust in archives. Their names are rarely spoken. Although celebrated and honoured in their day, very few are immortalised by statues, monuments, or tombs. But while the hazards of ocean sailing are ever present, these long-ago sailors faced much greater perils than those we fear today. The Earth is flat... the abyss awaits. Sea monsters will swallow the ship. Flesh will rot from your bones, Poseidon will exact revenge for intruding into his domain. Superstition lurked in every mind.

Captains could order a noose to hang you from the yardarm, flog a man until his blood ran onto the deck. 'Dereliction of duty' would remain a flogging offence until well into the 20th century and very few sailors survived the Draconian punishment of being 'flogged around the fleet' while those who did, having suffered up to 300 lashes, were maimed for life. So great was the fear that even cruel discipline could not preserve every man from despair, mutiny, or madness. And as if the fear were not enough, they journeyed as if groping in the dark, without compass, charts, or adequate provisions.

As with all great endeavours, each first momentous step becomes a ladder for others to climb...rung by rung. Across continents, to the top of the highest mountain, the depths of the ocean, to the moon and back. Until eventually any man or woman can choose to reach out into the world. See it, feel it, measure it, and marvel.

INTRODUCTION

Sailing away. That most ancient and persistent of all fireside daydreams. Cast off, lift anchor, loose the bonds, let go, break free. Whether sitting quietly in a darkened room lit only by a candle, watching a sailboat leaving harbour, strolling alone above cliffs overlooking the sea: the thought will eventually come to mind.

Usually it's a blue dream: azure sky, turquoise shallows, midnight blue in the dark, menacing deeps. The scene is cast in brilliant sunshine light. You are at the helm, calm eyes fixed on the horizon.

Now and again it will be an alarming dream. Huge chunks of ocean, sliced off at the wave tops by the wind, are smashing into your face. You are looking for canyons between a moving range of mountains, the slopes of which are that mythological ogre green and in the midst of an alarming noise comes the dread…should you choose the wrong route neither you nor your vessel will ever be seen again. There is no blue at all in a maritime nightmare. The sky itself is green.

I met Ken in 1979 when we were both approaching middle age. Thirty-five years have since passed as have the three uncommon adventures we shared. 'I'm building a boat,' he told me. Would that be a model, a canoe, a small river cruiser with a two-berth cuddy? I wondered. But this was no shed hobby nor the romantic appeal of twilight on the river Thames, it was to be a forty-two-foot, steel, sea-going yacht. With sails! For an HGV agency driver, living in caravan, paying his rent by working as a part time caretaker for a cricket club, it sounded rather unrealistic. With only 300 pounds in the bank? Utterly preposterous!

It was only when he took me to the boatyard where the keel of his boat lay waiting that I realised he was simply making a statement and not in the throes of a mid-life crisis.

Build a sailing yacht? From scratch? What a dreamer...but such a dream to have. Which was, I think, why I so dearly wanted to believe him.

And so the dream took hold, energised us, brought us close, tested us in all the ways and shaped the next twenty-two years of our lives together. Finally, in the years that followed, it prepared us for the shocking event that ended our adventures so abruptly.

As our boat rose from the ground, our relationship evolved with it. One may talk of the bond between man and wife, comrades at arms, blood-sharing brotherhoods, but just as intense and mutually dependent, is the bond between shipmates.

But beware! Romancing a boat builder is akin to taking up with a mountaineer. You can expect that at some point he will persuade you to share his passion, get to 'know him better.' Yet even when you have hiked up to cloud level with him, the wretch will tell you that it was 'a modest hill'...not even the courtesy of calling it a mountain! With boat builders, expect to add welding, carpentry, and painting to your other womanly skills.

Improbable as it seemed at the beginning, we earned what we came to call 'Our passport to play with dolphins.' It would take seven long years for us to build the yacht we named 'Imago'. We lived in a caravan, wore out several pairs of boiler suits, pared our needs to subsistence levels, and worked as hard as any labourers.

I often wonder if either of us ever 'grew up' or ever really wanted to. Perhaps we were prey to 'leftover adolescence,' a condition remarkable for its lapses in common sense. We could almost hear it as background music to our labours: that universal parental frustration: 'fools! They just won't take no for an answer. Why don't they build a narrow boat or a pair of kayaks? The idiots have never been sailing… not even in a dinghy!'

But to sail around the world! Could we realise that most singular of dreams, one that is unquestionably in the premier league of adventures. More importantly to us, could we construct a way of living that didn't depend on money, envy, or wishful thinking? Integrity to the DIY principle meant everything to us. Saving to buy a boat, being given one, winning the pools would have changed nothing. Our goal was to make what we wanted and be what we wanted.

As we enter our seventies, memories of our journey begin to fade and blur, as they do in lives that are nearly lived. For Ken, there is tragedy in his forgetting. Hopefully, this reminder of those fifteen years we spent sailing around the world will re-connect a few more neurons in his injured mind and that I too, before my wits wither along with the rest of me, will finally believe that however foolish, we were also brave. As Baudelaire says in his poem *The Voyage*... 'not knowing why' we did just say, 'let's go!'

CHAPTER 1

AND HERE ENDED THE FIRST LESSON

The first time we went to sea was in 1987, having excitedly marked way points for crossing the English Channel to our first ever foreign ports of call, either in France or Portugal. But we were severely punished for our inexperience and rightly so, barely surviving the ordeal of criss-crossing that seaway for nine dreadful days in huge wallowing seas and gale-force winds. Had we previously done any serious sailing, we would have known that big swells presage rough weather or its aftermath, though we would contradict anyone refusing to admit to just a twinge of dread at watching a huge freighter disappear into a trough or wondering how a small boat could climb a slope so close to the perpendicular without tumbling backwards.

It took weeks to recover from that ordeal: swaying rooms, hypothermia, hallucinations, dehydration, nightmares. I cannot think how we ever found the resolve to try again.

All we needed now was a hurricane to complete the meteorological repertoire! Some spiteful entity decided that was a really good idea and would finally see off this unlikely pair.

Imago was tied up to mooring buoys at the back of Poole Harbour. Winds had been fresh to strong for most of the previous day. In the early evening Ken returned from his temporary driving job, but when he looked across from the pontoon to our position out on the moorings, he realised that it was too risky for me to row over in the dinghy – not that I was disposed to even try, so he spent the rest of that violent night in the sleeper cab of the truck he was driving – leaving me alone on the boat.

The worst of the hurricane hit the SW of England just after midnight. It began with what was now a familiar sound: rumbling low pitched moans as the wind collected its forces, holding back like an aircraft preparing for take-off, before hurtling across the landscape. As the first impact slammed into the rigging, *Imago* shuddered from stem to rudder... so began yet another long night. Between shouting out words of encouragement to our noble craft and threats of unspeakable retaliation against any mooring rope that failed, I dragged on my wet gear. Curtains of rain soon obliterated the boatyard and the town lights. The air itself dense with noise and the sounds of destruction. We might just as well have been out in a raging sea as here in one of the largest and safest harbours in the world.

I spent most of that night squatting in the scuppers, hugging a 45lb anchor between my knees. Proper conduct I felt, since deputy skippers are supposed to 'do something.' But in reality, it had no more significance than as a 'girly gesture' of defiance. I can barely lift the damn thing clear of the deck, let alone heave it over the side! Perhaps I was relying on a boost of adrenaline that would instantly transform me into 'Desperate Delia.'

At the height of the storm, a boat moored alongside us lost her bow line, swinging her around, adding greatly to the strain on our own ropes. Several craft had broken away altogether, drifting in all directions around the bay. As the wind veered and the tide turned, a large catamaran locked together with a fishing boat tried to climb aboard *Imago*. Between this formidable pair of pirates, our dinghy was being tossed higher than the guard rails. Those few yachtsmen who were aboard their craft that night emerged briefly between squalls, feverishly working winches, tightening rigging screws. Later accounts described chaotic scenes in the outer harbour where over seventy boats had broken free. Several had been tossed over the harbour walls onto the roadway.

We escaped very lightly indeed, just a few more scrapes and dents to add to our battle scars and two broken oars from frantic efforts to repel those unwelcome boarders, unlike some unfortunate folk whose boats were smashed beyond repair against the harbour walls.

A bigger drama was played out at sea. A forty-foot catamaran had left Poole Harbour the day before, bound for the Canaries. Sophisticated as she was in terms of equipment, her roller reefing system jammed, threatening the boat with capsize and surely the loss of several lives amid the sixty-foot waves. A naval ship was brought in to block the worst of the seas and to pour oil, enabling the lifeboat to rescue the five crew, including a woman. The skipper stayed aboard to ride it out with his courageous escorts. We met up with some of the survivors a few days later. One image still haunted them all; the sight of the lifeboat balanced atop a fifty-foot wave crest, threatening to topple over then smash down on them in the trough below.

At the height of the storm, the needle of their wind speed indicator had trembled for more room. It was calibrated to the limit of the Beaufort scale force 12…a wild night indeed!

Shaken but undeterred, we spent the rest of that winter constructing a doghouse and reorganising the running gear. *Imago* had proved herself to be stalwart vessel. Now it was up to us to ensure her a better history… though not before another sharp lesson or two!

During our stay at Cobb's Quay in Poole, I worked as dish washer/ standby waitress at the Yacht Club which is where we met 'Dink' and her husband John. Dink (even today I do not know what her given name was) had worked in the catering industry for all of her life, mostly as a silver service waitress. Her tales about severe black uniforms, starched apron and cuffs, the loutish behaviour of pernickety guests, dictatorial chefs, over-inflated head waiters, were historical gems. We often sat together at the end of the day rehearsing for the wonderful hours of 'cockpit talk' we would later enjoy in harbours and anchorages all over the world.

There are 'universal mothers.' Dink was one of them. Her apron would have dried many a tear, wrapped many a graze. 'They don't use the crusts from the loaves, Dink. I can make bread and butter pudding, will you save them for us?' I think she guessed the reason why.

'Bread and butter pudding,' I said to Ken as I spread jam on them for breakfast! 'You'll do it, you know,' she said. It sounded like a mother's blessing.

The year passed quickly. We were ready to try again. This time the do-or-die. Even a hurricane could not erode our determination to continue on the path we had set our minds to those nine years before.

CHAPTER 2

'They listened and look sideways up
Fear at their hearts, as at a cup,
Their lifeblood seemed to sip.'

(The rime of the ancient mariner-Samuel Coleridge)

If we were ever going to experience the fears and joys of a long ocean passage we must first escape the consistently spiteful clutches of the English Channel: an unpredictable waterway with an 'attitude' that seemed determined to crush our spirits.

We left Poole Harbour at 6.30am on the 21st of August 1988. Folded into a mug in the galley cupboard was £300, our budget for a year. Our destination was the Canary Islands, with contingency plans to stop over in Portugal or the Cape Verde Islands if the weather proved unkind.

In a blustering wind, we headed west towards Plymouth, making excellent progress in a force 6. *Imago* registered 6.7knts, lunging through the seas, throwing rainbows from every wave – a wonderful feeling. By 7pm the following day, we sighted the Great Mewstone Rock that stands guardian in the bay. But the run in swept us too close to shore, forcing us to tack out to sea again. With an offshore wind slowing us down, we were committed to a harbour approach in darkness and in a heavy swell. We knew that, as novices, it was ill-advised, but the weather was again deteriorating quickly. We are not the first cruising sailors to be seduced by the proximity of land, its promise of sleep, respite, the thrill of safe arrival. Perhaps the nightmare of the previous year still lurked in our minds. The green pilot light marking the portside entrance was clearly visible. But where was the red light? There comes a dread feeling in my stomach that something is terribly wrong. The blackness ahead looks too dense, too solid.

Ken was at the bow. I called out to him but the wind was now soughing, carrying away both words and breath. But I can see he is struggling to drop the foresails. There is an unexpected sound of breaking surf. At last, both sails spill onto the deck and our speed is checked. As Ken gathered the sails into his arms, he looked down over the bowsprit…what he saw made him throw the sails onto the foredeck before staggering in a blind rush to the cockpit where he desperately turned the wheel hard to port. Amidst huge rocks and agitated water, the bowsprit is poised over the concrete slabs of Plymouth breakwater!

A cold logic invades our minds. All is lost. We are shipwrecked. In a few seconds from now, a decade of toil and self-denial will be undone as *Imago* embeds herself into those fearsome fangs of rock. For a frozen moment, we wait for the scrunch of steel against concrete.

What happened next was something we shall never forget (in the way that you don't forget seeing a UFO or a cow in a tree). It was as if *Imago* herself, despairing of our incompetence, decided to act on her own. Rising high on the next swell, she turned in her own length, lurching away as the mainsail caught the wind. As she did so, the skeg rolled over the rocks. We felt the grating vibration of it through the hull. But she was off! Crawling away from doom at a painfully slow 0.5knts. Surely in all our journeying we would never come closer to disaster than this (though a night on the Barrier reef would come a very close second).

But it was not over yet. Although both harbour lights were now clearly visible, wind and tide were in control, forcing us perilously close to the cliffs that skirt the entrance, eventually trapping us in bay just fifty metres from them. Ken dropped anchor when it became clear to us that engine power was not enough to get us away. It was a dire predicament, the anchor chain hummed with each rise and fall of the swell. Chain links snatched hard against the bow roller. We set to, tying three more warps to the chain shackle, but at any moment they threatened to part. In a last exhausting effort to avert disaster, we deployed a secondary kedge anchor, but that was instantly torn away and lost.

Whichever beckoned first, breakwater or cliffs, we knew we faced disaster. It was time to call the marina for advice or assistance. We heard the conversation that followed... 'a very long time since we have seen a yacht in so perilous a position as this... it's force 6 out there and they are dangerously close to the cliffs... we'll send out the marina launch and bring them in.'

While waiting for the launch, we inflated the dinghy before standing on opposite sides, ready to fling it over the rails and jump. By now our mouths were so dry that our tongues stuck to our palates and stayed there.

Once safely tied up in the marina, we sat together at the saloon table for a long time. Silent. Brooding. Ken was deeply dejected. Neither of us could summon up any thoughts about the future, but nor could we postpone a decision for very long before berthing fees swallowed up the money we had saved for the journey. This was a summit meeting, the agenda having as much to do with our future together as whether to continue sailing, especially if I was of a mind to call it a day. Even building *Imago* from scratch, employing all the skills he possessed, was not enough to preserve Ken from a feeling of failure. His boyish enthusiasm would evaporate, the dream that fired his restless spirit would be hard to re-ignite. It was this bounding puppy of a man I wanted to be with, not a wounded bear.

My own thinking was finished then, but it had to be a skipper's call. So, deploying the subtlety, intuition, and all round brilliance of most women, I tested him out.

'The only thing we did wrong out there, skipper, was to attempt an unfamiliar harbour approach in darkness.'

'Spot on, girl!' Ken reached across the saloon table to take both my hands in his. 'Sorry love, we won't do that again.'

With the word 'again' safely out, the meeting was adjourned. We went to bed.

Do-or-die then. We hope to be preserved. The sea is implacable. It would take us or spare us.

***

Even the noise of the engine couldn't muffle the sound of that thud. I hear it now, fourteen years later. Still feel the cold the helplessness. I thought he had tripped over the ropes that were hastily retrieved as we left the lock on the Canal-du-Midi, in France. I called out to him from my position at the wheel (some silly bit of banter which now makes me close my eyes in regret). I cannot leave the helm, a queue of boats are on the move, taking order to fill the lock we have just left. No answer, so a quick peep around the wheelhouse. Ken is sprawled in the side-decking, lying awkwardly as if he hadn't tried to check his fall. Unmoving. I want to be sick.

Manoeuvre *Imago* towards the towpath, click the engine lever into neutral, grab hold of two pegs and the hammer. Secure the bow first, then let the current swing her to the bankside before securing her at the stern, switch off engine: familiar mooring routines conducted at treble speed. Ken is making snuffling sounds, his breathing is laboured, he's not conscious. I call out to the last of the boats entering the lock. 'Medical emergency!' In English, with what I hoped was a French accent. The skipper replies in perfect, barely accented English.

'I'll tell the lock keeper.'

'I'm from Paris,' he adds, 'my English is OK.' I think he saved Ken's life. An ambulance arrived within ten minutes. Ken was treated where he lay for nearly half an hour. One of the paramedics came below to ask for a glass of water – I'm faint with relief, he's awake! 'For his dentures,' he says and I'm rigid again and my heart is pounding.

I have to set up the gang plank so that Ken can be transferred to the towpath on an inflatable stretcher, thence to the ambulance where he is treated for a further hour. I sit on the bankside, waiting. It's 80F, but I'm cold.

The attending paramedic finally emerged from the back of the ambulance. 'He did not hurt himself falling Madame, he has had a stroke, there is bleeding from his ears and his left eye.'

On the way to the hospital, sirens blaring, they tell me I have been calm and composed. 'It is 'elpful to be so like zis,' they say, so I suppose that numb was preferred over hysterical.

CHAPTER 3

ESCAPE FROM THE CHANNEL

Remnants of that hooligan wind swept the SW coast. Rigging clattered and whistled on all the small boats in the harbour, like a garden full of wind chimes. At night, warm and safe in our bunk, we imagined the bleak anxiety of those who were out in it, as we had been.

The cost of a visitor's berth in the marina, together with their charge for towing us in, seriously depleted our precious resources, yet as each day passed, our resolve hardened. This time, we would leap off, jump in feet first, casting off our doubts along with the mooring ropes. After all, we mused, our small ship was now a sound, proven, vessel, whereas other quirky Brits had crossed the Atlantic Ocean in rowing boats, even rafts, while purists, faithful to the art form of sailing, even scorned an engine.

Whether it was a symbolic farewell to British shores, or simply to lighten our mood, we decided to have a land based 'play day' in Weymouth, accepting the offer of a lift with a lovely young family who were holidaying from the Midlands. They had chosen Plymouth because their children wanted to see 'lots of boats.'

We sat on the beach among hundreds of people who seemed intent on sacrificing most of their clothes to the Sun God. A people watchers Paradise: posers, promenade walkers, sun shades, those entwined, a few alone but looking. Parents vainly trying to re-capture their own sea-side memories while their children imprinted their first: burying themselves in the sand, making sand castles, running the particles through their fingers. At the margin of the sea they generally played alone, squealing with exhilarating fear as they hopped away from a rogue wavelet. One curly-headed mite of a girl was seriously contemplating her first sea shell and accidently spilled a drink over her mother's freshly basted legs. The resulting mayhem and tears ended the tiny girl's moment of awe... science and wonderment snuffed out with a single slap. Adolescents marched up to their parents, demanding money before disappearing to buy plastic earrings at inflated prices or to feed the mouths of machines that simulated motorbikes crashing at 200 miles per hour. The beach hummed with irritations, drowning out the music of surf and seagulls.

During our travels, we would witness shocking examples of cruelty towards both children and animals, but the expression on that pretty young face stayed with us. Our own childlike remnants of wow and wonder about our world had also received a slap or two in recent weeks. The analogy was painful.

Away then. Conditions are rough. Four hours at the helm is too long so we reduce it to two. Even so, sleep is shallow and fitful. Numbingly cold. There are no stars, just inky blackness. Our navigation lights reflect back from a light mist. We sail towards a grey wall but never

27

reach it, though I cannot stop myself peering steadfastly into the gloom as if the grey wall might suddenly become solid. But with the passing of every hour, we are closer to rounding Ushant into the Atlantic Ocean. We feel a mixture of rueful satisfaction about escaping the channel and anxiety as to what might lie ahead for the next 350 nautical miles.

During the third night the sea is calm. Our course is parallel to the Bay of Biscay. An infamous stretch of water with a fearsome reputation, but we were to experience it at its most benign and were eyes-to-heaven grateful for it.

The colour of the sea is a deep midnight blue. It looks thick and glutinous. Along both sides of the hull we witness nose to tail slaughter: porpoise eat mackerel, mackerel eat sardines, sardines eat fry, all seemingly oblivious to what gaping jaws are following behind them. Carnage.

Despite feeling queasy and tired, we are getting our 'sea-legs.' An on-board routine begins to shape our days. Four small mackerel make a satisfying lunch though perhaps the salty air has spoiled the taste of tea. By the fourth day we managed to prepare Smash, dried beans, and corned beef. Our first substantial meal. A good sign that we are feeling better.

We stand well out from the notorious bay where Atlantic swell from deep waters meets the shallows that turn it into a giant's Jacuzzi. Even sixty miles off the coastline, changes in sea state are rapid: frequent squalls followed by night mist. A massive tanker passes a few hundred yards away, during my watch. Startling to see it suddenly appear from the gloom, my neck hairs bristle.

A nub of anxiety remains with us. Our second hand auto-pilot and radar have both failed. It might be minor faults, but we cannot find out until we are anchored somewhere. At this latitude, nights are perceptively warmer but dehydration and fatigue still bring on the shivers.

Not another ship in sight for well over thirty hours. We allow ourselves the luxury of three hours of sleep each. Alone at the wheel, familiar daydreams come to mind: a soft, four-poster bed, hedgerow greens to rest our eyes, a bath. So far we have neither washed nor changed our clothes, sleeping just as we are, ready to leap into action.

Perhaps one day *Imago's* crew will become relaxed and happy sailors. Those stories we have read make it all seem so easy-peasy… 'encountered a lumpy sea at 3am. All turned to and put a couple of reefs in the main.' The reality of that (unless a boat is equipped with in-mast furling/electric winches) is nothing less than an ordeal for both body and mind.

On we go. The horizon always higher than the bows, climbing a never-ending hill. But as we clear the bay, the weather becomes calmer, the waves assume a more predictable rhythm. As our spirits rise, our sailing improves, even the terminology is becoming more familiar. 'On the starboard quarter,' I cry, and it doesn't sound contrived any more. New obsessions come into our lives: satellite fixes (infrequent in those days), barometer changes, knots per hour, distance run.

We decided to break the journey at one of our refuge ports, Cape Finisterre, before the run to one of our dream places, Madeira. For two days and nights we have, as they say, 'seen no ships.' Just us with *Imago*, on the vast ocean.

As we gazed at our first genuine port of call, through gritty, blood-shot eyes, I think some of the beauty was lost to us, but it really was superb. Rugged bronze and copper hills with patches of forest covering the lower slopes. At the coastline, houses stood grouped in dense interlocking patterns gradually spacing out into single dwellings perched like nesting boxes, high in the hills. We picked up a buoy among the fishing fleet. Desperately tired, ravenously hungry…but we had got here!

***

They let me ride with him to the nearest hospital in Bezier. Three hours later the same Doctor emerged from the emergency treatment room. When he took hold of both my arms before speaking, I feared he was preparing to tell me the worst.

'Your husband is only sixty-six,' he said. 'A big, strong-looking man with good vital signs, he deserves a chance.' He then showed me the scans pointing out the white areas where blood had seeped into Ken's brain – so much blood that it was hard to discern any normal brain tissue. 'It is serious, Mrs Gogay, but don't despair.' A kind vocational Doctor. I watched the helicopter leave as it transported Ken to the neurological intensive care unit at the University Hospital in Montpelier.

CHAPTER 4

WINDS OF CHANGE

Cape Finisterre. Known locally as 'place of the winds.' We are both desperately tired, almost to the point of despair. So far, every land mass and harbour approach had led to a series of novice errors, resulting in chronic chest-pounding anxiety. Attempting to cross the Atlantic in such a state of mind would be truly foolhardy, especially as we faced the prospect of helming all the way. The second-hand automatic pilot now lay at the bottom of the Atlantic. Tossed overboard in a pique of frustration by Ken. Despite such a brief stopover, we remember Finisterre in a very personal way. We were to leave from there with the feel of a new beginning.

Here in this tiny fishing village we absorbed a different rhythm, a slower pace of living. We learned to moderate some of those 21st century stresses: timetables, deadlines, impatience, single-mindedness, open our minds to immediate, smaller pleasures, make a friend of time. It was chastening to realise how fundamentally we must change our attitudes from those we had relied on while building *Imago*.

Around the small harbour, men chatted amiably in small groups. A kinship community that polices itself and is unimpressed by strangers. We saw no tantrums among the children playing, adults appeared to command respect without resorting to threats or shouting.

Once we were safely tied up in the small fishing harbour, we each had a 'sailor's shower' (wet up quickly, turn off the jet, soap all over, wash off, just a kettleful mind, obey the mantra, water is precious). We ate in a café-sized restaurant, squid, followed by pork chops, a mouth-watering change from boat fare. Both food and presentation were superb, the service politely unobtrusive. Tables and décor are totally utilitarian: no gloss, no seductive lighting, and no embellishments. You pay for the quality of food sans gimmicks and we reckoned that to be the right way around. Not that we don't admire the 'art form' in all things, be they beautiful houses, sport, cooking, gardening, whatever is the best of its kind. But paying extra for ambiance wasn't what we were after just then.

Shops were like tiny living rooms. We would enter them feeling like guests. None of them advertise, we found the bread and meat shops by their smell. For anything else, we crossed the threshold to peer inside.

Throughout our stay, the wind howled around the harbour, as it usually does here. Feeling much restored in mind and body, we set out once more, hoping to carry some of the calm fatalism of Finisterre for as long as possible.

In fair winds, with eggshell-blue above and below, we made fine progress throughout the day and our course is set for Madeira. It's not quite so cold, but we are still wearing two jumpers under our waterproofs. No complaining though – we might be punished – sent back to the English Channel!

We are two days out when we notice the barometer drop just a little and hold. Within an hour, the sea state had changed from short and lively into a big swell. Soon we were sliding into deep troughs, struggling for the safest angle to climb the slopes before sinking down again, our stomachs protesting at the dipping and diving roller coaster ride.

By early afternoon, a whole gale developed. We encountered the biggest waves so far. Several exceptional waves, perhaps fifteen to eighteen feet high, smashed into our sides with an explosive sound. *Imago* takes on water over the rails, swamping the cockpit, twice we are 'pooped' by a following sea. With our newly acquired calm and as darkness fell, we decided to try lying-a-hull for the first time. We cannot hope to fight the wheel all night, though without the lessons learned at Cape Finisterre, we may well have tried to and suffer the exhausting consequences. Firstly, drop all sails. No easy task. Bolt all the hatches, then let *Imago* find her own position, broadside to the waves. The wallowing was fearsome, but she weathered it bravely. Placing pillows and cushions on the saloon floor and despite the noise, we slept for eight hours, only surfacing when a particularly large wave thundered against the hull. Occasionally the cockpit drains (four of them) couldn't cope. Water rose above the door sill of the hatch, squeezing through the slats before cascading down the companionway ladder into the saloon like a garden water feature.

The gale persisted throughout the next day, but having rested, we were coping well enough, even beginning to believe that one day we might become proper sailors! We were amazed to find that during the night we had been pushed twenty-four nm in the right direction. Still, we have taken a battering so best to check for damage, especially as the mizzen sail had jammed at the top of the mast and barely holding even a fistful of wind.

Rather than push on in such extreme conditions, we decided to turn and head for Lisbon. Our stints at the wheel are reduced to one hour at a time, but there are still 180nm to run… two more days and nights…

… Still the gale persists. Several times we reach a remarkable speed of 8.4knts with only the storm foresail and the jammed mizzen. This is positively steaming along, but it is too fast for these seas, they are majestic. As the tops break, the light pierces through, a deep, menacing green.

Below decks it's impossible to keep the boat tidy, adding to the feeling of discomfort and oppression: heaps of wet clothing, washing up clattering in the sink. But we have seen what *Imago* can do and it's more than we could ask. At times it was all fiercely exhilarating. Throughout it all, the sky remained bright blue. Odd to think of gales without stinging rain, grey-black clouds, through the scene was only marginally improved by being in Technicolor!

We would have to travel quite a distance inland to reach the City of Lisbon, so we anchored at Cascais, just within the shelter of the headland. We feel immensely relieved. Both we and our small vessel had coped well enough though we were not naïve about what weather conditions we may yet encounter should we choose to journey on.

Later in the day, we checked in with the Guardia Fiscal. Our bureaucrat was a charming, handsome man with a bemused smile. We managed, without language, to communicate our arrival, which he duly and solemnly recorded. He guessed immediately that we were 'ingles' though we saw no reason why (rather than American or German, let's say.)

Responding to what was now a familiar urge, (one we would experience with every landfall, all over the world), to sit over a modest meal on land, we found the nearest café. Only then could we convince ourselves of the reality of terra firma. The relief from constant motion seemed strange and unfamiliar.

Cascais, was also a small fishing village, though being so close to Lisbon, it was more commercial and cosmopolitan than Finisterre. Fish sellers, the vendors of trinkets and fruit, were generally West Indian women. Brightly dressed, charming, wonderfully relaxed about their work. Shoe shine lads, a few who beg, hung around fast-sell, music blaring, clothing stores. A place of atmosphere and colour, new and fascinating to us. Tiny picturesque bays with rocky outcrops and at last too, the blessed sun.

Being in season, sardines are on sale everywhere. At 250-350 escudos a kilo (about £1.00) they make a substantial and delicious meal, needing no more company than fresh chunks of bread.

Feeling much more content with ourselves, we took a train ride into Lisbon, a large and typical city. Ornate doors, Moorish shapes, hinting at its largely maritime history. Returning to Cascais, to stock up for the next leg of our journey: tins of sardines, rice, nuts, raisins, we were surprised to find that root crops and fruit were of very poor quality. But we did buy the biggest melon we had ever seen, enough to eat twice a day for at least a week! Most of the cars we saw were very dated (50s and 60s.) Clearly, they last longer in drier climes. The days are so predictably sunny – whatever do people talk about?!

On the debit side, perhaps explained by an open air abundance of fish and fruit, houseflies thrive and they seem bigger, bolder, and more persistent than their British cousins! Though there was no obvious rivalry between those who followed us home and the couple of Portuguese fellows who had joined us as non-paying passengers from Finisterre!

19th of September. 0800 hrs. We are truly committed now, ready to head out into the Atlantic once more, towards Madeira, 530mm west for our first sight of the 'Pearl of the Atlantic.'

***

Live or die. The first few critical days. Ken sedated, unable to respond to touch or voice. Too still. I listen to the rhythm of the ventilator. It looks as though someone has inserted a red pebble into his left eye socket.

CHAPTER 5

A DICE WITH DEATH

Madeira. Largest island of a tiny archipelago lying 530 nautical miles SW of Lisbon. No more than the eroded peaks of a volcanic ridge, jutting from the vastness of The Atlantic Ocean. An exciting destination for us, a heady feeling that we are leaving Europe behind.

At last we begin to connect with the sea. The first few weeks of our journey were awful. Fear. Wonder. Every familiar sense of self is under assault. We are no longer in control of our thoughts. Without those small but reassuring routines, that on land, bound our days comfortably together, we felt disoriented...even baffled. Just look out there, at that vast unrelenting seascape, water and horizon, featureless as a cloudless sky. We are enclosed in a bubble of water, on the very surface of our planet. At any moment we might be plucked into space.

Soon enough, just as a line-squall quickly comes and goes, the depression lifts. You have climbed the hill, legs a bit wobbly still, but at last, here is the view. The seascape we thought so barren reveals a subtle glory of nuance, music, colour and movement.

A sea state extracts the mood it wants from you: jocular, pensive, irritable, calm. It's a fabulous programme and we have the best seat in the house.

The ocean is an outstanding, tireless, performer, so take your choice: one day listen to a gut-wrenching aria, on another the 1812 overture, complete with sounds of cannon exploding against the hull. Dance to a waltz or to extra-heavy metal. Count those delicate watercolour hues, till you fall asleep...still counting.

Over the next four days, we basked in warm, bright sunshine, sunbathed nude on the foredeck. Early one morning we spotted our first whale as it blew a high jet of water at the edge of the horizon. Though several miles distant, we saw the massive tail fluke slapping into the sea. Estimating distance run and our track width with this sighting of a single whale, made for a sad conclusion: so few left, so many that the oceans could accommodate.

Years before setting sail, we had come across a fascinating account by a passenger on one of the first cruise liners, the SS 'Great Britain.' To pass the time between destinations, contributions were invited from guests and distributed as a pamphlet called 'The Albatross.' On the 4th of October 1862 the following observation was made:

... 'It is lamentable to think of the relentless destruction of these valuable inhabitants of the deep in these waters (approaching Patagonia). They are now scarce, also seals, sea lions, sea elephants and no wonder: at all seasons, and under all circumstances, were they pursued remorselessly and selfishly destroyed. The whales were followed from the open sea into the quiet bays to which they had resorted to calve, and there even attacked and slaughtered, old and young together'.

More than 150 years ago… still it goes on. There were times when we thought we might be among the last to see what remains of a world once so marvellously diverse and fascinating.

But here come the dolphins, plenty of them at least. Deep-sea dolphins, hundreds at a time, curving effortlessly from the surface in double and triple formation, such happy smiling jaws, whistling and clicking, as if beside themselves with a glee at meeting you. So very welcome, any time, one can never feel indifferent towards them. They are part of a unique relationship between which exists between creatures and humans when they encounter each other at sea. Migrant birds, normally shy and fearful on land will take temporary passage with you, searching the rigging for insects, perch on the wheel (comically side-stepping with its motion) sit on your hand, take a nap on your shoulders. There is an ancient knowledge bred into them… they will not be harmed on a boat at sea.

Encounters such as these are one of the highlights of any ocean voyage, they soften you. We always felt pathetically grateful for the trust, but it was impossible to overlook the reproach, indeed the pathos implied by such gratitude.

Abundance! Above the surface, below the surface… as far as the eye can strain to see. Flying fish, thrown up from the ocean like fistfuls of diamonds before taking flight in squadrons and small armies. Joshua Slocum described them best, in 'Sailing alone around the World' and his own enchantment with them…

'...shooting out of the waves like arrows, and with outstretched wing they sailed in the wind in graceful curves: then falling till again they touched the crest of the waves to wet their delicate wings and renew the flight...one of the joyful sights on the ocean of a bright day'.

Despite such enchantments, we are beginning to suffer fatigue. For two days we have stayed in the cockpit, day and night. We are at the fringes of the trade winds and shipping routes, the Canary current is swinging us along, improving our night speed to 4knts. The first ship we have sighted in four days is a cruise liner, we heard the music blaring long before she broke the horizon, we dare not sleep for long.

Whichever ghastly mind adopted sleep deprivation as a means of torture (may Neptune rot their bones), must have experimented on their subjects with the clinical detachment of a sadist. How many days before the body droops. How many more before the twitching irritability. Has the limit been reached when the victim pleads, or is it when their thoughts of death become a prayer for release.

When exhaustion does come, it quickly overwhelms us with its now familiar symptoms: loss of appetite, irritability, and despondence. Sapping our energy, eroding our spirits. We decided to reduce the passage time by a day and make for Porto Santo, 45mm north of Madeira. At 1300 hours on the sixth day, three pinnacles of land poked out from a hazy horizon. Geological monoliths, the very tip of a subterranean mountain jutting out of the ocean.

Arriving by sea offered a privileged view. Even through the heat haze, we could see the sheer escarpments, polished by erosion into massive gemstones. A clear bright day would bring out the colours, make it great spectacle, but after six days at sea, even drab is beautiful.

Revived by the sight of land, we plotted the long haul, round the point to the south end of the island. Just in time it seems: the sea is beginning to lunge at us as if preparing for a blow.

Anchor down at 20.00hrs. Splendid feeling. A note in the log book to record landfall and the fact that we are 1,000 nautical miles from Poole.

Now came the urge to set our feet on land to make it real. After testing the anchor by adding strain with the engine, we inflated the dinghy then headed towards the lights showing from a beachside café. The threatened blow had developed, though in the small bay we seemed to be sheltered from the worst of it. Still, it was a bit lively so we decided to attach the outboard and don plastic sandals so that we could step into the water to pull the dinghy onto the beach…

…I'm drowning…I remember summersaulting into the surf. Strange really, I'm not panicking. I can feel the edges of the capsized dingy with my hands. I try to push it away, but it rotates on top of me instead of sliding off. I am certain…with a detached, bemused awareness that I will drown. Bubbles of air from my last breath trail upwards to the surface of the sea as my fingers still keeping pushing at the fabric of the dingy, slipping and sliding on wet rubber.

Suddenly my head pops up into air. Coughing, spluttering, completely disoriented. Then I see Ken. He has a hold on the dinghy, shouting for me to cling onto it. The surf behind us is high enough to ride, smashing at my legs, tying them in knots. Another surge. Under again, but my feet touch bottom, and it rolls my body onto the shore. Grabbing at our belongings as they hurtle past; plastic sandals, torch, shoulder bag, spare rope, we finally haul the overturned dinghy onto the beach.

Whether with relief, shock, or a sense of the ridiculous, we started to laugh. A mite hysterically it must be said. We fall onto the sand with our mirth, rolling and waving our legs in the air as we slip and stagger to haul the inflatable above the surf line before turning it over to drain out the water. Ken lost one of his sandals. Torch in hand, he rushes off along the beach to recover it. I am convulsed with laughter. At that moment it struck me as the daftest sight I had ever seen! The hero returns in triumph, striding tall, dangling the sandal. We raise a cheer. Our lives are spared… our shoes too!

Stifling our giggles, we staggered towards the restaurant. It's getting late by then. Inside, a family group were finishing their meal; our proprietor is sitting at a separate table with his two lady staff, aprons off, drinking coffee. Pouring seawater from our sandals we entered in bare feet. No-one turned a hair!

Somehow, with gestures (helped along by the obvious signs of being wet through), we managed to convey that we had arrived by boat, capsized in the surf and that after six days at sea, we are very hungry (that last being the easiest to describe in sign language). At which point the proprietor beamed broadly, courteously offering to escort us to our table! Clearly our gestures had fallen short. By then we were shivering from cold and delayed shock, so we pointed to our feet, got him to feel our wet clothes!

Eventually we ate. Me in one of the waitress smocks, Ken in an assortment of clothes donated by the two men present. Tuna with rice salad by the light of a candle, music provided by a cicada, wind vibrating the door. At that moment, it was all very close to perfect. Our clothes were put out on the beach chairs to dry, later we would wade out through the surf and swim with the dinghy, back to *Imago*.

Waiting for coffee, warm and replete, we drew the gingham curtain back to look at the anchor light on *Imago* ... no light... no boat!

She is drifting. Ken rushed outside and spotted her, way across the bay. *Imago* has dragged anchor and is heading towards a rocky peninsula at the east of the island. He and proprietor run together along cobbled streets (Ken in bare feet), knocking on the doors of men with boats. All were out, fishing or enjoying a last pint at a bar. Unaware of what was happening, I was left on the beach, watching the boat light become dimmer and dimmer, while the threatening headland became blacker and blacker. As time passed, I wondered what we might salvage from the wreckage come daylight. Word gets around. Several people are now standing vigil. Peering. Pointing. By now, the anchor light has vanished. It is surely too late. The Portuguese family, who had dined with us, drove me to the far end of the island at alarming speed, but nothing. Their names were Adelino and

Theresa, our friendship, via letters, would continue for many years.

Back at the beach, a boat has been found. A fisherman has just tied up in the harbour and is persuaded to go out again. Someone rushed over to tell us that Ken is on board with him, but I am not reassured by the news. I thanked them though my smile was bleak.

Another hour passes. A cry goes up. 'There! The lights of the fishing boat, the white masts of *Imago* following behind!

Adelino and Theresa took me into their arms, laughing and happy, clapping their hands. 'It's alright? It's OK?' (the only English they knew.) Then we danced in a circle on the sand, hugging each other, before driving to the harbour to watch *Imago* come in.

***

Visiting is restricted to one hour a day, in the afternoon. As relatives enter the unit, each is supervised while washing their hands before donning white gowns. A doctor comes into each room ready to answer any questions and provide an update on their patient's progress. All wonderfully reassuring. They have tried to wake Ken from his drug-induced coma, but he became agitated so they put him back to sleep.

The difference in cleanliness, atmosphere, and openness between those usually encountered in British hospitals was striking, none more so than an air of calm efficiency of staff at every level. The hospital itself was set in beautiful landscaped grounds, dotted with well-tended shrubs and trees.

They tell me Ken will live. They cannot say what neurological damage has been done or if he will recognise the world he wakes up to.

CHAPTER 6

'If at first you don't succeed,
Try, try again. Then quit. No use
Being a damn fool about it.'

W.C. Fields

Although it was now well past midnight, several of the townspeople were waiting at the dockside to welcome *Imago*, taking her lines, securing her safely alongside the harbour wall. As Ken stepped ashore, they clustered round to shake his hand.

'I'll tell you tomorrow,' said Ken.

'Tell me what?' I asked. But when I looked at him, he was already asleep where he sat and soon so was I.

The story he told next morning was shocking. *Imago* had beached herself quite softly on sand, having been cradled in an offshore eddy. She was never in danger. When the fishing boat arrived at the scene with Ken on board, there was a young man on deck, flashing a torch, waving them over. As Ken stepped onto the boarding ladder, the fisherman tried to restrain him, grabbing at his shoulders. The lad began shouting, fisting his hand at the fishing boat skipper. He then put out his arm so that Ken could haul himself aboard. He spoke in English:

'He's trying for salvage,' he warned Ken. 'I'll stay on board with you until we get into harbour.' On the way there the fishing boat suddenly veered hard to starboard, at which the young man shouted, 'follow his line, quickly, quickly! There's an underwater obstacle, he's trying to wreck you!'

The following morning people drifted by, to wish us well. The café proprietor took coffee with us on *Imago*. As he left with our grateful gifts of honey and a music cassette, he told us the villagers were calling us 'The crazy English with the beautiful boat,' (we quite liked both labels!) Back at the beach, our guardian, who we now knew to be running an Aqua-sports business, had hosed down both dinghy and outboard, having housed them in his premises overnight. We found him trying to start the engine. He and Ken worked together for a while. It was such a pleasure to watch their instant camaraderie. A juxtaposition came to mind: the man a boy/ the boy a man. Can we pay him for his time? We asked. 'We must help each other,' he says simply…not so the fisherman. Later in the day he arrived with an interpreter to demand 25,000 escudos (£100). It was an outrageous sum, as much as he would earn in a month. *Imago* had beached herself safely in soft sand, had returned under her own power, yet he held us to ransom, simply for a lift there and an escort back, during which he had tried to wreck us.

'Your boat is insured?' he asks greedily. A dreadful predicament. We were more than willing to pay for his time, but we begged him to be fair. 'Por Favour,' I pleaded. 'Por Favour,' he sneered back. Totally unmoved, he then told the interpreter to threaten us with

47

the Guardia. This could end up becoming a very complicated matter.

Finally, we handed him £60 together with a pair of binoculars, given to us by a dear friend to help us on our journey. He gloated over them. With transparent greed, he 'reluctantly' agreed to accept both money and the binoculars. Hands were briefly shaken. Without another glance, we turned our backs. So far as he knew, he was taking the only binoculars from a boat that was about to go to sea. Monstrous. His callousness made us sick at heart.

But it was the goodness we encountered in Porto Santo that we would remember. Adelino and Theresa ordered us into their car to tour the island. A wonderful excursion into the high terrain, where goats find shelter in ancient dwellings built with rocks, crumbled with age and barely a man's height. A landscape scoured of all vegetation, save for the hardiest of succulents. We stopped at one of the dozens of small drinking parlours, some so isolated that the only customers appeared to be the goats. On again, high into sharply pointed hills. Hairpin bends, sheer drops, views to take the breath away. Back at *Imago* our new friends hugged, 'The English who are nice,' promising to meet again in Funchal, Madeira, when their holiday in Porto was over.

We would remember this small, unpolished gem of an island. Lashed by Atlantic gales, peopled for the most part by fellow sailors.

Having decided to sail to Madeira on the 3am tide change, we walked the two miles to the home of the Aqua-sports owner with a gift: a silver cigarette box that I had treasured for many years. Sadly, the wrong man was more richly rewarded, but to our delight he liked our poor gift. It suited his elegant home. We hoped he would remember it as an 'Englishman's gesture', modest as it was when compared with his unselfish kindness, his belief in the universal code of mariners, to help 'those in trouble on the sea.'

It was still dark when we sighted Madeira, a black, moonless dark. Perfect conditions for a glorious spectacle rising up from the Atlantic. A Christmas tree festooned with coloured lights, blazing and twinkling, casting a copy of its image onto the calm waters of Funchal harbour. An extravagant firework display, frozen a millisecond after ignition.

The city is a bustling place of commerce and tourism, tropical warm, much greener than its tiny sister island lying only a little further to the north. There appeared to be few restrictions about buildings and architecture: extravagant homes, imaginative office blocks, modest dwellings, shacks. Each with its own dignity. The houses spread out into the high ground, almost to the mountain tops, where they merged with the clouds. Behind the usual tourist façade that curves around the edges of most harbours, tree-lined streets and two roomed houses, made pretty by their owners. Small drinking parlours, some only ten paces apart, suggested a pivotal role in a masculine way of life, though we saw no public drunkenness.

Reaching Madeira, after so many trials, brought us a profound sense of achievement. We would never encounter a cruising boat whose crew couldn't tell a yarn or two about near misses, dragged anchors, critical equipment failure, or mind-altering fear. Perhaps our own near disasters had just been compressed together during our passage from England. If so, they were certainly enough to last us a while!

At last! Sun, lizards, bananas, avocado, oranges, brilliant flowering shrubs, and panorama. As promised, we met again with Adelino and Theresa who took us to their home for lunch. Barbecued chicken, salad, ice cream, and fruit. A generous elegant meal, enlivened greatly by a bubbling conversation using hand gestures and sign language! Bottles of wine were exchanged. Theresa presented us with two hand-embroidered place mats as gifts for our journey. They told us that the greedy fisherman had been roundly reprimanded for his behaviour. After lunch, we were bundled into their car again and taken to one of the finest high views on the island. We had met the first friends of our travels.

Mid-morning, on October 1st 1988, we waved farewell to the good people of Porto Santo and enjoyed a gentle, uneventful sail to the Canary Island of Tenerife. Heeding our bitter lessons, we lay a-hull six miles off the coast until dawn, before meandering down the west of island to the southern harbour of Gran Canaria. We could now look forward to several weeks of rest before our biggest test, the Atlantic crossing. Here was the place to meet experienced cruisers who had gathered here for the ARC (Atlantic Rally Crossing), an annual event for boats of every size, type, and level of experience. A chance to learn more about those sailing skills necessary to sustain our chosen way of life, which so far had lasted all of six weeks and a mere 1690 nautical miles!

***

A nurse was waiting for me outside the ward.

'I realise it will be a shock, my dear. We've put a tube in your husband's throat to help him breathe'. I thought, how kind it was to tell me. What she didn't say was that Ken had been shaved for the procedure, which was a bigger shock by far. I had never seen Ken without a full beard, his face looked smaller, more vulnerable. They said he was awake, but it was hard to tell. His eye was open (the bloodied one patched with a dressing) but he wasn't in a world we once shared. His hand in mine remained limp.

CHAPTER 7

NO ROLEX BUT AN UNLIKELY ALLIANCE

From largo to prestissimo, solo clarinet to massed trumpets, pastoral poem to hip-hop rap. After our most peaceful sail so far, the impact of a bustling tourist destination was like being woken from a dream state by a frantic ringing of bells. Nevertheless, it was a contrast that would confirm, in our minds, that the wonder and wow of childhood need never be lost, that we would find it again every time we went to sea. The curve of the Earth, stars and planets bright enough to mark out pathways on the surface of the ocean, sun-up, sun-down, all of it spread across the sky.

Within an hour of stepping ashore, we were stopped on the street by a time-share agent, a young lass from Scotland, Janice, anxious to earn her commission with an invitation card to attend a promotion event, advertising holiday homes.

We joined several families and couples in a hotel lounge to listen to the presentation. Overlooking the room was a glass-fronted office, similar to those found in supermarkets, from which the interviewers 'progress' could be monitored. The dark suited man assigned to our table, adjusted his sunglasses, looking us up and down, before remarking that Ken wasn't wearing a watch! Our interview was brief... no Rolex, no proof of substantial retirement funds, living aboard a boat: all reasons for being hopeless 'prospects'. After giving a flat-line signal to the office, he gave us a grim smile of frustration before we were escorted from the room by a bloke who was built like a night club bouncer. Even so, we left with a bottle of whisky and 200 cigarettes for our 'trouble.' Poor Janice, would she be reprimanded? We had explained to her that weren't interested, but her job was simple to gather enough people to fill the room. 'They need the right 'dynamic,' she told us!

It was a hard, hard sell, American style. High pressure targets, lavish staff incentives: Cases of Champagne, designer watches. But profits are enormous, including margins that allowed for generous gifts to be casually distributed, just to provide the right 'atmosphere.' Apparently the Spanish authorities frowned on such selling tactics, though the apartments themselves are tastefully appointed, the services exceptional...at a price!

At every resort on the islands, similar schemes for holiday letting are being built at astonishing speed, apparently in an effort to beat a Spanish Government deadline of 1990, they having sensible decided that beyond that date further development would outstrip the island's capacity to provide water, electricity, and sewage management. Nevertheless, most of the resulting architecture was remarkable, even experimental in concept and most attractive.

On all of the larger islands, shopping areas reflect a recent boom in all-year round tourism. Inevitably, some of the souvenir items look cheap and frivolous, but duty-free luxury goods are widespread also, to tempt a more discerning buyer, some being the very best of their kind: uncut gemstones, huge Lladro figurines, state of the art jewellery, and sophisticated electronics.

Yet some of the old ways persist. The daily fish catch still sold from barrows set up on the quayside, a boulevard atmosphere, enjoyed by residents as much as by tourists. International cuisine, including English breakfast, roast beef with Yorkshire, Paella, Chateaubriand.

Some of the islanders looked to be tourist weary but its benefits to the local community are evidenced by the cleanliness of pretty public spaces. Early each morning, beaches are cleaned of detritus and raked by a uniformed brigade.

We are very excited at the prospect of our friend Bill, flying out to spend two weeks with us (although I had turned down his proposal of marriage many years before, we remained devoted friends.) He will bring mail and news from family and friends. For two whole days we sat at the saloon table writing letters and postcards for him to take back to England.

We were then free to wander about, strolling around town, swimming, and rock pooling. The brightly coloured male crabs were enchanting to watch, as they chased the females across the rocks. 'Catch me if you can,' as she led them over the difficult route. Judging by such a profusion of crabs, the strategy works!

Small fish are plentiful in the harbour. Offshore boats bring in sea bream, dorado, and sardines. Very soon now the tuna run will begin. Every type of vessel, large or small, will join in the bonanza. Among the smaller tropical fish species, indigenous to these waters are many of the Wrasse, including, to our delight, those brilliantly coloured rainbow and Cuckoo wrasse, alongside blennies, damsel fish, and ling.

Bananas, bananas! We ate them every day, cooked in the oven with honey and brown sugar, sliced into custard, in sandwiches, or just as a fruit. Tomatoes too are cheap, large and succulent. Bought green, these two foods would last several days at sea.

The harbour was crowded with boats of every size, shape, and rig. Most were waiting for the ARC race, which would begin in De Gran Canaria and finish in Barbados. Any boat is eligible as long as it complies with certain safety regulations and is owner skippered. Some would take the racing aspect seriously, others just content to be part of a 200-boat flotilla. Many, like us, would be making their first passage across that famous stretch of ocean. The Pacific, though larger by many increments, is an island-hopping journey, once the Marquesas are reached. But the Atlantic is a different challenge because south east of the Cape Verdes, there is nowhere else to run for nearly 2000 miles. It's a total commitment to the half-way point where you know that you are 1500 nautical miles from any landfall, in any direction. An awesome feeling, the acknowledged endurance test for boat and crew, gateway to the rest of the world.

For an increasing number of people, cruising becomes a way of life. A grapevine of knowledge is passed on, from harbour to harbour. Most have done the crossing before, some of the boats several times. We found this very reassuring. No doubt we would meet up again with a few of them as we journeyed on. Though most of the yachts were en route, others would stay and live the harbour life for years.

At the end of that first week, Bill arrived, his suitcase filled with treats which even included a celebration dinner of steak and Champagne; nicely de-frosted during his four hour flight! We read our mail, over and over again... everyone so thrilled that we had made it thus far.

After a splendid two week holiday and all of us several pounds heavier, we joined our friend in the taxi to the airport. He insisted on leaving behind more groceries and extra treats to get us safely to the West Indies and his next holiday. I think we looked into his eyes for a moment too long.

'Stop that!' he said, 'I'll see you in the Caribbean.'

With only three weeks left to get *Imago* ship-shape for the crossing, Ken checked every piece of equipment on board while I visited other waiting boats to see what charts were vital for safe approaches into unfamiliar harbours. The large-scale chart we had would serve for most of the journey since most of it depicted water! Provisions, water, gas cylinders, diesel, check the rigging and sails, rest well, tone up our muscles with swimming. The weeks flew by.

Now we count in days. Grenada by Christmas?

Excitement and apprehension are an uncomfortable mix, but we are resigned to the fear. No matter how many times our stomachs get that squelchy feeling, we must learn to accept it as part of what any adventure is about.

Wherever cruising boats gather, so do waiting crews, all looking for a passage. Some for the love of sailing, others as a means to travel on meagre resources. The young and vigorous, eager to satisfy their own urge for adventure.

Qualifications vary (who were we to talk!) For some a first-time experience, for others earning their living as able crew, having particular skills as navigators or cooks. There were agencies too which charged profitable commissions for suitable introductions. Three young men called on us, but although having an extra watch was making sense, none of them was suitable. One relied too heavily on alcohol, another had never been aboard a vessel and felt queasy at anchorage! The last couldn't stake his grub. We liked the idea of providing passage in return for help with our heavy boat, but could not take risks about it. There were too many stories about incompatible crew arriving at their destination as sworn enemies, even tales of mutiny and violence!

It was different with Mr Jack. An immediate mutual liking (though it wouldn't last the distance.) Seventy-one years old, though even with the sloping shoulders of the elderly, still a fine figure of a man, six feet, three inches tall, a mariner all his life. We met him just days before setting out. He had flown over from England to join his son and family who were preparing for a much longer voyage to Australia in their thirty-five footer. On board, he found a haphazard, disorganised vessel. Though a happy but noisy family, he soon realised that he would not fit in with so great an age disparity in such cramped conditions. Deeply disappointed, Jack moved onto their second boat, awaiting sale in the boatyard. There he pondered whether to fly back to England or try finding passage on a quieter ship. Although he had sailed all his life, he had never crossed an ocean, but dearly wanted to. What could be a fairer exchange we wondered? Possibly his last chance of a long voyage for our first. Welcome aboard Mr Jack!

So we set off, to sail across the Atlantic. Thirty to forty days and nights at sea. 'The owl and the pussy cat' aboard their pea green boat…and Mr Jack. Let us hope that we will all, 'dance by the light of the silvery moon,' in Grenada by Christmas.

***

They have hoisted him from the bed onto a chair, packed him round with pillows to prevent him sagging to one side. His left eye is clearing – I can make out the pupil, looking like the dark centre of a red flower. Pale, passive, diminished. There is fear and bewilderment in his gaze. He is absent, not knowing himself, not knowing me. Wait to get home before you cry.

CHAPTER 8

THE ATLANTIC CROSSING

At 10.35am on November 21st 1988 we weighed anchor, wondering if, or indeed where, we would set it again. It would have been an earlier start, but I was violently sick several times, following a disturbed night of unsettling dreams, in which I would come on deck for my watch, only to find no one at the wheel. As we threaded a way slowly through the anchorage towards the breakwater, we were given the traditional 'Bon Voyage' salute. All manner of horns, hooters, bells, ship's sirens, blasting out a farewell. A heart-warming tradition.

Numbers attempting the crossing increase, year on year. For each of them it will always be remembered as a singular experience to have sailed this famous stretch of water. From dozens of anchorages vessels set out: large and small, sophisticated, basic, single handers, couples, families, some with uniformed crew. From mid-November through to early February, several hundred small vessels leave the shelter of harbour to do what boats are built for.

The crew of *Imago* are excited to be setting out, anxious as to what awaits them, determined to get there.

As we rolled in the swell beyond the breakwater, I wonder how our threesome will fare, how such a long journey, in fair weather and foul, will affect us. Whatever else, it would be memorable.

With another person aboard, Ken and I have a sobering weight of responsibility: Ken for maintaining equipment and running gear while I must provide at least one substantial meal a day, whatever the conditions. I fervently hope we have stowed sufficient provisions, treats and storm rations to last a possible forty-five days.

Setting out on a balmy, cloudless day, we hoped to catch an offshore breeze by late afternoon, a wind from the east within a few days. By the first dead reckoning, twenty-four hours from now, Tenerife will disappear behind us. Grenada, in the Windward Islands, lies 2,650 nautical miles ahead.

Not quite! It was well into the evening of the second day before the tip of Mount Teide curtsied its farewell for a last time before dipping below the horizon.

We soon forgot that our crew member Jack was seventy-one years old. He clearly delighted in sailing and getting the optimum performance out of a boat. What he brought to our vessel was caution, an enviable knowledge of general sailing theory and routine. It was this last discipline that was to serve us best. By the sixth day, both watch keeping and task allocation is so comfortably established that we would never deviate from it, in even the smallest respect. It's about who makes the mid-morning coffee, who washes up the breakfast things, what time to meet each day to discuss a safe nights sailing. When we eat, even when we clean our teeth! Most importantly of all, everyone is being courteous, looking to each other's needs, making sure that every watch change is a little early, if only by a few minutes. The last quarter of a night watch can seem interminable.

We have spotted just two yachts in five days – all faster and flying spinnakers, but we are quite content to be averaging ninety miles a day in little more than a fresh breeze. Yesterday we ran on what is termed a broad reach, all sails hoisted; wind a little abaft of beam, making good 110 miles. *Imago* loved it! She was teaching us that when running free, her movement through the water was smooth and snake-like. If her balance was out, she would stagger, bouncing like a dog held too tightly by its lead. There is a significant swell; the waves are long and broad, but nothing fearful, so far.

It was already made clear to us that experience brings greater confidence and that without an auto-pilot, three was a more comfortable number of crew for a long haul. Two hours on, four off, was such a luxury, indeed anything less would have made for a desperate voyage. Inadequate sleep had always been our undoing. Jack insisted that unless involved in essential chores or changing tack, we must rest, even if we didn't sleep. So Jack plays patience at the saloon table or delivers hymns in a tuneless hum while Ken and I generally read.

Before leaving Tenerife, I brought a whole stem of bananas, as did most of the boats that were setting out. Six days out we heaved at least 30lbs of them overboard! They had all ripened at once into a soggy, evil-smelling mush. Entirely my fault, I should have been de-ribboned, stripped of my buttons, drummed out. I had separated the hands from the stem for easy stowage, instead of leaving them on the stalk to hang in the cockpit, where they would have ripened in sequence, as nature intended. Nevertheless, I had to raid the treats locker for Jaffa Cakes, awarding them as 'medals' for heroic efforts made by master and crew to consume said bananas before the rot set in. You cannot fail to get the message when, 'Guess what's for dinner?' is greeted with a drumming of bare chests. Over they went!

But we needed goals and targets, as well as humour. The first of these being 25N by 25S, the waypoint at which the pilot books say that the all-important Trade Winds can be expected. A week into our journey. We have covered 500nms, according to the log, but only 420nms of the distance (allowing for tacks). Slow going. The sun is so bright that we all have squint lines around our eyes. Seas are swinging and confused which is making helming very hard work.

Now that we are in these latitudes, there is constant entertainment as we watch flying fish taking off on their incredible life-saving flights. Such marvels of evolution, with their bat-like pectoral fins, their sickle-shaped tails flicking the wave tops, keeping them airborne for thirty and forty yards at a time. Some are barely an inch long; adults may weigh close to a couple of pounds. Occasionally several squadrons of thirty to fifty fish take off together. With the sun flashing them into silver streaks, it's a spectacle. Despite such remarkable tactics, their predators simply do a torpedo run below the surface to gobble them up in the thousands. I lodged a polite request of Poseidon, not to re-incarnate as a flying fish!

For two whole days now, we have run with the wind behind us. The ship's clock is turned back an hour, the first of four changes before we sight Grenada. To increase speed we have set the big Genoa to the spinnaker pole and its working well.

We're there! 25N by 25S. Now we can expect the Trade Winds. A couple of squalls during the night and we are spanking along at 5-5½knts with *Imago* showing great style and balance. Helming becomes fingertip easy. As dawn breaks, we notice several bright blue fish with yellow tails. Big fish, over three feet long. They would keep station with us for the next thousand miles. Perhaps travelling alongside offered them some protection.

Those famous winds that drove the Clipper ships are either late or further south. The wind has dropped. The sea is as calm as an inland waterway. We could almost imagine that by peering over the side we might see the bottom of the ocean, lying 3,000 fathoms below. Nevertheless our spirits are high and we feel quite fresh – a sound ship.

The last day of November. A third of the journey behind us and still enjoying a very peaceful passage. I shall excel in the galley tonight: tuna bake, melon for afters. Although our twenty-four hour runs are well below the hoped for target of 100 miles a day, we are spot on course and sailing comfortably.

We can scarcely believe our eyes! More than 900 miles out into the Atlantic, but there it is, perched on the cockpit combing. A very large, very live, locust! It flew off before we could capture if for a closer look, but it was inches from us and unmistakeable – bound for Africa we supposed.

At our current rate of knots we are only meandering along. Nothing above force 3, though an easterly current is adding about ten miles a day. Had we continued to drift along like this, we'd be at sea for 200 days, arriving in Grenada as mummified bodies, having succumbed from hunger and thirst!

As dusk began to spread its way across half of the horizon, we played Barbra Streisand and Aled Jones tapes, getting ourselves into quite a moody-blue state of mind. Days race by. No sooner are the daily chores done it is time to reduce sail in preparation for the night run.

Getting tedious now… still the wind will not come. Wallowing along with noisy flapping sails. Several of the ARC racers have come and gone, their light air sails billowing out in front. It looks as though our Christmas schedule is off, which has dampened our spirits. Even the half-way mark is eluding us.

Tensions arise. At the daily 10am muster, held in the cockpit, attended by all crew to discuss the night's sailing and to announce the twenty-four hour distance covered, Ken remarks that on Jack's watches our course has deviated by several degrees and that his habit of humming loudly at night is disturbing our sleep. Ken doesn't get top marks for delivery, Jack doesn't take it very well.

December 4th. The clocks go back another hour. Today we caught a 3lb fish on a spinning lure. We think it might be a small tuna. Whatever it was made for a gourmet dinner: fresh fish in white sauce, cabbage, potatoes, followed by cooked apricots with evaporated milk. We all sat back like a pride of lions that had gnawed their kill to the bone!

December 7th – Collision!

We had watched another yacht approaching from astern for most of the morning. As she came parallel, some 100 yards off our port beam, we called across, waving, to wish her two crew a safe voyage. Ken and I then went below, leaving Jack to finish his watch. Shortly afterwards we heard him shout out, 'veer away! Seconds later a tremendous thudding vibration rocked *Imago* onto her scuppers. Although the passing vessel was on auto-pilot, a freak gust of wind brought her close enough to climb up on our port bow, smashing the spinnaker pole like a matchstick and tearing away a section of the guard rail. Our spreaders ripped a large tear in the other yacht's mainsail, a sound which brought the two on board scrambling into their cockpit from below. Both boats locked together in a vicious embrace.

Frozen disbelief! Speechless amazement! It just could not happen that two small boats could collide in mid-Atlantic, especially as *Imago* was motor-sailing when it happened. With a burst of incredible, fear-fuelled energy, Ken lifted the prow of the smaller vessel, announced that it was clear of any hull damage, and then pushed it away. Within a short time, they dropped their damaged sail and hoisted a replacement. Both boats resumed their journey.

Jack had been wrong to approach the yacht so closely as to deny it sea-room. He had also failed to respond quickly enough to take avoiding action. Calling out 'veer away' was more suited to sailing in the congested waters of the Solent, though Jack did point out that the colliding vessel should not have been left unattended at such close quarters.

But it was too shocking an event to be angry about and any further denial from Jack about his share of culpability might cause trouble between us all. So, after a quick flare up, it was never mentioned again.

Ken and I spliced and glued the spinnaker pole within the hour. That afternoon, more sombrely than planned, we all repaired to the foredeck with 'half way' painted on two sunburned chests and one belly (mine) and set up the camera with a time delay. Thus was the ceremony duly observed and recorded, though not in quite the spirit we had anticipated. Dinner too was a silent affair.

But halfway it was. Surely now the Trade Winds would come. We begged for them…cursed for them…and then they came.

***

With the help of a borrowed crew from the ever-helpful boating community, I've moved the boat closer to Montpelier. Ken is being fed through a tube in his abdomen. I talk and stroke… but nothing comes back.

CHAPTER 9

THE HAIRY SCARY, WET AND SOGGY, ROCK 'N' ROLL, YES. I'M SCARED TO DEATH BITS!

We have them at last! The famous NE Trade Winds that since 1812 carried the great schooners and clipper ships to and from the then known world. At this time of the year (November) they are described as moderate, increasing in both range and strength during the months of January and February.

And 'moderate' is quite enough for us! Having swept over the horizon during the dawn watch, they were blowing a consistent force 5 by late morning. Trade wind seas are the special event. Top of the bill. Star of the show. Predictable as the change of seasons and utterly magnificent. Dazzling blue and white. Crumpled up acres of aluminium foil, bright sunlight shooting out from each wave. 20-25knts off the stern quarter, everything up, your craft straining to leave the surface and fly. And on this glorious platinum sea your boat is doing all it was designed to do: flushing along at maximum hull speed, pushing for more. Ultimate sailing. It makes you feel happy.

It's exhilarating to sail in big seas, and noisy! White-caps everywhere, great patches of froth swishing past the hull. It can be difficult helming, wind and current battling for supremacy, confusing the waters, doubling up the waves.

Occasionally a great pyramid of water twelve to fifteen feet high, comes roaring in under the stern. *Imago* buries her bows in deeply, lifting her counter high in the air, before crashing down again. When we took them on the beam, each impact made the whole boat shudder. As the top of the wave disintegrates, spray falls likes a monsoon shower onto the luckless helmsman.

The more majestic and heaped up the waves become, the more *Imago* seemed to like it, but the strain on running gear is immense. The repaired spinnaker pole fractured again, this time beyond repair. We had to improvise some way of running safely with the wind behind us, so Ken boomed out the mainsail as far as it would go and balanced it with a small jib, securing each with a restraining rope to resist a gybe. We must now be satisfied with 4knts instead of 6 and accept that the ropes would chafe on the stays. Two days later the jib gave up – it simply ripped in two. 'Tis a known sailing fact that these things always happen at night! Hoisting sails is punishing work on a heaving deck and Ken was losing out on precious sleep.

The violent motion upset as all in those first few days, though none of us were actually sick. It is lack of sleep that begins to tell. Spirits are acutely affected by any negative event, then just as quickly bolstered by news of progress. A treat from the purser's locker today, to celebrate 115 miles over the course.

My word, these seas are awesome. Although confident that they pose no real threat, catering has become rather a torment. A plate of fried eggs disembarked onto the cockpit floor. After wafting about like jellyfish (and just as uncatchable) they finally slithered down the drain holes. Fried eggs are no long on the menu!

Provisions are lasting well though water remains strictly rationed. For most boats water makers are not yet common enough to be affordable. As daytime temperatures fall slightly, we encounter several short-lived but energetic squalls. Ken stripped off and washed in the scuppers. Rather pointedly I thought! So Jack and I took turns to follow suit. Truth is, that with water strictly reserved for drinking and cooking only, we had all begun to smell rather ripe.

Ouch! A missile has hit me in the ribs, doubling me over from pain and shock. Did it fall from the sky? Is it driftwood thrown up from this wild sea? Whatever it is feels slimy, flexible... alive! As it drops into my lap, flapping wildly, I realise it's a large flying fish, weighing a good couple of pounds. As it sashayed around the cockpit, thudding its tail in a drum beat, Ken and Jack rushed on deck with bleary anxious eyes, only to find me laughing at the novelty of it all. As well as providing an excellent breakfast, it has also served to test our emergency drill, having agreed at the outset that two hard slaps on the coaming was a call for 'all hands on deck.' The sound of traditional bell or whistle can easily be drowned out by engine noise or a screaming wind, but on a steel boat, a thump to the deck is unmistakeable.

Now that most of the waves are higher than the wheel house, many more flying fish are swept aboard. Most slide back into the sea through the scupper drains, but each morning there are usually enough, trapped by the stanchions for Ken to collect several of the largest for breakfast. Three minutes each side, delicious, with a taste and texture similar to sprats.

A day that started with novelty, ended with something sublime. At first glance they looked like aircraft, flying in tandem, a pair of bleached-white hyphens, high in the sky. But as the wings undulated in a graceful rhythm, long wavering tail filaments stretched out behind, we realised that they were tropic birds. As they faded, wraith-like, into the distance, they seemed to leave a blessing in their wake. An 'other-worldly' calm which left us deeply moved.

Night time weather assumes a predictable pattern of regular squalls. Every half hour or so the bright moonlight is suddenly blotted out – now grip the wheel that bit more tightly, bow your head, because for the next ten minutes you'll be standing under a waterfall. Moments later the surface of the sea is silver once more, stars distinct and bright. Sometimes the sea is flattened by the force of the downpour, droplets bounce and ricochet on the surface.

The 18th of December marks a month at sea. We shall all be glad to see land now, better still a quiet harbour. Despite the 80 degree heat, everything feels damp, stifling. Back go the clocks for the third time. As a gallant gesture, the hour is mine for an extra sleep period. The last hour will be left for when we anchor.

Counting each mile. There is a real chance now that we shall make harbour before Christmas after all. It should not matter when sailing an ocean... but it does. 500 miles to Grenada, 360 to Barbados, which is still an option if water tanks run low or we have serious rig problems. All the sails are badly stretched and chafed; at least a dozen slugs have been torn from their eyelets.

Two days later our spirits are lifted by the sighting of seagulls instead of stormy petrels ('mother Carey's chickens' as sailors call them). There to tell us that we are on the run in. We are all very tired, inside and out, in mind and in body. The night of December 21st earned a special note in the log. Words like, 'truly dreadful,' followed by a ruder word which we later deleted! Squalls came and went with vicious frequency, leaving behind a horrible swishing sea. We couldn't pole out the mainsail safely in such conditions, so all hands were needed to change tack several times in a strenuous effort to stay on course. Every stint at the wheel became an ordeal.

A couple of times I really felt I'd had it. Please stop this...I want to get off! Such emotional doldrums are quite frightening, especially so when the goal is within sight. Please don't let anything dreadful happen now...not after all this way. Travelling across an ocean in a small boat is to volunteer for chronic anxiety, whatever the weather.

We are all taking our share of the load, whoever feels stronger. Each of us has been hailed from our bunks over these last three nights to 'spot' ships in poor visibility. Several freighters have passed close by in recent days. Hang on tight. Don't let go! This is the

71

genuine run in and 'only two more nights' beats like a mantra in our minds. It's a little over 200 miles to Grenada.

Our course brings us to within thirty-six miles of Barbados. The horizon is too fuzzy with heat haze for a sighting, but when we switched our marine radio to 'all channels' we eventually heard the first lilting Caribbean voice.

Despite being so close to a landfall, there were several reasons why Barbados was never included on our route plan. Being the destination for the rally boats, with local venues set up in readiness for celebration parties lasting several days, there were plenty of opportunities for price hiking. Booking in cost $80 for the paperwork alone! Just a universal reaction towards perceived wealth associated with owning a boat. Nor did the prospect of steel drums, reggae, or the noisier consequences of rum fests hold any appeal for the exhausted crew on *Imago*.

Less than 100 miles left of our transatlantic voyage. We know we have made it now. As if to match our mood, the sea is especially beautiful today. In brilliant sunshine and a steady force 5, it looks like beaten copper, marbled at its edges with apple-green trimmings where sunlight pierces the waves.

Tomorrow we should sight land for the first time in thirty-three days. Waiting at the main Post Office in St. Georges will be mail from family and friends who have waited to hear that we have made the crossing safely. The temperature inside the saloon is a stifling 90F. We are close enough to smell nutmeg and cinnamon, the dank mushroom smell of tropical growth. There! Just off to starboard. The tell-tale cotton-ball cloud floating above a small smudge on the horizon. Making our way slowly to the south side of the island, we can see the first apricot-coloured beaches, palm trees, wooden houses dotted sparingly on the hillsides amid a lush green landscape. At 13:30hrs. December 23rd *Imago's* anchor chain rattles from its coils onto the firm sand of Prickly Bay. I have the half bottle of Champagne ready for a toast, the yellow quarantine flag, hoisted to signal arrival from a foreign port. But before raising our glasses, Ken walks to the stern and gently rubs the deck. A grateful salute to our brave and stalwart vessel.

***

Today we are mother and infant. Ken smiled! A six-week-old baby smile, fleeting, impersonal. I want to lift him from the bed, carry him away in my arms, put him to my breast. As the signal is sounded to leave, I raise my head from his chest. His gown is damp with silent tears.

The ruptured blood vessel has been sealed and life support equipment is no longer connected. Although Ken remains in a faraway place, the recording monitor shows that he is stable enough to take the first steps towards whatever level of recovery is possible, either here in France or in England.

Unable to speak the language, beyond some basic courtesy words, needing the support of family and friends, the possibility that Ken might be sent to another hospital far from sea or canal, are serious obstructions to what will be a long process. Whatever else, I cannot be parted from Ken and *Imago* both.

I make the decision to repatriate all three of us…back to England. Another long journey has begun. One that would be no less arduous and no less rewarding than our journey around the world.

CHAPTER 10

'You road I enter opon and look around, I believe you are not
All that is here, I believe that much unseen is also here.

'Song of the Open Road' (Walt Whitman)

Our time spent in Grenada would include some of the most indelible of our adventures. A cocktail of extraordinary events, several so bizarre as to leave us confused, disturbed, saddened, but also with enduring and deep regards for both the island and its people.

St. George's, the Capital. Bustling crowds, gregarious, haphazard, disorganised, and utterly charming! Dozens of street vendors 'working' the tourists. Christmas parties in full swing, everyone 'walking the walk,' adjusting to a different beat of music as they rounded each corner of the streets.

Most shops and institutions were closed for the holiday, but we managed to find a chicken, potatoes, even a jar of mincemeat with which to celebrate our first Christmas in a tropical climate. Only an English woman would do it!

All landfalls are beautiful after a long time at sea, though nothing could have prepared us for the colours of Grenada. Silver and gold beaches, lush greens of tropical growth, bright yellow coconuts, shrubs and creepers festooned with huge garish blossom and everywhere the national flower, Bougainville, lighting up the landscape like bonfires. And thick in the air, a pungent aroma of spices, herbs, nutmeg, and cinnamon. A continual round of nesting, flowering, fruiting, growing. A pulsating virility that matched the urgent sound of steel drums and reggae.

Early in the evening of that first day, Ken and I strolled along the beach, then sat for a while in a grove of palms. Our eyes still drawn to the sea, gazing out over the expanse of ocean, not yet able to grasp that we had crossed the Atlantic, or that we were 5,000 miles from Poole and England. As we sat there, quiet and still, a heron-like bird flew in to stare at us, as if about to ask a question, land crabs emerged cautiously from their holes, having scurried there as we approached, cicadas resumed their noisy courtship. We could not have wished for a more enchanting welcome.

Jack had decided to look for a passage to Venezuela. Although another watch keeper had been a blessing, he proved to be a confirmed misogynist, who despite his long marriage, spoke contemptuously about his wife, boasted about his 'other woman', and refused to listen to my summary at the watch change. For Ken and I, this was a useful way to get our night vision, point out approaching or receding vessels, new lights on the horizon and the course to keep. Twice Ken had heard Jack saying, 'run along now, dear,' or, 'off you go child!' He did manage to praise the cook, declare *Imago* to be a fine vessel, and acknowledge Ken's navigation skills. Being clearly delighted to have realised his dream, we left it like that and wished him well.

The 28th of December was a wonderful day. We sat on the harbour wall, a few yards from the Post Office to open our packet of mail. Inside were precious letters from family and friends together with small gifts and tokens for Christmas. They must all have wondered if we had arrived at our intended destination, after all those early dramas!

We read those letters over and over again, interrupting each other, reading bits aloud… mind hugs… we felt them and were as happy as any two can be. Next we bought the two local papers before visiting the tourist office, having learned that these are the best ways to learn about a different land and its culture.

Grenada lies 100 miles north of Venezuela and 12 degrees north of the equator. It is the largest of the Windward Islands in a group that includes Carriacou and Petit Martinique. At that time, the population was some 110,000. While agriculture, banana export, and spice production were the main sources of income, tourism was rapidly becoming the second largest industry.

Grenada, along with many other small Caribbean countries is deemed 'third world'… we overheard one overfed American call them 'eighth world', but that disparaging remark is far from the truth. Certainly progress is slow despite millions of USA aid dollars that were poured in, following the revolution of 1983, but the people of Grenada remain its richest resource and they will not be hurried or hassled.

Although tourism is such a vital part of the economy, Grenada sits low in the league of islands which benefit from the nine million tourists who holiday in the Caribbean each year. It was difficult for us to understand why that should be so for an island where so much cultural integrity remains. Part of the explanation may lie with high rainfall statistics. But although showers can be monsoon-like in intensity, most occur at night as temperatures fall slightly and are generally short-lived unless it is the rainy season proper or the edge of a hurricane passes close. The lushness of the islands depends on these conditions.

The island is divided into seven states, all having the names of Saints: George, Andrew, John, Mark, David, Andrew, and Patrick. The capital is the size of a small rural town in England, while the rest of the island is made up of villages and hamlets. There are no house numbers and very few street names beyond the town. Nevertheless, if you should live on 'Happy Hill,' even something as rare as a letter will get you to. Place names reflect a turbulent Franco-English history, both countries having fought for the same territory since its first sighting by Columbus in 1498. Imagine our surprise to find Windsor Forest, Arthur Seat, Halifax Harbour, Gretna Green, Hyde Park, and even Queen's Park Racecourse!

Television has very little impact. Most programmes are brought in from America, offering a daily fare that is limited to Perry Mason, The Flintstones, Beverley Hill Billies, and Magnum. But only the poorest lacked a radio. It was easy to understand why. Delivered in impeccable English, both commentators and disc jockeys spoke with such a friendly, intimate style. Music dominates the airways, throbs in every street and home and it's addictive listening: early pop, ballads, the latest and best of Reggae and soul. Regular BBC world service news broadcasts are followed by local news, such as who won the boys or girls netball or table tennis championships, or when a banana crop should be brought to the dock for shipment. All made for fascinating listening.

During those first few days, we went on some fabulous walks. Every bird we saw being a new enchantment, from the ubiquitous white egrets, perched on the backs of grazing cattle, equally common jet black finches, exquisite humming birds flitting between the shrubs in endlessly busy flights, to the huge thugs that are frigate birds, flying high circles around the harbour.

Wanting to see as much of the island as possible, we joined the huddle of citizens waiting to board a 'dollar bus'. Taxis are strictly for tourists, fares for them being a question of what a driver could extract from them, so, apart from a few single-decker public service buses, all other transport is by twelve seat mini-bus. That first day we took a seat on whichever was available, but soon learned to be more selective, choosing the most roadworthy looking vehicle, one with the least bald tyres and missing wheel nuts! Whoever said, 'one can get used to anything,' was a fool!

The driver of a Grenadian mini-bus is 'Lord' of his four-wheeled estate. There are no rules. Off we go…music blaring, packed together until it's difficult to breathe, but still stopping for anyone who waves from the roadside. These buses are the 'dollar lifeline' for the island. For any journey, just a dollar (then about 20p), be it one stop or twenty, one mile or six. Sacks of flour, bags of rice, even propane gas cylinders were collected and delivered, eggs, yams, bought by driver and passengers from roadside stalls en-route. Two taps on the roof signalled the driver to stop... and stop he does! Even in the middle of a hairpin bend! Our driver regularly leans far out from his cab, shouting and waving to friends and acquaintances, a business chat here, a deal struck there. Soon everyone is singing aloud to music blaring from a radio, thumping their knees to the rhythm. Once beyond St. Georges, the roads are appalling. Tyres are worn to shreds in just three weeks. A jolly carefree, petrifying journey!

Nevertheless, if you have a head for heights and nerves of steel, it's a breath-taking route, skirting the sea for much of the way and rising quickly into the high ground, close to the edges of the rain forest. On, and higher still, to where the road is simply a ledge set into the hillsides. It is here that Grenada keeps her secrets and displays her riches, in countless bays and inlets, nutmeg groves, waterfalls, tumbling tributaries, clusters of wooden dwellings. Everywhere the streams flow, groups of women are busy laundering clothes, rubbing them on boulders worn smooth by generations before them. A man unselfconsciously washes himself, another wades between the rocks, looking for crayfish. But how differently people interpret such sights. For us it was always as enchanting a rural scene as a pastoral painting, but when two American tourists joined us on the bus one day, they nudged each other, pointed rudely, remarked too loudly, 'don't they have washing machines?' Oh dear.

Despite such a wonderful Christmas, together with the delights of a new and exotic environment, it was soon time to consider the future for *Imago* and her crew. The reality of our situation looked rather bleak. 5,000 miles from home, only £60 in the kitty! *Imago* looking battered. A shredded remnant, all that is left of her stern flag. She needs new cordage, deck fittings, sail repair, before she can sail another mile. We did cry, though more from frustration than despair.

Jobs are strictly for local people. Quite rightly so. We began to understand why impoverished people look at tourists and think. 'It's all right for you, but we cannot eat beauty'. After so many years of toil, those desperate times as we learned to sail, a sad ending seemed inevitable. On the eve of 1989 we brooded for most of the day and went to bed before midnight, our New Year resolution being to face up to the consequences of a shattered dream...As we awoke to the first day of a brand-new year, two remarkable events occurred, setting the scene for our future travels and making our time in Grenada a finer prospect than we could ever have imagined, other than by dreaming.

***

Imago returned to England on a low loader, to a boatyard on Canvey Island, where she would sit for several months. I hoped that she would wet her keel again, sometime in the future. I already knew, with sad certainty, that she would never again be our home.

The hospital in Montpelier arranged for an ambulance to the airport and three seats on the plane. Two for the stretcher, one for the attending Doctor. It was all so fraught that I no long remember whether I returned by train or by air. Ken would remain a patient at Oldchurch Hospital, in Romford Essex, for the next eight months. The future was a blank page.

CHAPTER 11

LIGHT AND SHADE, BOTH PAST AND PRESENT

Having set aside the local paper until we had read all our mail from home it was mid-morning on the second day of the New Year before we came across an advertisement for qualified social workers. Being the profession I had left behind when we started to build *Imago*, I was curious to know how its principles were implemented on a Caribbean island.

A couple of days later, we boarded a dollar bus for an hour-long ride to the north west of the island. Minutes later, we were talking to the director of a children's project. It was an extraordinary, inspiring, meeting. We will give him a pseudonym, for reasons of delicacy and because of his truly worthy, if ultimately misguided intentions.

Under the auspices of an international children's charity, Peter had spent the last ten years in the Caribbean, setting up similar projects to serve 'street kids.' Young boys, usually aged between six and sixteen years, who were sleeping rough, not attending school, and tempted into criminality to survive. Peter had developed no less than three such programmes on different islands. When he first arrived in Grenada, he came across six such lads who had attached themselves to an elderly priest who was living in a derelict shed. Bowed down by such a responsibility, the priest gradually became alcohol dependent.

In just twenty months, Peter had leased eight acres of land from the Catholic Church, together with some run-down buildings, established a board of governors, and raised significant international funding. At first, he worked alongside the boys, clearing jungle, re-furbishing the buildings. By the time of our visit, there was a small residential unit, a community centre in town, an allotment area, where crops and animals, cared for by the residents, generated a modest income.

Peter told us that during his time in the islands he had provided assistance for nearly 400 boys and of the original six he had 'rescued' in Grenada, all now attended school and were re-united with their families.

Incredible work! Saint-like dedication! Totally captivated by Peter's enthusiasm we asked if there was any way in which we could volunteer our help, providing the project could cover our daily bus ride! We still had rice aboard, could catch fish in the harbour and with grapefruits at four for 10p, we could survive.

A week later we were invited to lunch with the Grenadian staff and a young American volunteer from The Peace Corp organisation. We sensed an 'atmosphere', but only wondered if it was a perceived threat about their jobs or fear of infiltration by the CIA, which remains a pervading suspicion, following the invasion of 1983, especially toward foreigners who ventured this far into the hinterland. Nevertheless, it was agreed that we would join the project to complete specific short term goals. Ken would extend the buildings programme and work alongside the boys to teach practical skills. My task was to set up a course in basic social work principles as well as supervising staff training and development, in preparation for a handover of the project to an all local staff.

Before we could begin our respective tasks, Peter would need to apply for temporary work permits, before contacting the Jubilee Trust in England, which supports training and education schemes in third world countries, by funding volunteers for their travel and living expenses. We would be paid £15 a week each – just enough for food and sufficient fuel to keep our anchor light running!

Well done *Imago*! What a beautiful ship you are for getting us here. It was tempting to believe that fate had somehow required us to travel to just this place, at just this time, to each do the kind of work we most enjoyed. We had only to survive another month, but with all our bulk stores gone and only £5 left in the kitty, it would be a long one!

But our particular fate had a habit of smirking and winking at our predicaments before intervening at the last minute! That following day, we met Brian, skipper of a luxury motor yacht. A charter vessel, charging its clients £2,000 a week! He anchored *Domino* close by, eclipsing us with her opulent bulk. Being himself a London man, both he and Ken got on famously. We spent the afternoon happily exchanging yarns. Early on the following morning he rowed over to us, 'my passengers have disembarked to fly home, so we have cleared the galley of perishables, thought they might be some good to you.' Perishables there were; butter, opened jars of marmalade, fruit. But also: tins of soup, baked beans, dried pasta. By adding a few basic extras, we reckoned there was enough food to last a month! Such are the vagaries of a wandering life!

Thus began what was probably the most extraordinary of all our experiences. At 5.45am each morning, after a hurried breakfast, we rowed about 400 yards to the harbour wall, padlocked the dinghy, before walking the mile or so into town to catch the 7am bus, ready for an 8am start at the project. The day ended at 3.30pm, leaving time to enjoy peaceful evenings at anchor. Over the next four weeks, Ken renovated the first floor of the centre in readiness for the training course, while I interviewed prospective students and prepared course notes.

The first hints of a disturbing undercurrent, was the behaviour of the boys on the first day at the allotment, when three of them took turns trying to grab Ken's testicles, then wriggling their backsides at him while shouting, 'Englishman! Englishman!' Fortunately Ken handled the situation without showing either embarrassment or anger, only telling them very firmly, not to do it again because it was disrespectful and not at all amusing. Later that day, as the group sat around eating their customary lunch, pig snout in a roll, they tried once more. Ken sensed that they planned to tease him again in some way, but he could barely disguise his shock when one of them calmly unzipped his trousers and began to masturbate!

'Go off into the bush if you need to do that,' Ken told him. Clearly, they were testing him out and were now satisfied. They soon warmed to him, never exhibiting such behaviour again, becoming more interested in learning how to use tools, wanting to make model boats, even persuading Ken to teach them how to use the typewriter in the community hall.

Dismayed as we were, by these early hints of a more unhealthy undercurrent, running beneath the purportedly charitable aims of the project, we set aside our misgivings to concentrate on the tasks we'd been given.

Over the next three months we barely saw the sun. Each evening and for much of the weekend, we sat together at the saloon table, planning the tasks for the coming week. While I prepared course notes and hand-outs, Ken drew up plans for a new chicken house, a shed, a means to deter parrots from stripping the fruit trees.

The course lasted eight weeks, finishing with a 'Grenadian style' graduation day. Certificates were presented by a senior representative from the Department of Education, following an afternoon of singing, role plays and a pot luck supper. It was pleasing to have so many parents attend, especially as it was a declared policy of Peter's that the project should be isolated from the community; a subject he had refused, rather crossly, to discuss with me and one I strongly objected to since it was already clear that there was a great deal of suspicion and hostility within the local community about sexual aberration at the unit.

Matters would eventually come to a head. As incidents of inappropriate behaviour towards both staff and boys escalated, the homosexual ethos became disturbingly apparent, not only to us but to senior members of the charity. On one particularly embarrassing occasion, Peter talked about a female impersonator he had known, illustrating his story by un-buttoning his shirt, squeezing his chest to simulate cleavage, then shaking his shoulders in a sexually provocative way. Another time when a local woman was discretely feeding her baby on the premises, he became enraged, 'I want her out of here…tits hanging out everywhere!' Group nudity, teaching condom protection (using himself as the model according to the boys), taking favoured boys to stay at his house overnight. His habit of wearing skin tight shorts also fell wincingly short of cultural expectations.

How to wrestle with such a huge moral dilemma? Such a sad betrayal of an internationally respected organisation. To lift anchor and sail away was a brief temptation but would condone the situation and leave us with feelings of cowardly guilt. Confrontation might cause the whole project to implode, destroying any further potential for good and might even deter further charitable involvement on the island. It would also mean letting down the students who had engaged so enthusiastically, so willingly and were ready to develop small projects in their own community: a baby minding rota, visiting the elderly, organising activity days with youngsters. For the lads who worked with Ken, it would represent an action replay of abandonment by a father figure.

And then there was Peter himself, a hugely talented man with admirable organisation skills, but also a complex egocentric personality, deeply deluded and surrounded by a totally demoralised staff who saw the situation just as clearly as did we, but were trapped into compliance, for fear of losing their jobs.

We agonised over such implications, before finally deciding that, as a married couple, we might have a positive influence in the short term but would never leave without submitting a report about our misgivings to a senior representative of the charity.

Another deciding factor, which relied on us for its implementation was a proposal to take several of the older boys on an extended boat trip to some of the neighbouring islands. We had already taken a few of the lads on weekend 'adventure days,' anchoring in a different bay each time. Thrilling, fun-filled days for all of us. When Peter approached the yacht charter company 'Trade Winds' with the idea of an 'off island' journey, they generously offered loan of a forty-foot boat to join *Imago* on a ten day journey up the island chain as far as Martinique. There was huge excitement on Grenada about the expedition, being the first of its kind. 'T' shirts with the project logo printed on the front were donated. The lads and their families busied themselves with fundraising events to pay for the return flight from St. Lucia. Ken and I would sail back alone and take our first holiday.

This was the wind of change we were looking for. Peter wasn't slow in garnering this opportunity to present a different view of the secretive, distrusted project, but we cared not a jot. This trip would have far more impact in terms of social service than highbrow theories about repairing the consequences of maternal deprivation or the dynamics of group interaction.

Although the Windward Islands are so closely grouped together, the majority of Grenadians, excepting a few fishermen, had never left the island, even though their own neighbouring island of Carriacou lies only thirty miles to the north. A journey by boat represented a once in a lifetime adventure for these youngsters, who for various reasons had experienced the very least of life's good things. To be a part of that would be a highlight in our lives, too.

The itinerary included overnight stops at Union Island, Tobago Cays, St. Lucia, Martinique, and Dominica. During the three days of their stay in St. Lucia, the lads would spend a few hours a day working in the community, as an exchange gesture.

Dignitaries, townspeople, relatives, and journalists, lined up at the dockside to wave us off. Both skippers gathered their groups of boys for pre-sail instructions about on-board behaviour, safety rules, assigned duties, emphasising that they were ambassadors for their country. For the final word, both skippers 'borrowed' the status of Captain to make clear that, 'a Captain's word is law!'

It was a hugely successful trip. Each of the boys took a turn at the wheel, worked the winches, kept to the galley rota, promoted Ken to an Admiral, played at being pirates. Ken too was in his element, glad as I was, to be at sea again. The lads cannot yet work out why Ken never resorts to hitting them, no matter how much they tease him or sometimes deliberately try to provoke him. They were used to violence and could dance away from a threatening hand as quickly as a scuttling crab. It was something about Ken's demeanour that earned a respect that was much more subtle than just because he is a tall man.

On most of the Caribbean islands, children are expected to work incredibly hard from a tender age. Punishments are harsh. The howling screams we sometimes heard through the windows at the project, which we first thought were screeching parrots, or an injured dog, had been calmly explained by Peter, to be the beating of a child with a 'tamarind switch,' made from the supple branches of that tree.

Watching the boys crowded together in the dinghy, rowing themselves between the boats at anchor, squabbling over the fishing tackle, actually 'playing' was something very special. Each pronounced himself an 'expert' fisherman, but with so much confusion, noise, and tangled lines, no one catches anything! Except once, a garfish about a foot long, rejoiced over, cooked by culinary artists! Eventually, looking rather crisp, it was divided (very equally) into six portions, amounting to a teaspoon each.

The youngsters were allowed to venture into town in the evening, with strict instructions to be back on board by 10pm. Preparations for 'meeting girls' began at least two hours before setting out. Each took a shower, doused themselves liberally with perfumes, and combed each other's hair, before 'dressing to impress.' The saloon reeked with musky odours, forcing us into the cockpit for the rest of the evening. Not even a fly dared venture below!

After seeing the youngsters aboard their plane we thanked Brian, our co-skipper for his contribution to what had been a thoroughly rewarding time, before setting out for a leisurely sail, back to Grenada.

Sorely in need of a break, following four months of unrelenting labours, the prospect of living a quiet harbour life for a week was an appealing one. Now we had time to visit some of the other cruising boats, enjoy a few hours of 'cockpit talk,' always the best of sailor's pastimes! Not only to swap yarns but also to learn tips about the cruising life, heed warnings, and seek the best advice. Sailors are not a fraternity that seeks superiority by withholding their knowledge, and much of what we learned would serve us well, gift us the confidence to journey onwards. The very first boat we boarded offered up a golden nugget of wisdom which we cherish to this day. The woman happened to be doing her washing, in a bucket, as do the rest of us. Having long regarded Terry Cotton towels as an abomination, she introduced us to squares cut from flannel bed sheets. Not only were they far more absorbent, they also washed as easily as handkerchiefs, never getting that manky smell of old towels. Brilliant! Back on *Imago*, we disposed of those 'abominations' we had aboard, bought a flannel sheet, blessing her name thereafter. Although our towels today have the added sophistication of being children's cot sheets, we have never used anything else.

Imagine if every British hospital did the same? Every household? The water saved, less detergent, softer on the skin, more space in the linen cupboard, time saving, cheaper. What if the whole world? It could be called the 'linen revolution' – such an easy, dainty step to take, on the road that must be taken if we are to preserve our small place in the universe. Nice logo for a 'T' shirt... 'Ban the bath sheet!' Seriously.

We have a friend. His 'street name' (everybody has one), is Polar Bear. A local boatman who likes his rum! He is also loved by all. Pride of his life is his rickety, brightly painted day boat, with its tiny crooked mast, its shreds of a sail that had long since bowed to the wind. Despite his addiction to the local rum, he is proud, dignified, and content with his life. He makes a few dollars ferrying tourists and cruisers across the harbour though he is usually the last chosen. His boat is cluttered and looks doubtful, even for a fifty yard trip! But the *Seagull* engine alone is worth the risk. It must be forty years old. Sometimes it runs, in a din of vibration and belching smoke, often it won't. Either way, it matters not to Polar Bear who simply unlashes his stern paddle, grasps the tiller and swishes his boat along. A small string bean of a man, with the sinewy look of a distance runner. He picks us up every Friday with our shopping and calls us Mum and Dad. Our friend is a singer of hymns. Late in the evening we hear him, laughing with delight in the cuddy of his fourteen-foot home. We know he is laughing at himself and the world at large. It made sense.

The rest of the harbour folk also call us Mum and Dad. News travels faster over water than a garden gate. We are hailed by boats from America, Switzerland, Denmark, and Norway. All of them intrigued by word of the inter-island trip with the boys, wishing they too could help in some way but most having a schedule to keep. I think they were glad to see us demolish the myth:

that boats invariably mean wealth and leisure. Most, like us, are just about surviving.

Polar Bear was also, in his garrulous way, a teacher and a teller of tales. On his first visit with us he brought a large bunch of bright red, thick-leaved blossom called Sorrel. Boiled until the leaves become pale, the fluid then strained off, sweetened to taste, becoming a delicious healthy drink that is as vitamin rich as our own blackcurrants. Tea and coffee are expensive, as are all imports. An 8oz jar of coffee cost a staggering £8, cornflakes nearly £2 a box, but there is no need for such indulgence when oranges are 20p for six and there is the elixir of coconut milk.

Locally grown onions and carrots are popular staples, but it was the wealth of unusual (to us) tropical vegetables we wanted to try. We bought them from the market, set them out on a tray, then rowed over with them to Polar Bear who seemed nothing less than delighted to name each one and how to prepare or cook them: yam, breadfruit, callaloo, plantain, sweet potato, dasheen, small green bananas. Like all good students we would return later in the evening to offer him a plate of our culinary efforts for his approval. Occasionally, like any good teacher, he would laughingly chastise!

But however delicious the drinks and vegetables are, it is the fruit that makes living in a tropical climate such a pleasure. Grapefruit, lemons, limes, oranges, golden apples (tasting like pears), star fruit, melon, guava, mango, and bananas. All picked green, fresh, and succulent.

Land is sold by the square foot. Densely cultivated to provide sufficient for family needs leaving a small surplus to sell on. It is a frugal, labour-intensive living, especially during the dry season when even the locals wilt. The day begins at 5am when the produce is picked. The bundles, mostly carried aloft on the heads of women, are walked to the nearest tiny shop, or to a pitch by the roadside. There she will remain, often with her children beside her, until the last leaf is sold. Richer by just a few dollars, they then walk home, in time for the twilight cool, when they will cook, before working the land again until late at night.

Yet 'poverty' is not a word that belongs here. A desperate word. Later on during our travels we would see the real thing. Certainly life is basic. Outside of town the majority of homes have no electricity or internal plumbing. Water is collected from standpipes. But the land is luxurious, abundant, life-sustaining and nowhere did we see a child with the pot belly of starvation.

Nevertheless, wealthy tourists, fabulous yachts, the pervasive psychology of advertising, all have a strong impact, resulting in an almost resentful envy of Britain and America. The most able in the community, politically and intellectually, are secure enough to advocate keeping every tradition in the culture, but the people we talked with dearly covet the cars, the fashions, the gadgetry, or even a little money to spare at the end of the week, just as Britain's agricultural classes did at the turn of the century.

***

December 2003. Ken has languished in hospital for six months. He still doesn't know my name (the marks he makes with pencil and paper just scrawls), but there is recognition in his smile. Severe hip/knee contractures have developed. An electrical devise is in place to prevent them, but staff are unable to monitor it regularly. At visiting times, I find it has slipped off, or has trapped his foot. His tracheostomy prevents him calling out in pain. We spend our time squeezing each other's hands, manipulating his fingers, Indian-arm wrestling, to strengthen his arms. One hand is curled into a fist, the other splayed out. I wonder if he can see or smell the food when the trolley passes his bed. I take his wheelchair to the end of the ward, leave him there, back away from him, gesture for him to come towards me, (like dog training without the 'sit' command)! He succeeds and his smile is that of a delighted child.

It's the start of our third adventure together: building *Imago*, sailing her around the world, and now, using that same willpower and optimism, embarking on the most rewarding journey of them all.

CHAPTER 12

EXPLORING GRENADA. A BLIGHTED PAST. 'MAMA'S.'

Imago has been anchored in the lagoon, close to the harbour of St. George's for more than four months. Even the street vendors, selling straw hats, conch shells, and baskets of spices, no longer pressed us to buy.

Although the charts for the next leg of our journey lay ready on the saloon table, there was still much of Grenada to explore, as well as remaining tasks to complete at the project.

Peter announced that he would be leaving as soon as a replacement could be found. He was clearly very angry and bitter about it. The atmosphere deteriorated, leaving staff anxious about their jobs, unsupported and demoralised. Which was exactly how we were left feeling after he sacked the cook's helper, a young impressionable girl. When he found out that she was having an affair with the Peace Corp Volunteer, he dismissed her on the spot. Having been doubly seduced by the promise of going to America with him, her distress at being spurned just made Peter angry, but everyone else knew that the wrong person had been sacked. It seemed the cruel actions of a misogynist. Having spent years in the islands, he knew perfectly well how important any job was and that the loss of extra income for her family was likely to result in punishment.

Ken continued working with the boys while I supervised the students as they set about their community work, meeting with them at the end of each day to discuss their plans. Not wanting to become embroiled in matters concerning the changeover, we knew that our time in Grenada would soon end, that it was time to prepare for the next stage of our journey. But before then, we were determined to see as much of the island as possible, to complete what would always remain a richly rewarding experience.

Although above ground level, it was built like a cellar with massive blocks of stone, wedged together with pebbles and volcanic mortar. We entered through a low arched doorway. A tiny grilled window was set higher than the tallest man could look through. The last remaining slave pen measured about eighteen feet across by fourteen feet wide. It accommodated over 100 men, women, and children, who were kept there after transportation until the plantation owners came to examine them as suitable estate workers. Casualties were high.

Hundreds of bats rustled and squeaked at the intrusion. The walls oozed, wet and dank, as if still leaking out the misery. The pen stands some fifty yards from the old estate house, now crumbling into dereliction. Two elderly Grenadians peered out at us from a room on the first floor where they were living out their last days. Ex-slaves themselves, they took over the house as retainers. As their children moved out, one by one, the rooms were deserted.

We stood outside the house for a long time, conjuring up sounds and images from a blighted past, imagining the carriages, lights, parties, the slaves about their labours. The contrasts were morbidly depressing. Inside the pen, if you could bear to stay for long, the moaning from the past might overwhelm you. Just a handful of greedy, arrogant, families who left behind an ugly, shameful legacy.

Our next excursion was to the high ground in the north of the island, overlooking Grand Etang Lake. A place in which to sit and gaze. Meadows and pasture land sloped gently towards a smooth expanse of water, stretching over several acres. Tethered cattle and goats calmly grazing between palm trees. Peaceful. Still. For the first time since leaving home shores, nostalgic thoughts of England entered our minds, though the wistfulness came more from the atmosphere around us than from homesickness. Without oak trees, willows, hedgerows, and meadows grass, it could never be England.

To round off such an agreeable and thought-provoking day of exploring, we sat on the veranda of the 'Nutmeg' restaurant, overlooking the harbour. After ordering our usual fare of chicken roti, washed down with a half of local beer, we settled down to watch the 'Cabaret' performances of several, strikingly handsome, young men, who home in on unescorted female tourists or elderly couples. We came to call them, 'professional friends.' Most tourists are pleased to have a conversation with local people, being a way to learn more about a foreign destination, even a little flattered at being approached. But these young men are at work! And are very, very, good at it!

'How you be enjoying Grenada Mamma?'

'Hey, pretty lady.'

A bespectacled middle-aged woman looks up from her plate, only to be dazzled by a Hollywood vision with flirting eyes and a huge smile. She will soon order him a meal and a couple of beers. He will show her around the island if she would like. If all goes well, there could be presents for the 'lovely young man.' A well delivered hard luck story may even earn a cash gift. Despite the artifice, there was nothing to suggest coercion or intimidation. Both parties taking equal gain from such encounters.

Roti had become our favourite snack. A staple found on most of the islands. It has a similar history to that of our Cornish pasty, providing a nourishing meal for the workers on the estates. A yeasty dough rolled very thin, with fillings of chicken, beef, or fish and vegetables. A nourishing meal for less than a pound. Back on board, we rounded off a splendid day with a mug of locally grown cocoa (pared from tight round balls) and a couple of mangos.

At these latitudes, there is hardly any dusk as we know it. Once the sun has set, at about 6.30pm, darkness descends quickly. It is light again by 6am. The night time temperature falls by only five degrees, so after changing into shorts and T shirts, we spend our evening on deck, watching the town lights, the passage of freighters on the horizon, the stars, until it is 9pm and bedtime. The town comes alive and is busy again by

6am. Night-time fishing boats were already lassoing the bollards on the quay, sorting the catch into baskets. Most of the fishing vessels are day boats, open to the elements. Powered by small outboard engines, they work the outer reefs for pan fish. Larger diesel-powered boats bring in yellow fin tuna. Huge fish of sixty pounds or more, hauled inboard by hand. Off shore, commercial catches are brought in on the Carriacou Trawlers, distinctive wooden sailing craft originally constructed by Scottish craftsmen and their descendants. They were sturdy, solid looking vessels, constructed from huge planks of timber, expertly shaped by adzes and hand-made tools. A sailboat capable of weathering the roughest seas anywhere in the world. Even the inch-perfect flare of their huge bowsprits suggests a proud resilience. Each of these beautiful craft is 'personalised' in paint: greens, blues, and yellows. You could love a boat like this a lot more than a car or a horse.

It seemed to us that every man on the island is a fisherman before he is a farmer. On several of the beaches the long nets are still cast. International aid to the fishing industry may have added more sophistication to the tradition, but essentially it is unchanged. Buoyed nets are carried out beyond the surf by rowing boats and launches – some fitted with high-powered Japanese outboards. Several of the strongest young men don snorkelling masks and goggles before diving alongside the sinking nets, undoing tangles, moving obstructions, herding the fish. Although flimsy looking, the net is large enough to cover some 100 square yards of sea surface. One of the older, more experienced fishermen shouts his call. The circle is slowly closed. A dozen men and women haul rhythmically, sometimes singing. As the net drags closer to the beach, the water boils with small fish. Women and children emerge from the township to converge at the shoreline, ready with plastic buckets, large marlin hooks, and wicker creels, to begin bartering for anything from three fish to fifty, which they carry away on top of their heads. A colourful, noisy, community activity, taking place every day, all year round.

We are gradually working our way through the fruits, vegetables, and spices. Mango and grapefruit are huge and sweet. We wear our glasses when eating them or be blinded by the spurting juice. Local people wade into the sea to eat them so that they can wash the surgery liquid from face and body. Star apples, guava, avocado, golden apples, and tamarind. The variety of vegetables seems endless: callaloo (tasting like strong spinach), becomes a firm favourite, along with sweet potatoes (like boiled chestnuts). We also try cristophene, yam, breadfruit, dasheen, wild celery, plantain, fresh ginger, and ochre.

Rice is the staple food, generally mixed with dried peas which have been soaked overnight. Another family favourite is 'oil down' for which any vegetable, together with chicken or beef is cooked in coconut oil, blended spices, bananas, breadfruit, then slowly simmered until the whole becomes a nourishing stew. No part of a chicken is wasted. Backbone, neck, feet, innards, all goes into the pot to make 'back-a-neck-a-fig.' Bulk is added with dumplings. Not the fluffy, suety dumplings that are so familiar to the British, but the dense, chewy West Indian variety that are so solid they must be speared with a most determined jab of a fork before being gnawed at! Bananas are called 'figs' of which there are several varieties. Those that are familiar as a fruit, several others which are prepared and eaten as vegetables. One of these has a name we are quite taken with… bloggoes!

'You go Mama's before you leave us,' said Polar Bear. He was talking about the most famous restaurant in the Grenadines.

After warming up with a half pint of local beer, we began… three hours and eighteen dishes later, grasping the tables edges to help us rise to our feet, we slowly ambled home. A gastronomic experience! Each small dish was carefully explained by Mama herself. A statuesque, handsome woman with an aura of proud distain. She was evidently used to a variety of reactions as she intoned the main ingredients: monkey, lambi (conch meat), armadillo, beef liver, yellow fin tuna, Callaloo soup, curried goat, and sea urchin. Having given 'Mama' no cause for contempt or irritation, she eventually warmed to us (just as well, since she looked capable of tucking us under each of her arms before marching us to the door). Having earned her nod of approval and paid our bill of around £10, we winked at the green lizard that had been watching from a chair leg at the opposite table, through our meal.

With that memorable farewell to the green and fertile island of Grenada, where we had lived and worked for almost a year, it came time to sail again on a journey that would largely take shape through the people we met and talked with, rather than from any carefully planned route.

As we set about our preparations: stocking food, stowing away objects that might hurtle about in a gale, checking rigging, and patching damaged sails, it always felt like that first time. Nervous. Excited. Wondering if we could learn enough, soon enough, to compensate for our inexperience, yet already longing to be out on the ocean once more.

Leaving behind the tropical rain forests of Dominica, the volcanos and mineral springs of St. Lucia, and tranquil evenings anchored off Carriacou and Tobago Cays, we sailed south to Venezuela.

***

The nurse has given Ken sheets of paper and a pencil. Has written our names for him to copy. His efforts are an illegible scrawl, but his trying overwhelms me in some deeply maternal way. These are his first steps. He still doesn't know my name, but his smile is the one I know. Personal, intimate. I return it with the smile 'he' knows.

He cannot concentrate for long before his eyes glaze over and his mind drifts into a fugue state of lost identity. Friends have visited but are sad to be unrecognised. They think he is lost, but I have seen and felt something reconnect, and I'm certain there is more to come.

CHAPTER 13

A STRANGE, ENCHANTING PLACE. THE GREEN FLASH. ROBBED.

A day's sail brought us to the arid rock-strewn outcrops which make up the islets of Los Testigos. An important breeding area for hundreds of Frigate Birds and where, for the first time, we watched Pelicans plunging heavily into the sea for small fish. Following a successful dive, they gulp and nod their heads before puffing out their huge bill pouches to align their catch before a mighty swallow. A miss appears to embarrass them. Rigid with surprise, sitting for a while, hunched up, looking down their bills as if slightly bewildered. Graceful acrobats in flight, soaring and gliding like bulky herons.

Used exclusively by visiting fishermen, an occasional yacht, populated by only a two-man custom post, the islets are almost deserted by nightfall. As the moon rose, silhouetting the looming shapes of craggy boulders, monsters appeared. Dinosaurs, giants, vast heads, monoliths, and pillars. An eerie, ancient place. We stayed up late, gazing out on a tropical night sky, embedded with a dazzling confetti of stars, speaking together in whispers, in keeping with the mystery of the place.

The green flash is real! We have seen it with our own eyes! A wonderfully rare event. You may see it once, twice, never, or as often as a dozen times during a circumnavigation. Green flash sceptics must now be numbered with 'flat-Earthers' though both debates have raged for centuries. First mentioned in Egypt, some 4,400 years ago, little more was heard of the phenomenon until the late 19th Century. The matter was only settled by a Doctor Briscoe, who in 1978 published the first photographic evidence. This was a serious blow to those who claimed, after a hard passage, that 'sailors could be forgiven for mistaking the gin bottle for the sextant!'

Having decided to stay at anchor for a further night in such a magical setting, we just happened on those optimum conditions necessary for a sighting. Bright calm weather, a flat line horizon with not a trace of haze or cloud. Look for a setting sun that is as crisply outlined as an orange-red balloon. Concentrate your gaze for that moment when the sun finally dips below the horizon to catch the millisecond of brilliant electric green, as the last of the orange rind reflects through the top layer of the ocean. The best explanation we have found is that of refraction, most of the spectral colours being absorbed or scattered by water vapour, oxygen, and ozone, to leave the green, and such a green, to dazzle and intrigue us. (Ref: 'The green flash lives!' Yachting Monthly…1983).

After two, lazy, other-worldly days, in this tiny archipelago, *Imago* turned south. Early enough to see the sun rise, but already a working, feeding, and nesting day for the frigate birds, who bade us a screeching farewell that sounded more like 'shove off' than 'bon voyage!'

Only hours later, the tip of a skyscraper pierced the horizon. A skyscraper! Such a startling contrast: from wooden houses with corrugated iron roofs, now to a city of condominiums, hotels, fast business, and faster cars. Having adjusted to the ambling pace of the long Atlantic voyage, the small island life in Grenada, and now thrust into the frenetic bustle of a city, it was all strangely unnerving.

Although the island of Margarita is part of Venezuela, its character is altogether different from that of the mainland. A distinction arising from its wealth and Freeport status. Fast becoming an international watering hole, it has embarked on an orgy of building and tourist development. The whole population, except the fishermen, is fully engaged in catering to an economic explosion, whether it be stalls, pavement vending, or construction. The island rises from an enormous continental shelf. In these warm waters fish congregate to breed in vast numbers. The distinctive two-man fishing boats number in thousands.

With eighty bolivars to the pound, we emerged from a currency exchange bureau with a wad of banknotes too thick to fit into a wallet, 2,800 of them, (£33)! Having come here to do some serious stocking up, we spent a whole afternoon compiling a shopping list. Tinned foods, as always, were beyond our budget, but everything else proved to be cheaper than any other place in our travels. A litre bottle of spirits 80p, cigarettes 20p, and a long bus ride 10p. By far, the best value for a cruising boat was the cost of diesel. In recent months there had been much political grumbling about rising fuel costs, but there would be none at all from *Imago* or her crew, as we filled all three tanks and several Jerry Cans with 150 gallons, at the grumbling price of 11p per gallon! Five gallons of engine oil rounded the bill up nicely to £25!

For the first time on our travels, we ate meat several times a week. Good stewing steak cost just 35p a kilo, so we simply kept a stew pot going by chucking in vegetables. Clothing, shoes, and leather goods packed the shelves and draped shop doorways, the whole island a gigantic bazaar. Having spent many years resisting the temptation to buy anything other than basic food or boatbuilding materials, and despite gleefully chastising each other for outright decadence, we did of course succumb. A pair of shorts each for 80p then Ken, exceeding the bounds outrageously, bought a pair of flip-flops for 50p! Nevertheless, we were grateful for the opportunity to stock up with flour, rice, dried vegetables, tea, coffee, and a few boxes of packet-soup for our night watches.

Having already been warned by the yachting community in Grenada that dusk brought out human predators as much as it did mosquitos, we never ventured out after dark. Despite the prosperity and the cosmopolitan makeup of the population, though it could be argued as the reason, this was a violent place, especially around bars and nightclubs. Close to our anchorage, four holiday-makers were robbed at knifepoint on a crowded beach. Very sensibly, they meekly handed over their clothes and valuables, returning to their hotel in beachwear.

It was here that we met two of the most famous sailors in these parts. The first being 'Crazy Eddie' of Hurricane Hugo fame. In a far from seaworthy boat, he meanders his way through most of the Caribbean Islands year on year, east to west. Eddie was rarely sober. When Hugo struck, he was in Guadeloupe. Every boat in the harbour battened down securely, setting out extra anchors, adding more chain, while Eddie steadily consumed his three bottles a day. As the hurricane approached, marching in on dense, roiling pillars of cloud, he went on a binge. As he slept it off, his boat was hurled into the mangrove swamps. Three days later, as the devastation was being cleared, the voice of Eddie, with its southern American drawl, cut into channel 16, to say, 'Hey, I hope you are all OK out there – must have been a blow, folks… I got mangrove leaves all over me!' Yep! It was a 'blow' alright. Eddie had slept through the worst hurricane in a decade!

For Eddie it was just another piece of notoriety… having already been barred from most of the islands for barroom brawling. When he is eventually 'asked' to leave Venezuela, he will, as always, clear the harbour and set his self-steering, before going below with several bottles. Days later, he will stagger on deck to see where he has arrived. A sad, colourful remnant of a buccaneering breed. A harmless ocean vagrant, safer on water than on land. The sea would not judge him.

The second character we heard about was one of a very special breed of sailor – the single hander. His was an extraordinary story. Half way through his solo Atlantic crossing in a twenty-two foot boat having barely two feet of freeboard between waterline and deck, he 'lost it'. He may never remember the extra month spent at sea, or why his mind and memory deserted him. He couldn't recall anchoring in Grenada after two months at sea; until he came up on deck the following morning to find himself surrounded by land, his boat swinging gently to the tide. Having run out of water, fuel, and provisions, he arrived in a very poor state. It was doubtful whether he could have lasted many more days before dehydration, with its delusional consequences, took its final toll. We were working at the project when he came in, though we know that the boating community rallied round to care for him. Somehow he found the courage to sail again, but the month spent drifting on the ocean stayed locked in his mind.

Joshua Slocum's inspiring account of 'Sailing Alone Around the World' remains the definitive description of a self-reliant man who could describe his lone adventures in such an easy-going, confident way. Yet even he would experience times of overwhelming despair and mind-numbing fear. He too would shout at the wind.

A well-stocked larder brings joy to any woman, afloat or ashore, which is to say that our stop-over at Isla De Margarita served us well in that respect. But it also alerted us to the sad fact that there are many more dangers to contend with than the sea.

It was with a genuine sense of relief that we now set a course for Curacao to the west. One of the ABC islands as they are known: Aruba, Bonaire, Curacao. It was our first longish passage since the Atlantic run, but we quickly re-established our sailing routines, settling *Imago* down for night-time sailing and keeping a sharp lookout as we closed to within fifty nautical miles of land.

You can feel a bit 'peculiar' at sea. Not 'all over the place dotty' you understand, but always prey to three obsessions: sleep, food, the moon.

Adult cats, month-old babies, and the very elderly only sleep. Sailors plunge gratefully, instantly, and usually unwashed, into a coma! Having logged all the familiar sounds of a boat on the move, all that will prise you from it now is a change of note from the engine, the blunt clap of a flogging sail, or the smell of coffee at the watch change.

Food. No matter how thoughtfully you have provisioned and however many treats you may have secreted away, you will still gloat and fret over food. Imaginary menus can fill a whole afternoon with conversation. Every small detail: taste, colour, and texture. After one such debate, we concluded that there are at least a dozen ways to cook and present a pork chop!

The moon. It just feels less lonely out there when the moon is up. We found ourselves waiting on her, knowing her phases, and missing her short absences acutely. The most memorable moments during long passages will include a night in company with a full moon. Ghosting along on a twilight ocean, thinking and speaking in whispers, humbled with awe. She rises above the horizon like the light from a huge ship, so suddenly sometimes as to cause you to flinch for a moment, just as you do when it really is a cruise liner... how are you supposed to identify a green or red light on that floating Christmas tree, that festival, that carnival of

111

lights! Both moon and sun have 'character.' The sun is bold, raw, and blatantly masculine, the moon is comforting, maternal, and serenely feminine. Archetypes, though they are, humankind have long imbued the natural world in such a way.

The Caribbean Sea is sometimes the most uncomfortable passage of all for circumnavigators. Even in fair weather the sea is always 'lumpy.' Tide and wind play bagatelle between the islands, bouncing into one before swirling round the next.

Dawn on the sixth day brought us to within a couple of miles of the harbour of Willemstad, though we had seen plumes of fire from dozens of oil derricks during most of that night. We stood off, waiting for the daily exodus of fishing boats to time our approach while the famous pontoon bridge was open for them. The bridge protects the harbour from rough seas and a very fast local current. From his hut at the end of its long arm, the bridge master drives the pontoon across a 200-yard gap many times a day to service this busy commercial port.

Both derricks and oil terminals are surprisingly discrete. Sculptured figures loom over the harbour like alien guardians, an aura about them that reminded us of the stone giants gazing out from Christmas Island. In recent years, Curacao has alerted itself to the benefits of tourism and has much to offer to its visitors. The Dutch influence is unmistakable. Clean, pastel-coloured, and charming. In a fascinating blend of Caribbean and European culture, all points meet at the floating market, where boat vendors from Venezuela act as a ferry service, supplying fresh fruit and vegetables to the island. With its panoramic coastline, cosmopolitan varieties of food, and unspoiled countryside, Curacao is a welcoming, different, and hospitable destination.

We moored alongside the quay wall. Passers-by were soon chatting to us. One evening, we met Rudi, master of one of the huge tugs that tow or nudge liners and freighters into the harbour. Ken and he were soon happily engaged in 'man talk': pistons, injectors, and revolutions per minute, which inevitably led to the offer of a tour inside the bowels of his floating engine. The seventy-foot tug is Rudi's home, business, and mistress. To judge by the polished brass portholes and the completely oil-free engine room, she is a lot more besides.

Over the usual yard-arm brew (rum), he told us stories of salvage attempts in desperate conditions, bone-brittle coolness in North Sea storms, the touch and go thrust of the business, steaming at the limits of his 1400-horsepower engine, to scenes of disaster, keeping radio silence so as not alert competitors, in what is a 'no salvage - no pay' gamble against a raging sea. Military style heroics are often in vain. The crippled ship goes down or is smashed beyond claiming. Nevertheless, if the outcome is successful, the hard-earned rewards can amount to King's Ransom. It was a privilege to meet such a brave skilled seaman.

Boarded! Robbed! Roused by a commotion taking place on the dockside, I scrambled up the companionway ladder into the cockpit, only to see a melee of men shouting loudly, angrily pushing each other about. Thinking that Ken must be amongst them, I cleared the space between *Imago* and the dockside in one leap, before rushing amongst them, joining in with the shouting and pushing. One of the men held me back, but in a surprisingly gentle way. He kept pointing to a black refuse bag, as if that was the cause of the fracas. Shouts of 'Police! Thief!' were making me nervous. Ken wasn't in the group. Had he been arrested? The men had restrained a man and were marching him away. Well thank goodness English is one of the universal languages, though it took more effort on my part, to realise that the good people of Curacao had been outraged into action. One of their own had been seen to board and steal the contents of a black plastic bag from the cockpit.

'But there's only rubbish in it,' I said.

'No, no, madam. Thief. Bad man. We are sorry this happens when you visit us.'

Handing back the bag before shaking my hand, the group marched along the dockside with their citizen's arrest. We would encounter nothing quite like that example of public spirit, anywhere else in the world.

Ken had remained asleep in our bunk throughout the whole commotion! So I roused him of course, not a little irritated that I had confronted several men who might have been attacking him, dressed only in my nightie! But then again I had rolled out of the bunk in a state of fear and panic, not even noticing that he was beside me! The punishment wasn't too severe considering that I now had post-trauma shakes. I just ordered my 'Knight in less than shining armour,' to make me hot sweet tea and listen to every detail of the drama.

It was now time to decide whether or not to head south towards Panama and the Pacific Ocean before the onset of 'Northers,' (fierce and often dangerous squalls, which are at their peak in March.) In the end, we decided to head that way but delay any final decision. We were not yet confident sailors and without radar or self-steering, a journey across the Pacific might well become a foolhardy test of stubborn endurance. Decidedly not the right attitude when crossing an ocean.

The Caribbean Sea was kinder than usual, as if lulling us into a false feeling of confidence, but then when water found its way from the engine exhaust outlet into the manifold, reality overruled naïve optimism, on what had been a wavering decision all along.

Having only sufficient funds to pay the canal dues, no sure prospect of finding employment, work to do on the engine, and spares to buy… the risks weighed heavily. One usually becomes less 'derring-do' with age? Our quirky fate was also having a say in the matter, keeping its secrets yet smiling broadly as it looked into our future.

For the moment, we would stay on the Atlantic side and divert to Jamaica until we felt better prepared. As we changed tack for our new course, an American Coastguard Plane thundered over the horizon and 'buzzed' us. We assumed they were already aware of us. Our sudden change of direction supposedly made them curious about intentions. They were probably taking photographs before checking out *Imago's* description from our last port of call. Switching to channel 16, in case they called us up, we waved from the cockpit, trying to look relaxed… and guiltless! Next day it appeared again, a little higher than the masts, with a noise that made us cower down as we steered. Surveillance had been stepped up in the drug war, especially in this area of the Caribbean and had come as a great relief to yachtsmen. The area off Colombia had been a worry to cruising boats for decades: piracy, disappearances, and smuggling. We were already giving this 300 mile 'drug triangle' a wide berth of ninety miles, though like all small vessels, it still felt like running a gauntlet.

Not having harbour charts for Jamaica and now wholly reliant on sail, it was predictable that we should get into a spot of bother…which we did.

Kingston harbour is fringed by sand bars, tiny atolls, and convoluted reef systems. A scuba diving boat spotted us heading towards the shallows and sped over to warn us. By the time they reached us, a diver had surfaced within yards of our starboard side. When he stood up, the water barely reached his hips! His eyes were obscured by goggles so we couldn't see the expression on his face, but he was clearly just as agitated as we were, flinging both arms out as if to shoo us away. Three Jamaican lads leapt aboard. By whipping the mainsail through several short-angled tacks, they managed to steer us into deeper water. *Imago* grounded, very gently several times, just to let us know that this was indeed an alarmingly close encounter. As we rounded the reefs, into the main channel, several wrecks could be seen, bows or sterns rising from the depths like tombstones as grim warning.

***

'We have to start thinking about a placement for your husband.'

116

Chilling words. Placement? Did that mean a nursing home? An institution? I want Ken home with me. Teach me how to suction his tracheostomy, show me how to set up his feeding apparatus, give me advise about what is needed for incontinence management. It's different for us. He could never be a burden. We have sailed the world together, he's my Captain. I cannot leave him to dispassionate hands, however careful and competent they may be.

'We were hoping to locate a rehabilitation placement for him, Mrs Gogay, but his nursing needs are too complex.'

The task is set. We have to prove that we can manage to live together despite his severe disabilities. Visits become dedicated therapy sessions for both mind and body. Ken is mending, coming back to the world in dozens of small ways. He can identify a set of cutlery: the knife, the fork, the spoon. He can tick most of the right boxes on the charts I bring him. A Flamingo is a tree, a fish, a bird, a flower? Bacon is made of pasta, steel, pork, paper? Which is the odd one out of the following: oak, primrose, larch, Birch? But what joy it was that he knew what a 'tick' was!

CHAPTER 14

TRAPPED IN PARADISE

Travellers should never presume too much about a country, beyond their own encounters with it, since what they see is merely a glance, and what they feel is only personal to them. Every country in the world is 'characterised' in some superficial way: friendly, clean, organised, stiff upper lip, or cruel. In the case of Jamaica, we imagined her character as that of a fabulously beautiful woman, who had been spurned in such a way, as to leave her angry and vengeful. All we could hope, was that someday her lover would return, to beg forgiveness.

The island itself is large by Caribbean standards. It is also stunningly beautiful. White-coral sand, exotic vegetation, big rivers, waterfalls, and caves. Ringlets of spring water run down the sides of rocky outcrops. At the south-east end, the fabulous Blue Mountains rise up behind Kingston in a lofty range of smoothly rounded peaks, its slopes covered with low lying vegetation and scrub, as if clothed in vast folds of turquoise velvet, giving them a uniquely feminine quality when compared with the shaven, chiselled grandeur of other mountain ranges. It is here, on the slopes and in the deep valleys that exclusive coffee and high-grade marijuana are grown.

Our stay in Jamaica was an unhappy and anxious time. Had we not been a co-operating couple, we might have suffered 'cabin fever' in the weeks we were there. Afraid to venture into town. Not daring to explore such sights as would have gladdened our eyes and hearts.

It was only after we had left that we learned from other yachtsmen that very few cruising boats anchor near Port Royal, heading instead for the main tourist destination of Montego Bay, 100 miles to the NW. We only wondered how authentic it could be to stay in what is virtually a cordoned off playground.

But here we were and here we stayed, one of only three cruising boats lying at anchor, in sight of the 'Buccaneer Town' of Port Royal, once headquarters of the pirate Captain Morgan and his infamous crew, later of the British Royal Navy. The whole turbulent history of Jamaica is embodied in what was once known as 'the richest and wickedest city on Earth.' As well as the military battles between Spain and England to possess the rich spoils of Jamaica, it has also suffered several catastrophic natural disasters. 2,000 people died during the earthquake of 1692. In 1702, a fire destroyed every house and business in the port. Hurricanes in 1712, 1722, and that of Gilbert in the last decade, have devastated the area. Who can judge what such a history will make of a people?

The customs official who cleared us in was genial enough, as well he might be, since he was probably quite rich! After making out a complicated booking in receipt that included 'overtime', travel allowance for a round trip of twenty miles (we learned later that he lived just a few yards from his office), and jumped up the official rate of four Jamaican dollars to eighteen American dollars, he smilingly said, 'welcome to Jamaica, have yourself a good time.' The next vessel to book in was an immaculate, shiny, motor yacht, several times larger than *Imago*, so perhaps we should have been grateful for our rather more battered look and our rusty bits, since his fee was a whopping thirty dollars! At least our bureaucrat had the decency to warn us not to leave anything on deck. 'If the fishermen need a piece of rope,' he warned, 'they will simply cut it from your halyards.' By the following day, both outboard and tender had been stolen from the motor yacht. After that, we hauled ours aboard each evening. An unwelcome, irritating, chore.

Bus drivers operated with such gay abandon that we opted for the ferry service, a pleasant half hour journey across the harbour. The city itself is a fascinating sprawl of decaying buildings, ad hoc settlements, and old and new architecture, but there is a tense, almost palpable, New York kind of atmosphere.

Even the smallest business premises have an armed guard at the door; every frontage is grilled and padlocked. Purchases are delivered through cages or metal shutters (asking for what you want when you can't see what is being sold is frustrating. You could be asking for a tin of beans from a flower shop)! In all supermarkets there were at least two armed guards wielding what looked like pump-action shotguns and a separate counter where handbags and holdalls must be checked in first, to be re-claimed when leaving. The first time we wandered in, we were hustled and bustled a bit until it was realised that we hadn't known what to expect. Very often we seemed to be the only tourists in town... a rather vulnerable feeling. Although never openly abused, we heard plenty of muttering and hissing whispers, and I had never been more glad to be walking alongside a big man.

It probably happens to every traveller sooner or later. We strayed into a 'no-go' area in downtown Kingston. Within minutes, we were robbed! The classic heist, one that takes place in every city in the world. Ken keeps a hand on the wallet in his pocket at all times, but we were being watched and followed... in the second his hand came out to point at something, three very large women pushed him against a shop window. The crowd around them pressed in further, separating him from me. The wallet was gone in an instant, passed through several hands, before the young lad ran off with it.

Disaster! Although we still had a small amount of money aboard, we would now have to travel with minimal provisions for the next leg of our journey.

The whole of that day was a complete nightmare. While still in a dazed and frightened state at being robbed, we just wanted to escape, but had now lost our bearings. We turned the next corner, only to come across a scene that has never left our minds. A huge derelict horror-scape, where charcoal burners live and work. Gathered in squalid campsites around the fires and sleeping on wooden platforms, young children were already coughing away their lives, spitting out the smoke and soot. Hands reached out to us 'give us a dollar.' The mentally ill with nowhere else to go, pathetically naked, gazed at us in total despair, some so sick that they stripped off their rags at the edges of open manholes, washing their bodies obsessively, over and over again, while passers-by scolded or jeered at them.

We were not seasoned travellers – such sights saddened and shocked us. While no less disturbing than those one would encounter in Eritrea, Sudan, or Ethiopia, in a country where millionaires take their holidays, this was a contradiction too far.

We retreated to the boat, only venturing into town once a week to buy vegetables from the sprawling open-air market where hundreds of vendors display their goods, on benches or heaped up on ground sheets, careful to carry with us only small amounts of money, keeping it loose in each of our pockets.

Reading the local newspaper and listening to local radio stations only increased our anxiety. During the first ten days of our stay, there were twenty-six murders, and many more reports of serious assaults involving rape, beatings, and stabbings. The factors are no doubt complex, an amalgam of cultural and political history, though one that appears to account for much of the violence is an endemic use of drugs. Not necessarily of marijuana, the effects of which seemed peaceful, even jolly, but of crack cocaine and its ugly sister, heroin.

A few days before deciding to leave and not much caring about where to, we met a British pilot and his wife who were spending two days between flights on their small yacht which was permanently tied up at Port Royal under the watchful eye of a paid minder. Although they were planning an early night so that they could reach the best diving sites next morning, before the tourist boats set out, they happily accepted our invitation to join us aboard *Imago*. Later that evening, we admitted that we might have resorted to dragging them aboard, kidnapping them even! Being just so glad to have someone to talk with!

We all agreed that Jamaica has much to offer, but could be a dangerous place for the independent traveller, especially those of a 'certain age' who don't have a 'hip-hop' or 'Reggae' style. After we had re-counted our unhappy adventures, our two delightful acquaintances said they too had been robbed and now always brought their provisions with them. But the diving was spectacular enough to keep them coming back.

'What you are seeing', they told us, is the 'big man' syndrome. Every young man wants a gun or a knife, to be the leader of a gang, the wearer of the gold necklaces. Those who have lived in America return to visit, posing in smart designer clothes and shoes, riding around in expensive hired cars with an arm hanging out of the window to show of clusters of gold bracelets. They are envied, imitated, and feared. Our BA pilot shook his head sadly. 'We think they could be living in Paradise if they could only curb the corruption, but they all want to go to America.'

Such 'cockpit talk' as we were having, not only added to our sailing knowledge, but also offered up new ways of looking at the world. Even those 'forbidden' subjects, religion and politics, are allowed, though generally expressed as pondering or wondering, rather than as dogma. Far removed, as such gatherings are, from normal social situations: neighbours, family grudges, quarrels, and garden fences, conversation without gossip, was itself a new and rewarding entertainment. Having visited Jamaica for many years, our companions had a broader view of what had shaped it history.

'It's a matriarchal society. Men were separated from women during the era of slavery and in many ways remain so. The women have become very strong, minding the children, selling their produce, choosing men who will put some dollars on the table. When the woman becomes pregnant, the man will move on to 'make another baby' with a different woman. The men justify their ways with biblical quotes about 'sowing their seed,' being 'fruitful and multiplying'. A chosen woman must, above all, prove her fertility.

The pilot's wife was sad for the children. 'When the next man comes along, the other children are often resented. They may even have to live 'under the house' (rural dwellings are raised on stilts to afford protection from heavy rains, reptiles and insects.) Most will never know their fathers. While it was undoubtedly slavery that influenced this somewhat Catholic approach towards reproduction and reshaped so many old-world societies, we all felt things could change without compromising the positives that are also embedded in the culture. A time might come when the sins of the fathers no longer demand either eternal damnation or further retribution. One day it might even be acknowledged that the ending of slavery was the finest moral decision in history. One that had cost many thousands of 'other' lives.

Having so convivially failed to 'put the world to rights', we summed up our feelings by asking each other whether we would 'thump the next Italian' for what the Romans did to the British. However facetious that may sound, it made us all feel more hopeful that time might eventually dilute the legacy of anger and resentment.

Even so, for the visitor who takes sensible precautions and can afford guided tours, Jamaica has an abundance of natural treasures. A mile-long tunnel of huge bamboo, tall enough to create a canopy overhead, mineral springs, caves. Peer over the edge of Lovers Leap, a sheer drop of 1600ft from cliff top to sea, said to have been names after a suicide pact between slave lovers forbidden to be together. Dunn's River Falls, a beautifully stepped waterfall that cascades right down to the beach. A five-hour train ride from one end of the island to the other. For the romantic, an eight-mile glide down the Rio Grande on a hand built raft is guaranteed to prolong the mood.

And so passed an evening that would change our lives and salvage our dreams. After briefly recounting the years spent building *Imago*, our time in Grenada, and our current indecision about whether to continue or not, our pilot friend suggested that with Ken's practical skills and my social work experience, we might find employment in the Cayman Islands. Although grateful for his suggestion at the time, we couldn't know that we would be heading for a place that we would come to regard as our second home.

We left at dawn. Looking back, we could see the green and orange smog layer that rises, California style, above the town. We have very little in the way of stores or funds, but were simply glad to have escaped with our lives. There could be no denying that we were on an adventure, if that meant not knowing what may happen next.

And so it was, that we plotted a course for the Cayman Islands. Tiny specks on a map of the world lying just ninety miles south of the continental-sized island that is Cuba.

***

I'm nervous. Everyone present at the meeting today has the power to decide Ken's future. I'm trying to appear calm, composed and above all…competent.

'You do understand, Mrs Gogay, that your husband will require fully dependent care?'

'I do, yes,' I reply. Feeling that I'm in a courtroom, answering a question under oath that I don't fully understand.

Social workers, occupational therapists, representatives from a care agency, and Ken's hospital consultant were presiding. They each discuss their roles in what would be a complicated care package. Two carers at each visit, a hospital bed with an air flow mattress, a mechanical hoist, liquid feed machine, suctioning equipment, incontinence pads and wipes, urine bags, sheaths, wheelchair, and shower chair. They will also have to approve the accommodation at the sheltered housing complex where I am now living. These are the people I shall rely on. I know I cannot do it alone. I listened with admiration as each discipline discussed the part they might play in constructing a workable plan, and I'm beginning to hope and believe that they will re-unite us. It was as if a dreadful storm was abating, the sea calming enough to put us back on course.

Ken is present at the meeting, slumped in a wheelchair, his limp body supported with pillows, wearing a hospital gown, a blanket wrapped around him. I wonder if he minds the way he is being described. I wondered too whether it was the smiles we exchanged that swayed those present to give us our chance.

I was harbouring small secrets. Ken had written a note to say he loved me. A week before the meeting, he had recalled his signature, scrawling it several times on his writing pad. It was hard to contain the joy of it... he's slowly coming back.

'I think Ken will be in safe hands,' said the consultant. I cried.

CHAPTER 15

TO SEEK BUT NOT TO FIND

'What's it like out there? Where was your favourite place?' These are the two questions most often asked of ocean sailors, each of which are surprisingly difficult to respond to, especially when they are posed by strangers, who know nothing of our likes or dislikes or that so much of what we experienced was new, immediate, difficult to define, and impossible to explain, even to ourselves.

The answers are deeply personal, shaped and coloured by the people we met, the sights, and the creatures, but mostly by the weeks we spent at sea, where matters of choice and definition become irrelevant. In every sailing account we have read, it is that sense of awe and insignificance which stays in the mind as an indelible, calming, reflection. A lasting gift, an emotional placebo that will come to mind whenever there is need of solace. A state of un-being, a meditation. We can only join with those others in saying that there is 'something out there,' needing neither tribute nor ritual to make its presence known. Offering up a different truth that is unknowable and therefore unnameable.

'What's it like out there?' We know the meaning behind 'that' question! Tell us how bad it can get: the strongest winds, the highest waves... a near-death experience too if you can manage it! So we tell about the hairy scary bits while believing for ourselves that they are the least significant, most quickly forgotten part of what being at sea is all about.

As to the question of a 'favourite place?' Again no ready answer comes to mind. Is there really somewhere on the map of the world at which to point a finger, declare it to be the finest place on Earth? To do so is impertinent. Is it a place for which to forsake your own country? Are its people so different from all others? Does the beauty transcend that of the Scottish highlands, the fens, estuaries, dales, farmlands, the suburban blossom trees that joyfully herald every British Spring? If only to us then, the ocean itself was that special place.

Some questions have a more sceptic tone: 'Why did you do it? What were you looking for? What were you escaping from?' To answer 'nothing' was the only available word we had that didn't sound too fanciful, as it surely would if trying to describe a relationship that sympathetic others find in rocks, trees, on the summit of a mountain, or with the universe itself. As to questions of courage and determination, *Imago* herself had already tested our endurance during the seven years building her. Indeed she took us to high waves of euphoria and the low troughs of despair even before those we would encounter at sea. Perhaps like all adventurers, we were simply restless spirits who needed to experience the strange magnificence of being alive, on a planet that is revolving around a star. Still, we try to answer, but trip and stumble over words that are better left to the vision of poets.

But there was a land to cherish. Even after twenty years, we think of it as our second home. Had we sailed from Jamaica into gale force winds and heaving seas, we might well have lost our resolve to continue sailing. To fear both sea and land would surely overwhelm us. But it was a fair wind on a calm sea that carried us to the Cayman Islands. *Imago* herself seemed intent on restoring our confidence. She glided along like a damsel fly resting on the surface of the water, perfectly balanced, wings aloft.

'I'll wait for you,' she appeared to say and so she did, for two whole years.

Grand Cayman. Beverley Hills of the Caribbean. An exclusive holiday destination, tax haven, off-shore banking capital, offering some of the most spectacular diving sites in the world. Such wealth, acquired so recently, might have overwhelmed the character and traditions of these small islands, but they have managed to remain Caymanian first, while playing generous host towards its rich expatriates and tourists. An enviable collaboration in a world where rabbits from different burrows rarely play together!

The architecture is a fascinating mix. Many of the private homes are large as hospitals, some glitzy and tasteless, others sumptuous but stylish. A few are embarrassingly ostentatious. Most of the condominiums were built to satisfy the American market as well as for mega-rich investment bankers. The buyer walks into a tastefully furnished, air-conditioned, marble-tiled, fully draped apartment, with pool and sometimes a tennis court an essential part of the complex.

After booking in at the customs quay, we were advised to anchor in North Sound if we planned to live aboard for the duration of our three month visa. This was very helpful advice, since fierce 'Northers' are a regular weather feature during the winter months and no vessel could hold in surfing waves that explode against the harbour walls before rising twenty feet into the air to drop fish, coral, and driftwood onto the harbour road. As soon as these quickly moving weather systems are forecast, all vessels, large or small, relocate to the alternative anchorage at South Sound. But it was always a hasty exodus, so if we did find employment, we might get caught out. It is this shallow expanse of North Sound that gives Grand Cayman its jigsaw piece shape. The rugged, iron-shore reef that surrounds it serves to protect this pancake-flat island from the scouring effect of Caribbean storms as well as providing a habitat that makes it one of the premier diving sites in the world. The only escarpment is a sixty-foot hill at the east end of the island, just a bulge, no more an obstacle than a speed bump.

Having always determined to earn the means to travel with *Imago*, remain independent, and open ourselves fully to the vicissitudes that are the stuff of all adventures, we accepted that we might have to survive on rice, fish, and pulses, but to maintain our vessel, possibly for many years and thousands of miles looked light years less than feasible.

Truth is, we never set out with a plan other than to build a boat together that was sound enough to sail the oceans with two complete novices aboard. Sailing around the world was not a challenge we set ourselves in a way that has been described by the fastest, the soloists, the oldest, the youngest, and the record setters. An official circumnavigation is a somewhat bureaucratic affair, what with meridians, precise log keeping, passport stamps and whatever else is required for ratification. Hats, shoes, and socks off to those dedicated trail-blazers who make the improbable possible: sailors of the Southern Ocean, climbers of mountains, explorers, astronauts, and the many others who were never seen again. To pursue a goal with such brave determination, to overcome the tension, the teeth-grinding frustrations, is an awesome strange endeavour that has both enriched and emboldened the human race since that time when men first stretched animal skins over wooden frames or hollowed out a tree.

We rested at anchor, relished the feeling of safety, stillness, but were nevertheless deeply troubled. *Imago's* equipment was too basic. The Atlantic crossing had alerted us to the possibility of shredded sails and equipment failure. Even the lack of a frame to secure saucepans on the hob was risking serious injury as well as making cooking an ordeal. If *Imago* encountered 50knt winds, we carried neither a drogue nor heavy rope to trail off the stern. No radar, life raft, no emergency beacon except a few RNL1 flares (years out of date) and a limited supply of charts. Not being a sponsored boat, we could never reply on spares being shipped out to us. Surely it would count as foolhardy to continue. Yet now that we had truly set out, we dearly wanted to travel onwards. Our time in Cayman would decide the issue once and for all.

'Anyone aboard'? A gruff shout from the shoreline. A man on his own waving to us. He wore baggy shorts, scout length socks, a short-sleeved Hawaiian shirt, and flip-flops. Clearly not a Caymanian as they are very particular about their appearance. Since he looked so much like every other cruising sailor we had met, we quickly rowed over to him. A good yarn to two would surely lift our spirits.

Our tender at that time was six-foot fibreglass dinghy. The man wasn't particularly tall, but he had a chunky build so Ken decided to row him out to *Imago* first and then come back for me. Dropping someone in the drink on first meeting them isn't the way to make friends. Fortunately our visitor didn't appear to notice that the dinghy was bouncing along with less than two inches of freeboard!

His name was Garth. A Canadian bear of man. Stocky, hirsute, hearty, with a sixty-a-day growl of a voice and a pronounced swagger that failed to disguise for one moment that he also possessed a bear-sized heart.

'Was told you built this boat.'

'But we've only been here a few days,' said Ken.

'This is an island!'

Two hours and many yarns later, Ken returned Garth to shore, after arranging to meet him at his aluminium fabricating and glazing workshop next morning. While waiting for a work permit to be processed, Garth would allow Ken to use the firm's tools and machinery for any work needed on the boat, including fabricating a spare anchor. It would also serve as a probationary period for Garth to assess Ken's skills. This left me feeling very confident indeed that all would be well.

'I've been offered a difficult commission,' Garth had said. 'Two massive pyramids to sit atop the newest, most prestigious condominium on Cayman.

'They're only decorative pieces really but I've cost them at 85,000 U.S. dollars,' (£50,000)! That sounded like a colossal sum for 'decorative pieces' but was put into perspective when we learned that each apartment would sell at 1,250.00 dollars!

'Did Garth mention wages?'

'I didn't ask,' replied Ken.

It was exhausting to have such good news. I went to bed early, leaving Ken at the saloon table… drawing pyramids! Drifting off, I imagined the pleasure he would take in working out the angles and fixings for those huge, one-ton edifices. He would be so proud to leave such a substantial example of his skills on the island of Grand Cayman.

***

Preparations for the nursing/caring environment had taken several weeks to organise. I am already aware of and grateful, for how carefully and skilfully those various professional bodies had co-operated to enable us to be together. I had never been so proud of the British ethic with regard to the disadvantaged and of the NHS and always will be.

Today is the 1st of March 2004. An auspicious day. The first twenty-four hours of whatever time we may have together. The hospital bed stands ready, with its inflatable air mattress onto which Ken will be stretchered. The containers of liquid feed, the delivery pump, ready at the bedside, surgical gloves, suction tubes, incontinence supplies, mechanical hoist with its sling, tracheostomy equipment, swabs, wipes, skin cream, disinfectant, and syringes to deliver a measured intake of water directly into his abdominal tube. My bed is angled so that I can see his face and body.

Pinned to the walls is a list of contact numbers for all the supplies and advice we shall need, together with recording charts to monitor fluid intake/output, overnight feeding, suctioning frequency, and bowel movements.

Out flat is sparsely furnished. Charity shops and the Salvation Army have provided the essentials, most importantly a long narrow table on which to accommodate all the nursing paraphernalia. The lounge has become a nursing room. What should have been the bedroom is my small den come sitting room.

All our portable belongings have been collected from *Imago*: favourite pictures from the saloon, mementos of our travels, her bronze commissioning log engraved with Ken's name as owner and builder.

I cannot tell him yet that she is up for sale. It was a decision that sat too close to being both right and wrong. We never thought for a moment that she would cease to be our home, but leaving her to languish, continuing to pay yard fees while she rusted away among other derelict, forgotten boats was unthinkable. She must go to sea again, live again, just as we would try to do. Just before Ken was discharged from hospital, I put up our favourite photograph, where he could see it from his bed… *Imago* sailing under Tower Bridge those seventeen years ago.

How long will we have? Weeks? Months? Years?

Waiting for the ambulance, I could feel a familiar low level tension seeping into my shoulders and my chest. That same momentary self-doubt, every time we lifted anchor. We had always felt sea-sick when setting out though never at sea. Exhilaration, uncertainty, and expectation…the ingredients of fear.

CHAPTER 16

'What a difference a day makes.'

Esther Phillips – 1975

What a glorious feeling it was, to wake up this morning in a more hopeful, energetic, frame of mind. Our journey so far, had been one of unrelenting anxiety and way too much drama.

At 8am we met with Garth at his workshop, to agree together on the costing of material to fabricate a fisherman's anchor. Although we had a CQR aboard and a smaller anchor in reserve as a kedge, most of the workboats in the Caribbean still used this most basic design. A good enough recommendation. It would prove to be highly versatile anchor, easy to set and retrieve.

Garth looked up at me. 'Are you looking for work as well?'

'Here? Yes, it would be wonderful if Ken and I could work together again.'

Garth chuckled. 'I don't think we will get a permit for a lady welder in Cayman, but after what you did in Grenada, you might want to talk with Olive Miller. She runs most of the voluntary organisations here. She might have something for you.'

At the end of the day, Garth invited us back to his flat for a meal. His wife, Rebecca, was gracious about having unexpected guests, but Garth's handsome black Labrador appeared less than bouncingly happy to have his evening routine disturbed. He ignored us, sitting adoringly at Garth's feet, waiting for him, and only him, to fill his dinner bowl.

We shared a simple elegant meal of conch fritters, salad, and crisp, warm bread. Being an abundant harvest from the warm waters of the Caribbean, Conch has long been a staple food which local people prepare in a variety of traditional ways: stewed, marinated, as a thick chowder soup, and ground like mincemeat to make burgers. Its briny taste reminded us of cockles and winkles.

The shells themselves are big as bowler hats, each having a uniquely patterned pearlescent opening, painted in the colours of tropical dawn and sunset, some pastel, others vivid: pink, copper, orange, and violet. Garth described how a hole is chipped into the apex of the shell, exposing the main ligament, which is then severed to release the mollusc from its shell. Best not to think of it in a raw state, looking like a lump of wet offal and trailing its 'innards'! The same goes for octopus, squid, and whole pig heads. A few months later, having immersed ourselves in such Caribbean delicacies, we realised that such squeamishness was merely a cultural bias. A really 'oops! Silly us, typical tourist. A haggis, kidney, liver, tripe, black pudding, and jellied eels, moment!

We were grateful for Garth's advice about cooking conch. To simply chuck it into a frying pan would make it tough as a strip of Perspex.

'We'll cook you turtle meat next time.'

They both grinned at our questioning frowns. 'Don't worry, they come from the Turtle Farm where they are bred for release and local consumption. It's a conservation project.'

The flat was spacious. Air conditioning hummed in the background. We wondered if they could adjust to a cramped saloon and stifling heat, even as we invited them to eat with us on board.

'We have only two guest meals.' I warned them, 'spag bol or home-made curry.'

Just before winding up a thoroughly enjoyable evening, I said something that would have made my mother wince. Having noticed that Rebecca was about my size and height, and wondering how on Earth I could present myself for an interview, I took her to one side to ask if I could borrow a skirt and top for my meeting with Mrs Miller!

Although it had been important to look respectable in Grenada, I had passed most of the clothes I possessed then, to one of the women at the project. Nothing redundant has a place on a boat.

'We have to be careful about weight on board,' I explained. 'We only carry shorts, cut offs, T shirts, two pairs of flip-flops and a pair of slacks each to show respect when we go ashore. It's need over want every time.'

A brief rummage in her room-sized wardrobe (ranging from gowns to sophisticated casuals) produced two pretty blouses, a linen jacket and a calf length skirt. I would look smarter than I had in the last ten years!

'Did you know that Olive Miller has an MBE and is a magistrate?' said Rebecca.

'That makes her sound rather formidable.' I smiled. 'I'm really glad I found the nerve to ask for your help.'

I would remember that remark, even as Olive and I talked. Formidable? If that means astute, direct, no nonsense, she certainly was, in a 'what you see is what you get' sense. Yet she possessed a deeply caring, compassionate dedication to her work and an extraordinary list of achievements. A truly remarkable woman. As worthy a candidate for Dame-hood as we would ever encounter. Formidable indeed!

Diminutive in stature, she was a grey-haired, bosomy lady in her late sixties who was married to a Caymanian and was deeply religious. She lived according to her beliefs and had a voice and sense of humour so 'Essex' that to my ears it sounded Cockney. She was Secretary of the National Council of Voluntary Organisations and manager of the Pines Retirement Home where we now sat, sharing tea and biscuits in her office. Her history was that of a brave, committed, visionary woman, with the energy of a combustion engine and a blatant disregard for anything 'airy fairy' or impractical. 'Just get in there and do it' was her style. Unescorted, she embarked on a ship from England to Jamaica at the tender age of twenty-four. A few months later, she was directed by her mission to move to Grand Cayman, taking on a post as full-time youth worker. During her forty-four years on the island, Olive and had helped establish the High School, introduced pre-schools, raised sufficient funding to build and staff a retirement/ nursing home, set up an all-female fundraising group and its young people equivalent called 'Candy Stripers.' Still the list goes on: a boys and girls brigade, initiating three of the biggest fundraising events in Cayman: 'ValenPines Ball' (in support of the 'Pines' retirement home,) an annual garden party held at the British Governor's House. A 'Radiothon' broadcast by the local radio station.

I listened in awe. If I could assist such a woman in any way whatsoever it would be a privilege.

'The only position we have at the moment is for an activities director.'

'I'm not sure that would be appropriate for an ex-pat, Mrs Miller. In the UK it's about bingo, fish and chip suppers, and sing-alongs. I really don't know enough about Caribbean Culture for me to be useful in that way.'

Olive looked at me for a long moment, holding my gaze with her bright, compassionate eyes. 'That's an honest answer,' she muttered to herself. 'Perhaps something else will come up for you. But if your husband is going to work here, perhaps you'd like to join the 'Pink Ladies' a volunteer.'

Pink Ladies? I didn't like the name, and still don't. But this was a small island to explore, after which I would be idling about on the boat while Ken laboured. So, with sinking heart, notions of the 'Women's Institute, Mothers Union, baking, jam-making, knitting and sewing, I heard a synthetic two-faced voice saying, 'I'd love to Olive!'

So I donned a pink tabard and was sent to work serving lunches in the hospital cafeteria, preparing sandwiches for fundraising events, and was warmly welcomed into an energetic group of fantastic, capable, and fun-loving women who never once insisted that I bake a cake, thus leaving me with an unblemished record, as far as Victoria sponges and scones are concerned!

A few weeks later, Olive came into the cafeteria to tell me that she had applied for a work permit for me to manage the retirement home and to re-establish a telephone counselling service that had lapsed when its last team leader left the island.

That same evening I broke the news to Ken.

'If I take this on, I must offer to stay for at least two years. It's not something to dip into for a few self – serving months, just to earn some money. It wouldn't be fair to Olive or the residents.' I waited anxiously for his response.

'This is something you'd really like to do isn't it?'

There was passion in my voice. 'I think you know the answer to that, Ken.'

'Well, we're travellers now, Pat, we can go wherever we want, stay as long as we want. This is the chance we didn't have before setting off. If all goes well, it will mean easier sailing, with better equipment when we do move on.'

Having imagined a longer, more serious debate, with my impetuous skipper, I realised, as clearly as he, that we had indeed run very close to the wind since leaving England and that unless we grasped this opportunity, if only to set up a 'shipwreck fund', our Odyssey would become a torment. We needed a lot more than just a fisherman's anchor! Even a forgiving sea might eventually lose patience with us.

While waiting for the tragi-comedy that would mark my first day as manager of the retirement home, I borrowed a bicycle to explore the island from end to end. It would offer up such enchantments, such vivid delights that now, today, I still visualise them. Contorted bleached-white driftwood, where mangrove roots had failed in their struggle to prise a way through the iron shore rock, sighs and hissing from blow holes in the reef, as seawater builds up pressure before belching out high plumes of agitated spume. Humming birds, tarpon thrashing in the shallows, even sunlight flickering through mangrove leaves as they trembled in the breeze was a joyful thing to see. Heading out early one morning to explore the small reserve called the 'mastic trail,' a rarely seen Blue Iguana meandered across the road in front of me. As I slowly, carefully, applied the brakes, it paused for a moment. Turning its head towards me, a tiny dinosaur, it fixed one eye to mine with a look of utter contempt, before continuing its slow amble. Deliberately slower. I was certain about it, though whether arrogantly or primly is difficult to swear by. We would relish such encounters. Even in England we were stilled if a squirrel stopped to look at us!

A small trail led into the bush. Screened from any sound that didn't belong there, I entered an eerie, 'Triffid' world of dense foliage. Twilight. Forbidding. Mysterious. The big trees, especially mahogany, were long gone, together with the thousands of turtles, once so numerous that sailors called Grand Cayman 'turtle island' claiming that they could walk to shore from their anchored ships by walking over their shells. Each were plundered for more than a century by passing ships and pirate vessels to provide wood for mast and spar repairs, a living supply of meat. If, as rumour had it, Blackbeard's Treasure was buried somewhere on the island, this place of limestone boulders, caves, and impenetrable hollows would be the ideal location.

But there were more available treasures. Bundles of moss, hanging from branches, palettes of green and yellow lichen on trunks and rocks, huge bromeliads and ferns. In one of the caves, a snake raised its head as I entered. It was home-sharing with a hermit crab that was as large as a saucepan. The crab quickly withdrew it claws, becoming just a shell, lying empty as if carelessly thrown: a tactic that probably accounted for its size and venerable age.

I felt like an intruder. I was. An iguana, a snake, and a hermit crab had told me so! The call went out. Elite troops alerted. Which was when the attack began! Insect repellent appeared to be more a provocation than deterrent, or else the sustained action that followed was carried out by commandos.

This wasn't just the irritating sound of a mosquito pestering close to your ear, but a horde of hundreds, nay thousands, a descending cloud, a high-pitched clamouring for blood! Much of the interior of Cayman is swampland. In the rainy season, frogs, mosquitos, and land crabs celebrate their own carnival. 'Fogging vans' patrol the tourist venues every evening to spray a mist of diesel and water into the air and onto the surface of the swamps. The elderly residents of the retirement home told of children walking to school holding tin cans of burning coals between twigs, wafting the smoke over their faces. Cattle were sometimes smothered to death as mosquitos filled their nostrils.

A few months later, having settled into our respective jobs, we could afford some of the more expensive attractions on the island. 'Sting Ray City' is a 'must see' destination. A shallow sand bar lying close to the outer reef, where these wonderful creatures, large as dustbin lids, gather to be hand-fed strips of squid. They have become habituated to this daily feeding bonanza, gliding between the legs of squealing tourists, allowing themselves to be lifted out of the water by local tour operators. To touch such beautiful animals, to feel the surprisingly small puckered mouth gently suck a piece of squid from your fingers is thrilling.

We would visit 'Hell', the Turtle Farm, museum, Seven Mile Beach, Smith's Cove, Cayman Kai, and the rocky coves and secret beaches of East End, but would wait to share them with friends who had promised to visit us. We know of few destinations that offer such a satisfying range of holiday pursuits: lazy days on the beach, high-class hotels, sophisticated nightlife, the thrill of water sports, helicopter rides, a submarine descent, and diving or snorkelling in a Disney World of coral and fishes.

***

Moments before opening my eyes on that first morning, I was aware of him. Even as the vagueness of sleep focused into wakefulness, I knew he was lying in his bed, here in this room. Some aura or presence, quite different from the emptiness of grief now charged the room with a stronger pulse and altered the atmosphere, filling the space with its proper density.

With a tracheostomy in place since his life-threatening stroke ten months before, Ken would not speak again for a further six months. We must rely on this 'psychic' awareness, together with those non-verbal expressions of gesture and touching that all living creatures possess.

Dogs, elephants, whales, and dolphins too, they say, employ these subtle yet eloquent ways of communication. A dog with sad eyes sits at the master's grave, a mother knows the moment when she should raise up her wide-eyed child, elephants grieve over the bones of their relatives, whales stay with the ailing, monkeys clasp their dead infant, antenna touch, bee to bee. Even a blue iguana can deliver a telling rebuke!

Science has yet to fully understand these pre-cursors of language, though anyone who has shared their life with an animal is in no doubt that each has a personality beyond what training or habit can account for. Ken and I would include mice and caterpillars too!

For hours at a time, we had sat in companionable silence in the cockpit of our small boat, sometimes in calm seas, too often rigid with anxiety. During night watches, alone at the wheel, we each felt the comforting presence of our sleeping partner. Without that invisible aura, we would be denied the unmoving oblivion of 'sailor's sleep'.

Two agency carers arrived at 7.30am to give Ken a bed wash, cream his legs and feet, before laying in a slide-sheet to roll him on his side with a foam block between his knees. I'd already shaved and creamed his face, removed his night sheath, emptied the urine bag, logged its colour, clarity, and volume. As the carers worked, I dismantled the feeding apparatus before syringing 200ml of water into the peg tube hanging from his abdomen.

Twice during the night, when Ken's breathing sounded laboured as mucus bubbled in his chest, I suctioned it out from the hole in his throat using a long flexible tube, watching as it collected in the containers of the electric pump. Throughout the procedure, Ken gazed up at me with relief and satisfaction, like a suckling baby.

I knew I must look and move with confidence, but until it all became part of the rhythm of our days and nights, a low-level panic hammered in my chest as I followed the instructions from the hospital staff. The warnings too…only insert the tube until you get a cough reflex… if you feel resistance, you may damage his trachea. Call us if you see any blood…I prayed I would never see blood.

'Use it or lose it. Nature abhors redundancy.' Months in hospital had changed Ken from a tall, fit, properly weighted man into a thin weak, helpless one. Those strong legs that for so many years had braced him firmly in pounding, wallowing seas, were now as thin at the thighs as they were at the ankles. I tended to them in an abstract way, not really looking at them…as if they didn't really belong to him at all.

Without physical and mental exercises, any potential for improvement is doomed. Joints dry out, muscles that relax and contract help blood to circulate. The smallest of new achievements made a huge impact on us both. Later that morning, I wrapped the loop of an elasticated strap around each wrist so that he could pull it towards him. Then around his ankles to do the same. 'Well done you!' I told him. But then I had to leave the room, cry a bit. The strap had barely tensioned.

I didn't ask until the week before his discharge. It seemed such a pointless question at the time, but people do always ask, even when a loved one is on life-support following terminally catastrophic injuries.

'Will he come round?'

'Will he get better?'

So I asked, 'Will he walk again?'

The answer was delivered kindly. It could have been that blank hopeless statement, 'He'll never walk again.' Instead the nurse included a word that lodged in my mind.

'I'm sorry, Mrs Gogay, it's very unlikely indeed.'

'Unlikely' wasn't quite the same as 'impossible.' Was it?

CHAPTER 17

A TREASURED ISLAND

Any frog-like depiction will serve. Quirky ones, photographs, caricatures, children's toys. Twice a year for twenty years, at Christmas and on her Birthday, I have sent Olive Miller a greetings card featuring frogs of the world. A dense collage of them, packed together, staring out at her accusingly. As well as the usual affectionate greeting I include the last line of a well-known hymn.

'All things bright and beautiful, the Lord God made them all.'

Although Ken and I share a passion for the natural world, that embraces snakes, rodents, hippos, and warthogs just as much as the 'cuddlies', we are not obsessed with frogs. Nor by pigs or penguins for that matter. But they will always serve as a fond and amusing reminder of my first working day at the retirement home.

The door to the office stood wide open. I could see Olive sweeping the floor with dustpan and brush, stamping her feet, muttering as she swept.

'Nasty little things!

Not at all what one might expect of an MBE. JP! At first I thought she was sweeping up cockroaches, which isn't such an unusual chore in the tropics. But jumping cockroaches? Moreover, cockroaches do not squelch underfoot, they crunch. Squatting onto my haunches I picked one up that had been stamped on. It was like trying to prise chewing gum from a pavement. Transferring the goo into my palm, I found myself staring in horror at a once perfectly formed, newly emerged frog, now looking like a viscous lump of spit!

'Olive! They're frogs!'

'Yes, I know that,' she said crossly as she continued to stamp and sweep. Small as the buttons on a man shirt, some still with vestigial tadpole tails, they continued to jump about frantically, some landing on Olive's shoes, only to die in a different way. Vibrated into a coma first, before suffering a fatal concussion against walls and chair legs when she shook them from her feet. All I could do was pick up survivors between thumb and forefinger, rush out through the door and place them on the grass outside. It was a tragi-comedy worthy of a Monty Python sketch! But if nothing else, it was early evidence that we would work well together: she trampling, me saving with equal flowing energy! I love reminding her and she has long since joined in with the absurdity of it all.

For the first few days, Olive continued with her administration of the 'Pines', allowing me time to read her carefully detailed handover notes and to introduce myself to an all Jamaican staff, residents, and the qualified nurse-in-charge. Olive then left me to it, re-locating herself at the NCVO offices in town in order to concentrate on her other myriad projects. It was just as well that I didn't see a job description beforehand, I might have baulked at such an unfamiliar range of responsibilities: old-fashioned ledger accounting, public relations, secretary to the board of governors, keeping minutes, recording history, fund raising, and paying salaries. Duties which kept me busy from 7am till 4.30pm.

The home itself could serve as a model for care of the elderly. The main entrance led from a vestibule directly into the main lounge, so that rather than being hidden away, residents could watch the coming and goings of staff, tradesmen, and relatives. Each had their own room in which they could keep furniture and pictures from their homes. My very first impression was the absence of odour that is often associated with the elderly, such as stale urine or lack of personal cleanliness. Everyone was dressed nicely, buttons and zips done up properly, hair combed, and men shaved every day. All the considerate ways that serve to maintain dignity and self-regard.

Caymanians were accustomed to looking after their own aged parents, but when the main island became an offshore banking hub and premier tourist destination, the quickened tempo of daily life catapulted Grand Cayman into the so called 'developed' world. In the process, it was not only the hammock that became an endangered species but also the bedrock of deeply held religious values. In this sort of context one has to wonder what it is in the first world that has 'developed'.

Relatives would visit regularly, but seemed reluctant to engage with staff. When I spoke with Olive, she explained that the discomfort came from feelings of guilt and that it would take time to change the public image of The Pines as a 'dumping ground.' Having always believed that demonstration is more persuasive than preaching and that changing opinions is best done in small increments, I asked staff to engage when they could and note any concerns. We could prolong some of the more furtive, overly brief visits, by offering hospitality by way of a drink and a biscuit. I wanted the community to know that their loved ones were being cared for in a wonderful home and that they should be glad of it. If care of the elderly is poor or impatient, the proof is in their eyes, their posture, as it is with all impoverished, dispossessed people. Shoulders bowed with misery, eyes glazed and distant.

During the time it took to process my work permit, Ken had completed the pyramids, which having been craned into position now graced Cayman's newest building, overlooking Seven Mile Beach. The aluminium structures reflected the bright sun like welcoming beacons to every passing ship. Both they and the cruising yacht *Imago* were striking statements of Ken's skills.

Working with the elderly was so different from what I had been used to. I had found my niche in the UK when engaging with families and adolescents. Perhaps I had picked up some negativity from College days. Very few students had opted for geriatric care, preferring to work with sad young people than sad old people. But I loved every minute of those two years. It was fascinating, sobering even, to learn about the Grand Cayman of yesteryear. Small wooden houses, always with a porch. Hammocks set between palm trees and still used indoors by those who had spent their working lives at sea. Rope making, thatch palm roofing, woven hats, open air 'caboose' style cooking, horse riding to school and into town, weekend fights in George Town between North Side lads and East End lads, most of whom would eventually go to sea to earn their living. Meanwhile, back on the islands, the waiting women, bereaved women, and total war with mosquitos.

Cargo boats were mostly schooners back then. There are said to be a thousand wrecks between Jamaica and Grand Cayman, most of them lying crushed and broken in the five-mile deeps. The wreck of the ten sails figures large in Cayman folklore, remnants of masts and spars still visible on the reef. They say it was a bleak, stormy, moonless night. The lead boat in the fleet signalled a warning to run back out to sea or be blown onto the outer reef. Each of the following vessels appeared to misread the signal, as meaning 'all clear ahead.' One after another, the ships foundered and they, together with all hands, were lost. It was Cayman's 'Titanic' affecting not only the main island but also the sister islands of Cayman Brac and Little Cayman. As with the tragedy of 'Titanic', it was caused by an error of judgement and happened at night.

At least one of the schooners was carrying wages to pay off their sailors in port, along with provisioning funds. For several years thereafter, sovereigns were gleaned from the beaches, together with new coinage still stacked in their waxed covers. But the Cayman Islanders were sea-faring folk, not wreckers. As one of the oldest residents, Captain Henry Watson, told me,

'We found them and we kept them, but it felt like blood money.'

Having completed the pyramids, Ken was now transferred to the largest construction company on the island. Instead of labouring in the relative shade of a workshop, he was outside all day at the hottest time of year while still underweight after the Atlantic crossing and his work with the boys in Grenada. Temperatures hovered close to 100f. Humid air pressed down like a heavy weight. A huge yellow sun deleted all the blue in the sky.

At the end of each day, we returned to *Imago* as limp as wet rags. It was as though we hadn't stopped, except to sleep, since the day our boat was set upon her chocks eleven years before.

Yet it was our time in Cayman that re-ignited our dreams of journeying onwards as committed cruisers. As we each adjusted to the climate and the demands of our jobs, feeling safe and eating well, we slowly recovered our energy and found the time to enjoy our leisure hours.

Seven Mile Beach is for sunbathers and swimmers. There are no rock pools, though the sand itself is soft, fine, and the colour of apricots. We preferred Smith's Cove which was also favoured by local people. We swam out to large outcrop of rock, some 100 metres off shore to snorkel above huge Parrot Fish (so named for their beak-like mouths) weighing thirty pounds or more. Even on the surface we could hear them crunching audibly on the coral. Huge Tarpon cruised past while juvenile. Barracuda practised 'stalking'.

'Don't wear rings or shiny bracelets,' we were told, or they will think you are a bait fish and attack.

Venturing further out to where pale green and turquoise waters change to midnight blue, we gazed down into 'drop-off' zone that descends suddenly, as if from a cliff top, into the black deeps. Reef and nurse sharks roamed around the sheer sides. It made us giddy to peer into such depths despite knowing that we were floating on the surface.

It is a misconception to suggest that there are no 'seasons' in the tropics, though it is true to say that it is a more subtle event when compared with the dramatic resurgence witnessed in Britain. Instead of everything happening at once, each species seems to have chosen its own time. The Tulip and Orchid trees flower annually, producing a visually shocking profusion of red blossoms. Christmas time is when many of the shrubs are at their best. An English gardener would give up their favourite rake for some of the hedges here. The landscape of Cayman cannot be described as majestic. There are no craggy slopes or mountains such as those we saw in Grenada and Jamaica, but there is a certain charm about the flowering trees and shrubs, the oleander hedges surrounding the airport, the unbelievable perfection of hibiscus blooms as large as posies. Seeds flung from pods that have dried in the sun seem the favoured means of propagation and these come in capsules that are sometimes longer than a twelve inch ruler.

Land crabs (and frogs) mate at the beginning of the wet season, leaving hundreds of flattened 'messes' on the busy roads. They stalk the banks of the creeks like futuristic moon buggies with hydraulic legs. Some of the 'boss' crabs stand eight inches off the ground. They are harvested at night, by torch light. We tasted them. Delicious.

Cayman has a busy harbour. As well as local fishing boats and supply vessels travelling to and from Florida, cruise liners regularly anchor in the bay, three at a time, as if planning an invasion. Most of the passengers being elderly, overweight, and American, it was quite entertaining to watch them being carefully deposited ashore from tenders with a well-timed push on an expansive bottom, causing much bosom clutching and whimpers of anxiety, as well as brave determination and merriment.

Investment bankers are a wealthy lot, but even their mega-riches can be eclipsed by even greater opulence. It was the first time we had ever set eyes on a so-called mega-yacht, though we had admired the fine lines of the magnificent 'Sunseeker' yachts as they were towed from their yard in Poole, Dorset. If a motor yacht can be described as 'over the top', then this was surely it. A hundred feet long, capped and liveried deck hands, above deck electronics which might have been supplied by NASA. Pylons of antennae, fully enclosed wheelhouse, not even a rust stain on the anchor chain! Compared with a tall ship, it looked like 'bling.' Perhaps it was the two black helicopters strapped to the deck that made us wince, but at least they weren't labelled 'his' and 'hers'! We never did find out who owned it, though wondered, with not a shred of envy, if this is the boat, what kind of house? What make of cars?

We spotted the advertisement in the 'Cayman Compass' which is Cayman's main newspaper. 'Kittens, five weeks old, free to good homes.' Having both had cats in our previous lives, we couldn't help but go and look. Six in the litter. One black, two white, three covered with black and white splodges. We sat with the owner, watching them play. Although we had never thought of having a pet aboard, we now looked at each other with raised eyebrows... why not? Our soon to be 'ship's cat' raised his head from the pile of squirming siblings, made his falling over, tottering way to where we sat, patted my foot, became ours, and travelled home with us tucked under my T shirt, fur to skin, bringing into our lives an animal character so unique and loveable that we mourn him still. He would travel with us for the next nine years.

***

Baby care. Baby talk. Legs lifted up, one by one, trousers rolled on like stockings. 'There we go love, 'roly-poly' now we'll pull them up.' Arms eased into shapes that will fit into sleeves.

'Now where have those fingers got to...there they are!' As Ken rolled back onto the slide sheet I leaned over to kiss his belly. Still do. Maternal love. It poured out of me, responded to his helplessness, his smile, to his trusting infant eyes.

But four months of interrupted sleep, the intimate caring needs of double incontinence, would overwhelm me. One morning I couldn't get up. My body was trembling. Just one night too many: suctioning, personal care, a constant state of shallow, semi-alert sleep, listening for any sounds of distress from that other bed in the room.

Exhaustion is a strange 'other-worldly' state. It's not a 'can't do' or a 'won't do,' it's a 'don't care what happens next' distancing from the real world. In the hospital, I slept for three whole days. Doctors gathered at the end of the bed. 'Open your eyes for us, Mrs Gogay.' I couldn't. 'There's nothing of her,' one of them said. It was true; I weighed less than seven stones.

Ken was admitted to a nursing home for six days. They were kind enough to bring him to the ward for a visit. We sat holding hands. I promised him that we would soon be together again, firmly believing that I was telling him the truth and wanting nothing else in the world but for it to be true.

After he had gone, I lay there wondering how any of us finds time for work or recreation when the list of daily doings includes: hair brushing, nail trimming, mouth care, eye care, skin care, washing, dressing, ear cleaning, going to the toilet, cooking, eating, housework, mental and physical stimulation, shaving for men, make up for women.

Which has more weight? A vow? A promise? A pledge? Would it count as such if you try yet fail? 'I promise I'll be there,' but you break a leg or the car won't start. 'Till death do us part'… how temporary and provisional, indeed how weightless, a promise can be. The practical demands of dependent care, exacting as they are, proved far less debilitating than of carrying the weight of responsibility for someone's entire well-being and at times, their very life. If the situation had not changed so dramatically in September of that first year, six months after Ken's discharge from hospital, I doubt if will-power alone could have preserved my promise.

Every afternoon I wheeled Ken into the lounge of the sheltered complex to socialise in different surroundings and to play the simplest form of card game, Rummy. I went into the garden for a few minutes while Ken spread out the cards for the next game. One of the residents rushed out to tell me that had pulled out his tracheostomy tube. It was lying on his chest, the ugly red wound in his neck plainly visible. It had happened before when I cleaned the opening twice a week, but had always been easy to re-insert it gently into place. This time the wound had closed.

Ken was breathing through his mouth. He seemed calm. I pulled the emergency cord, briefly explained what had happened, and asked them to call for an ambulance.

'Can I have his name, date of birth, address, and a full description of the problems please?' In a coldly formal voice I replied, 'This is a life-threatening situation – we need an ambulance as soon as possible. Then you can have all the details you want!' I let myself down with such a frigid tone. Fear taking over. Not now... not like this.

'We've had this before,' said the paramedic.

'We can usually get it back in, I could try.'

Ken still calm. 'It's the first time the wound has closed; perhaps it is best done in hospital. Ken doesn't seem to be struggling, please don't.'

To my huge relief, the paramedic nodded. 'We'll get him there as quickly as we can.' Some professionals can be quite affronted by even the mildest of contradictions from a lay person, but even as we spoke, he was attending to Ken, assessing him, and reassuring him. 'How are you feeling, Ken?'

'I feel OK.' And the voice I hadn't heard in sixteen months startled me.

Tracheostomy care was by far and away the most challenging aspect of Ken's nursing needs at that time. Even the district nurses called in to see how the wound and inner tubing were cleaned. Every few weeks we used our allocated taxi-card scheme to transport Ken to the hospital in his wheelchair so that the inner tube could be replaced. Several times our appointments had not been relayed to the ward and we were sent home again. On other occasions, no record could be found for the size and design of the device. I felt badly let down, close to panic and feelings of helplessness, until I too became a patient. I never complained. Not once would I dare risk a judgment that Ken's nursing needs were too complex for me to care for him myself. Nor would I ever lose the gratitude I felt for the medical skills that led to his survival.

Ken was admitted to A&E at 3.30pm. It was 10pm before a consultant was called in from another hospital to make an assessment. Student Doctors came and went. Did I know the type/number of the tube, they asked. I didn't take my eyes off Ken for seven hours while they came, and looked, and went away again.

'Do you think the wound should be covered in case of infection?' I asked. The student was clearly affronted by the veiled criticism, but a dry dressing was soon applied, so I really didn't care about deflating his puffed-up feelings.

When the consultant did arrive, she said, 'Well, if Mr Gogay has been this long without showing signs of distress, I don't see the point of replacing the tube...but a proper dressing, please. Admit him and monitor him carefully.' Oh heavens! What if the students had simply forced it back in!

I left. Went home. Opened a bottle of wine, lit a candle, played an Aled Jones tape, faint with joy. We are going to experience everything there is to know about mending a mind and working towards an optimum level of recovery. Anchors away, skipper!

CHAPTER 18

MIRACLES, MAGIC, AND A PLANE CRASH

Having mentioned to Olive that lying at anchor exposed us to fierce, even hurricane weather, which might prevent me from being 'on call' in a readily available sense, should anything untoward occur at The Pines, 'she, who was known by everyone on the island,' found us a mooring in one of the creeks. Since our brief tie-up against the harbour wall in Curacao, it was the first time in nearly two years that we were moored to the land, able to step off at will without having to haul up the dinghy at night, or keep an anchor watch with every shift in wind speed or direction. We could walk along the bankside until 'mozzie time', leaving a smouldering repellent coil aboard to deter squatters of the irritating, flying, bloodsucking kind.

Whoever described tropical islands as 'Paradise' was probably the breed of estate agent who would extol a beehive as 'a desirable residence.' Beautiful, exotic, and enchanting, though they are, fire ants, the 'pin in your skin' bites of no-see-ums, monsoon rains, humidity, the wrecking potential of hurricanes, and the absence of

Unicorns, make most islands decidedly more worldly than ethereal.

At six months old, the kitten we named Dudley, was on the threshold of cat-hood. Instead of 'killing' our bare feet, he now brings us adolescent-sized gifts of moths, mangrove leaves, snakes, tree frogs, and lizards. The foot-long snake he brought aboard slithered about somewhere in the bilges for several days before I sneaked up on it, basking in the rope locker. He leaps from the companionway ladder into my lap, wriggles his way to my neck where he suckles like a new-born. An endearing habit that continued for all of his life with us. It was time to take him for a ride in the little red car we bought. A thrilling novelty which robbed him of his libido. We hoped he was still confused about what happened to it, or should that be 'them', and why he found himself so fuzzy and wobbly when he woke up to find himself back on the boat. To relieve our guilty feelings, we 'talked him through' such a breach of trust. 'It's for your own good,' we told him, as most parents do, and like most adolescents, he glared and growled at us. Now and again we catch him a small fish, preparing him for life as a 'proper' ship's cat and the joys of manna from cat heaven that are flying fish!

Meetings at anchor tend to be transitory. Hello is the same as goodbye, but now we are making friends, several of who would remain so for the rest of our lives and theirs. Our landlords at the nearby boatyard were Ray and his companion/helper known as 'June Bug.' Before retiring, Ray had owned the yard and built his house there. Both his story and hers were extraordinary and tragic. One of them prevailed, one of them didn't.

Ray had been a US bomber pilot during the Second World War. Returning from a mission to his base in the UK, his aircraft, peppered with bullet holes and flak damage, was struggling to stay aloft.

Then the fire.

Flames and smoke engulfed the plane. A hideous death awaited Ray and his three crew. What happened next tortured his mind, lodging there so deeply that he resorted to blotting it out with alcohol. But even a bottle of rum and several bottles of beer a day failed him, indeed it only served to make the memories more vivid, compelling him to tell it all again, over and over. We always wondered if he was really as laconic as he sounded, about those few minutes...

'We got two choices gentlemen. We burn or we drown.'

'Ditch her skipper... beddah way a' dying than burnin.'

So Ray transmitted a Mayday alert before pitching the plane into a dive, towards the Atlantic and certain death. Here, Ray would pause in his telling, drawn back in time to a silence more pervasive than even the flames or the rattling of the fuselage, as each man contemplated the ending of his life.

Then the miracle.

As the plane dived, the flames were suddenly extinguished. An impossibility. The rush of air should have stoked the fire like bellows. Ray skilfully aborted the dive, climbing as high as he dared before continuing on towards UK shores, landing the plane heavily but safely onto the runway.

Ray's de-briefing was received with amazement bordering on disbelief, but when each of his crew was interviewed separately, corroborating the events in every detail, it was agreed that something had occurred to contradict all that was known about this aspect of aeronautical science, so that even the most sceptical had to accept the only other explanation.

A miracle.

A few months later, Ray and his crew were invited to an audience with the Pope, during which 'Divine Intervention' was ratified. But neither the miracle nor the Pope's blessing could liberate Ray from his memory of that demon-dance with death, that suffering descent towards the Atlantic Ocean.

June and Ray shared an extraordinary relationship. An amalgam of couple, mother and child, brother and sister, bosom buddies, adopting each role, as and when, to meet each other's needs. June herself harboured hurts and bruises, some from irascible men but mostly from her own indelible memory of sitting for hours at the bedside of her dying child. Hoping for her own miracle, yet knowing that the horrific injuries from the car crash could not be overcome.

Did this sensitive, intelligent, mutually supportive pairing evolve from their shared pain? Had they once been lovers? They never said, we never asked, though it was clearly some kind of loving. They finished a daily crossword together, sitting closely, heads nearly touching as they pondered the clues. Later in the day, June would patiently deal with those disagreeable, sometimes disgusting, consequences of alcohol dependency.

More than a decade later, I would have cause to remember her patience and compassion and like her, delete the word 'disgusting' from both my mind and vocabulary. June was one of the only four women we came to know, who could teach the world without saying anything. Each of them a matriarch, the 'wise woman' of a tribe.

Most evenings we would be invited in for a mug of tea after finishing work. One evening we found them already chatting with a long-time friend of Ray's who regularly spent his annual holiday with them. He too was a prodigious drinker. Jene-Jene, as he was known, stood up to be introduced and shake our hands. We found ourselves in the presence of the biggest human being we had ever seen (morbid obesity being less common then than it is now). Six feet six inches tall weighing some forty stones (it would have discourteous to ask, but he appeared proud to tell us)! He was absolutely colossal! Thankfully the hand that was bigger than my head, closed on ours with surprising gentleness. American huge. American loud. Consumer of whole baking trays of lasagne, loaves of bread, and beer by the gallon. While it is morally reprehensible to judge anyone by size, colour, costume, gender, fetishes, or persuasion, Jene-Jene was not someone we could warm to. His size 'fed' his need for notoriety and he was rather ruthless about it, boasting of threats to sue airlines when they asked him to pay double for the two seats he occupied, unconcealed glee that a diving school had to have a wet suit custom made for him, having promoted the course by including the loan of a wet suit, charging pub-goers to pose with him for a photograph... not our mug of tea at all. At least he was a generous lodger, paying June good money to provide gargantuan meals. 'All you can eat' restaurants must have shuddered at his approach. He saw it as a challenge. He liked to swim, so we agreed to go snorkelling with him. Once semi-submerged, he became almost graceful, due to his buoyancy, like a Blue Whale is graceful. But in knowing that his bulk wasn't a medical or hormonal condition, but rather his insatiable appetite together with an emotional need to be 'larger than life' was off-putting. It was impossible not to compare him with a Biafran or a Sudanese peasant without shuddering.

'She 'Obeah' woman.'

'Obeah?'

'Shush,' whispered one of the long-term residents, lowering her head, glancing round as if fearful of being overheard. She pulled the collar of her blouse closely around her neck, as if suddenly chill.

'She do magic things, voodoo... kill you dead.'

Our newest resident was certainly 'difficult.' An aura of fear, like a force-field separated her from staff and residents alike. They shunned her. An unfamiliar, culturally sensitive situation such as this required guidance. All the caring staff were Jamaican women who were certain to know more about it than I did. I arranged to meet with our senior carer.

'I've noticed that staff cross themselves before entering this lady's room. Can you help me to understand how best to care for her here?'

I watched her carefully. Normally a mature, confident woman, she now appeared to be genuinely afraid, sitting stiffly in her seat, eyes lowered, and fingers clasped together in her lap.

'Obeah woman. Devil work. Put a curse on you Miss Pat' ('Miss' being a social term of respect in the Caribbean.)

'If we all work together, we can be stronger than her. Would it help if there were always two of you in the room with her?' The carer nodded slowly, clearly unconvinced, still afraid. Her demeanour made me feel both ignorant and impotent. The social work tenet of resisting judgement was being tested here. How to respect both carer and Obeah woman?

Anywhere else, our new resident would simply have been regarded as a cranky, cantankerous, self-absorbed, old, and so-and-so. For years she had been cared for by neighbours, who fetched and carried, fed her, and feared her, until they could bear it no more, begging social services to relieve them of her demands and threats.

Every tragedy, every sickness, was attributed to her 'Devil work.' Being admitted to the Pines was a challenge to her power. She wanted to return home with such passionate determination that she led our friend Marian and me to make a serious error of judgement.

Marian lived in a beautiful house at South Sound, close to the sea. Director of the 'Pink Ladies', a talented organiser, homes in Canada, Spain, and Florida Keys, and a dedicated volunteer. She would take cigarettes to the only known murderer in Grand Cayman and visit those few disadvantaged in the community. Having once been skipper of an all-women racing boat, she wanted to help us in any way she could.

Obeah woman screamed, wailed, cried, and howled. 'Take me home. 'Just a visit, please, please, just a visit.' So Marian and I decided that we would take her in the car, let her be at home for a couple of hours, thinking it might calm her. She immediately took to her bed and refused to return!

'Chicks, chicks!' she demanded. A neighbour brought her some that were a few days old. We had to leave her there while she plucked at them, clutched them close to her chest, mumbled over them, picking them up then dropping them down. Happy, content, triumphant!

The carers were overjoyed. The qualified nurse was furious. We both had to accept that we were at fault in not advising her of the outing, even though volunteers regularly took residents out for home visits as part of volunteer activities. In this case, and probably deliberately, the staff had not passed on our message. Obeah woman knew exactly what she was doing when casting her spell on two expatriate women! She was eventually re-admitted, protesting loudly, to a specialist wing dealing with dementia and end of life care. But she had won! We could hear it in her cackling, Shakespearian witches voice. Obeah?

Though clearly glad to see the back of the sorceress, none of the staff was prepared to talk about her, as if she might still hear them no matter where she was. The only comment made was shocking enough to silence me too and wishing I had never asked.

'Why did she want the chicks?'

'She make spells with them…pull off their heads!' True or not, it sent a shiver down my spine.

Throughout these overwhelmingly Christian islands, ancient lore persists as a potent force for good or evil, healing or curse. To pooh-pooh such an influence is to deny an ancient morality that served to account for both the tragedies and miracles of life. Witchcraft, voodoo, Obeah, shamanism, black magic, white magic, seers, soothsayers, healers, and necromancers. Each attempting to engage the Gods in human affairs or to express the kind of awe we ourselves had experienced at sea. Missionaries themselves preached similar contradictions: a loving and vengeful God. Heaven and Hell. Salvation and damnation. Promise and threat. Punishment and reward. All of mankind teetering on the tip of a moral precipice.

For an island as small as Grand Cayman, having a dedicated airline (Cayman Airways) seemed extraordinary, but without this vital service, it would never have attained its international status as a banking hub and premier tourist destination. The runway bisects the island, from South to North and can accommodate most freight and passenger planes except a 'Jumbo'.

In addition to a scheduled passenger service, private jets made frequent visits. The end of the runway bordered the sea, and for the passengers, the sight of Cayman from the air was of a green and turquoise gemstone set inside a ruffle of surf. That is, until the evening when the airway's 100 per cent safety record ended. The view was seen, the aircraft landed. But it failed to stop in time to avoid tipping into the sea. Both the hospital and the Pines were put on full alert to deal with potential causalities. Staff at the home prepared trestle beds in the lounge and corridors, liaising with the hospital to set up a triage system. Fortunately only two passengers suffered minor injuries, though others were treated for distress and shock.

Happening so soon after 'Obeah woman', it was spooky! A few months later, I took a three-day break to Cuba with Marian. I don't enjoy flying at the best of times, but in a small twelve-seat plane that could glide a bit, I felt safer. That is, until one of the passengers remarked in a whisper that our pilot was none other than he who had been demoted after his plane had tipped into the sea! Was 'chick woman' having another go at me?

***

With extraordinary concentration, Ken lifts up his bed sheet, holds the top in front of his face, runs his fingers along the edge, folds it, shakes it taut...over and over again. The actions are important to him. They have meaning. His whole understanding of the world he now inhabits is the top edge of a cotton sheet. I saw it again in hospital, another stroke patient doing exactly the same. My own mother doing it when she was ninety years old. Is it a mending thing? A way of controlling a small part of his forgotten world? I could only wonder if it was a remnant of that childhood fascination that causes a toddler to stretch a worm to breaking point, chase a butterfly, touch and taste everything within reach: soil, grass, pebbles, and toys. But neither they nor Ken will ever remember, ever be able to explain. Some instinct told me never to interrupt this behaviour or try to distract him from it. A couple of years later, he began to ask me to paint his fingernails! However often I said 'we'll see', he kept asking. Finally I asked our carers to bring in any nail vanish they no longer used, and bless their hearts, each one of them sat with him, offered up different shades of red and pink for him to choose from, and painted his fingernails. My virile and exceptional lover was beside himself with joy! He was ecstatic when I trimmed and filed his nails, to then have them painted was the topping on a cupcake!

But it ended his twice-weekly respite care at a day centre. Several of the pre-Beatles ladies were horrified, even his sister was disapproving. They said cruel things to him about it, refusing to sit near him, and I had no idea of what was happening. The senior care worker at the centre telephoned me at home.

'Why does Mr Gogay wear nail varnish?'

'Because he wants to,' I said calmly. Being the truth, I felt no need to fabricate a reason. Despite this opportunity to tell me Ken was being bullied, he let it pass. A few days later, the taxi arrived to take Ken to the centre, but as I wheeled him to the door he was violently sick. Finally he said he didn't want to go any more. It highlighted the difficult, often frightening consequences for stroke patients who struggle to translate thoughts into language. An inability to express emotions in socially acceptable ways gradually erodes their sense of self, especially when messages from the outside world they are trying to understand are hostile or impatient towards them.

But for Ken to have made his own decision was nothing less than a huge step forward in his recovery. A false picture of Ken's personality had been formed, all because he was wearing nail polish – but perhaps we are all guilty of judging people in this way.

Everything about those early stages was a revisited childhood. Ken was now four years old. Saying no! Expressing his urge for independence with a tantrum, avoiding playschool with a 'sickie' or a 'tummy ache.'

The nail-painting phase ran its course over the next few months. Gradually I 'forgot' to do it. Eventually he forgot too, though he never went to a day centre again. How different it would have been for him if the organiser of the day centre had really understood about being non-judgemental, had understood Ken's needs, defended him, instead of recoiling along with others. How thrilled Ken would have been if this strangeness had caused them to simply admire his nails while waiting patiently for that particular obsession to run its course.

It was our carers, so often overlooked in the hierarchy of nursing, who seemed better able to understand what was happening. Specialists who care for patients with dementia do understand and usually respond very differently towards bizarre behaviour. If a person is locked into a disturbing memory, they know that reassurance, acceptance, or just taking time to listen is a better palliative than a pill. Responding with 'never mind.' 'You're talking nonsense.' 'It's all in your imagination,' sends a cold stark message. You, the patient, have not only departed from the real world, but also from the last remnants of the only world left for you to imagine.

I remembered an elderly lady at the retirement home in Grand Cayman, who became highly agitated as her dementia entered its paranoid phase.

'I've lost them... the children!' She put her head in her hands, rocked with anguish, wailed, and moaned.

'Where are you?'

'The railway station, can't see them, can't find them!'

'I'll get someone to look for you... there they are! They're safe, what a terrible worry for you.'

'Oh thank the Lord! Praises be! My grandchildren!' She held out her chubby grandmother hands. Holding and stroking them made me cry.

A month before Ken's discharge from hospital, I had taken in Polo Mints. Holding one firmly between thumb and forefinger, I rested it on his tongue for him to suck. His eyes closed in ecstasy. Although unable to eat, he was still producing saliva, which along with mucous, collected in his tracheostomy tube. He was having regular tests, ingesting a dye to assess his swallow reflex. If the dye diverted from throat to tube, he would remain dependent on a liquid diet delivered by tube directly into his stomach, perhaps for the rest of his life. Talk now was of a permanent breathing devise and learning to use a light box to communicate – but he had 'swallowed' the taste of the mint... I'd seen it!

In March 2005, six months after rejecting his tracheostomy tube, Ken underwent an endoscopy to remove the abdominal feed tube. We had been to the radiological unit no less than five times before then, only to be told that his swallow was too weak. I just didn't mention that for the last three months, Ken had been eating yoghourt and drinking tepid tea. I fully understood that replacing a feeding tube could be difficult, even harmful, but the increasing restrictions of 'health and safety' regulations had already become an irritating public issue. Together with fear of litigation and inappropriate claims for compensation, even professionals were becoming overly cautious. So we went home, after yet another failed test and added mashed potatoes and lollipops to his diet, waiting patiently for a 'pass'.

That day came. As the spigot was extracted from his stomach wall, held firmly in the forceps of the endoscopy tube, it appeared in his mouth. As it clattered into the receiving bowl, I felt momentarily sick with relief and joy. We had never weathered a hurricane at sea, but I imagined that it would feel like this.

CHAPTER 19

SUICIDAL JELLYFISH AND OTHER STORIES

Whatever it was that inspired our friend Bill to bring us a decoy Mallard Duck, we confidently recommend it as an essential item to have aboard a cruising boat! Not only for the quirky fun of it, but also because he proved to be the most undemanding of pets. Having exchanged the confines of a freshwater environment for life as an ocean adventurer, we were bound to name him 'Sir Francis', thus combining nautical connections with huge respect for our 'Drake'.

Using the strongest of our nylon fishing lines, we tethered him about three metres from *Imago's* stern where he sat and bobbed, loyally turning with the tide, looking properly authentic and feathered but thankfully, 'quackless.' Sir Francis became an instant celebrity: gazed at through binoculars, stalked with a harpoon gun, approached with a landing net, shot at with a catapult. Children rowed out in dinghies to throw him bread, while every adult wanted him for dinner!

Bill was a retired postman bachelor, my friend before he was 'our' friend. Having never wavered in his belief that we would build and sail *Imago*, our guest cabin in the bows belonged to him. As long as we didn't take him sailing, Bill was the perfect companion/shipmate. Enthusiastic, happy with simple meals, a walker, prepared to wash his own clothes in a bucket labelled 'Bill', delighting in evenings of 'cockpit talk' to which he brought a dry British humour that became dryer still with each tot of rum! Our dearly loved friend was a functioning alcoholic, which to our minds confers 'mariner status.' He knew that we would understand both his dependency and what a holiday meant to him, which was a more than usual evening session which kept him 'topped up' until 6pm the following day. *Imago* was normally a 'dry' boat, but we couldn't let our 'mate' drink alone. Yes, we did have to undress him down to shorts and top a few times and roll him into his bunk, but it was just another gesture that marked him as our friend.

At home in the UK, Bill led a solitary life tending plants and vegetables in an average-sized garden yet on a market-garden scale. A well-known character at boot sales, customers looked to him for the healthiest plants, his encyclopaedic knowledge of all things horticultural, his dry poker-faced wit. Unusually, Bill was never belligerent or paranoid in drink, but his day-to-day isolation was only relieved by his evenings at the pub. Year on year, whatever the weather, he rode his bicycle to the same pub. We wondered how anyone could fail to understand his need; an only child, his parents dead. But we were his family and he knew it.

However! What we thought was an 'inspired' gift was nothing of the sort! It was a 'message.' Get rid of

Dudley! Settle for a pet duck. Bill did not like cats. You can always tell. A perfunctory, stiff-fingered double swipe was the closest he could muster up as a 'stroke.' What a two-faced gesture that was. He really HATED cats (diggers, crappers, knotting up the carrot tops with their twisting rolling preparations for a lie in the sun). We excused his vehement 'sod-offs' when Dudley's paw sneaked towards his dinner plate (never ours!). The frisson between them became an art form. Dudley would simply persevere with flat eared, wide-eyed determination. On his next visit, Bill brought us a brass plaque 'beware of the cat'. A salve perhaps for a) loss of face, b) reluctant admiration for a better player.

'Why is it always my plate?'

'Why do you think?'

Above all, Bill was my 'mooching' friend. We cycled the length and breadth of the island together. It was he who spotted the yellow plastic parcel wedged between the rocks of an East End Bay. Wrapped tightly with tape, weighing about 10 kilos, either jettisoned by a drug boat or lost along with its crew. Worth a fortune, Cannabis of course, which along with alcohol is the acknowledged palliative in the Caribbean. More recently it has been augmented by cocaine, heroin, and pills. Modern lifestyles don't seem to suit the human spirit, but in a land of sunshine beauty such stimulants seem out of place.

Bill was a perceptive commentator despite having an unusual approach. He simply compared what he saw on his travels with what changes he was seeing England. Hardly a scientific assessment one might think but surprisingly pragmatic.

'They're doing that on the football pitch now.'

'What'?

'Lifting up their shirts, hawking and spitting.'

We were in the pharmacy section of the Supermarket... 'Look at all those creams to relieve Jock Itch. Even that's a pop star gesture now...scratching their tackle all the time... Michael Jackson seemed to suffer terribly from it.' None of us commented on the even wider range of skin whitening lotions – it made us sad.

'Why don't they do that in the UK?'

'Do what?'

'Collect water in the cellars during the rainy season.'

Indeed, why not, they call it 'grey water' and use it for flushing lavatories, watering plants, washing clothes. Usually it lasts for the whole of the dry season. Yet in the UK, a country renowned for its wetness, comparatively short dry spells result in hose-pipe bans and water shortages. In the summer of 1976, when even the Thames turned green with algae, 'third world' standpipes were installed. Something to add to the bath sheet ban: a water catchment cellar beneath every new house built. We had crossed the Atlantic with 100 gallons of water. Thankfully the maths are simple: three people, thirty-three days, a gallon of water per person per day for washing, drinking and cooking. It was an attitude to water conversation that would last for the rest of our lives.

Sun, beaches, organised tours, comfortable accommodation, good food, 'ethnic' beer, entertainment, and solicitous service, the agenda expected of a relaxing and enjoyable holiday, especially when it is that precious two or three weeks' relief from workaday responsibilities. Unfortunately that very desire to unburden oneself can lead such uninhibited behaviour that the host country is obliged to accept economic gains over acute embarrassment. Perhaps having an agenda is in itself inhibiting since the only ingredients that make the difference are the blessed sun and not having to plan, prepare, and cook meals, which is joy enough for most women!

Travel manners are a real issue for many countries. We ourselves felt shock at seeing a young woman with undeniably impressive thoracic adornments filling her car with petrol while wearing the skimpiest of bikinis. Men would enter a restaurant bare-chested, complaining loudly when asked to cover up or leave. Behaviour that would be offensive in your own country is surely insulting.

Later in our travels, we would hear of yachtsmen washing their sails in a private swimming pool, eating a small village out of food at a Birthday Party, parading naked in a non-secular country. In street talk, this is 'dissing' (disrespect) and shames the flag that is flown from the stern of a yacht.

We ourselves were guilty of cultural incorrectness in some of the countries we visited and indeed it is difficult to avoid such lapses altogether (some of which were hilarious) but we shall hold our hands up to them as they happened, leaving fellow travellers to decide for themselves if they can be avoided.

At the same rocky cove where we found the cannabis, Bill spotted a 'specimen' piece of driftwood. The sea had delivered it up gently, retreated politely, and left it for us like a shyly offered gift: clean, laundered, bleached, and starched. A sculpture. You could lose yourself in it as when gazing at clouds, making of it whatever you willed. We walked back to the boat as if we had found a chest full of treasure. Today is sits among the cowries, rocks, volcanic glass and smaller pieces of contorted driftwood in a large aquarium tank in memory of reefs and wonders.

Being a horticulturist, Bill was fascinated by the tropical flora in general, the coconut palm in particular. We spent a whole evening of 'cockpit talk' extolling this 'heavenly' tree. Bill called it the 'manna' tree: food, water, roofing for a house, a flask, copra, a drinking vessel, a remedy for kidney ailments, furniture. A very different fruit from the coconuts sold in Europe. When still green the 'milk' is cool, refreshing, the flesh soft as jelly. The elderly residents swore by the medicinal properties of coconut milk. To 'cleanse the blood', to relieve urinary problems.

As well as 'Stingray City', we saved the submarine trip, Hell, and the Turtle Farm, to share with our friend. 'Hell' is a unique area of iron-shore rocks that rise up in sharp pinnacles like a meringue topping, impossible to walk over, a huge cheese grater, ferocious fangs of rock that would pulverise a body, rip a boat to shreds. At the end of the viewing platform is a small post office where tourists are invited to send a quirky postcard from 'Hell'.

At the Turtle Farm we all learned about the fascinating life cycle of these endangered species. As they swam around in outdoor tanks, we delighted in the newly hatched Hawksbill, Ridley, Loggerhead, and Green turtles thrashing their tiny limbs like terrapins. In another tank, juveniles coursed through the water like Olympic swimmers. The final tank, large as a swimming pool, held the breeding pairs, cruising with intent, some weighing more than 400lbs, hissing and sighing at the surface. Huge, prehistoric, and glancing at their audience with baleful, ancient, knowing eyes.

Inside a humid, temperature-controlled building, eggs collected from the beaches are laid out in glass-fronted drawers to await hatching before transfer to the pools. Most of the stock will be herded gently back to the sea, protected by their handlers from the usual massacre and mutilation carried out by frigate birds and gulls, wheeling, diving, and screeching in frustration above them. Turtles are such endearing little creatures, thrashing their tiny limbs in that un-co-ordinated way of most infants, including human babies. As a conservation project, it really does have an impact. Perhaps one in a hundred survive instead of one in a thousand.

Cayman Islanders love their turtle meat. It's sweeter than beef, tender, succulent, and let's face it, no more 'offensive' than a young lamb? The peoples of the world eat piglets, calves, pigeons, dogs, rats, goats, capons (castrated domestic cocks), sea urchins, armadillos, foie gras, caviar, insects, shark fins, whales, seals, bird nests, and turtles. Apart from shark fins and foie gras the 'yuck' factor is just a cultural bias. The problems only arise when such tastes become 'fashionable.' Caymanians didn't decimate the turtle population, it was pirates, trading vessels, and explorers.

The submarine descent was expensive but offered a fascinating experience. First, it cruised in the shallows where we saw a turtle browsing on sea grass, huge shoals of tropical reef fish, fronds of black coral, parrot fish grazing on man-sized barrel sponges. Elkhorn, brain coral, sea fans, pink coral. A sunken freighter lay tethered at the edge of the drop off, awaiting the storm that would start its inexorable descent into deep crushing oblivion and the fate of so many ships before it.

In most cities of the world where a traveller would wish to explore it is the taxi-driver who will have 'the knowledge.' On islands it is fishermen. They are sailors too and their knowledge is just as broad and particular as those more used to monuments, short cuts, and place-names. A local fisherman will know which bait or lure to use, inshore currents, signs of unusual weather, tradition and taboo, uncharted rocks, and 'sea secrets' such as the lobster march. There is no special time for it to happen they say, but they have seen it. Hundreds of lobsters inexplicably gather 'en-masse' to form a marching column and re-locate like an advancing line of soldiers. On either side of the column, the biggest crustaceans guard their troops while they march, keeping it in line like sergeant majors.

But no-one on the island, not even the fishermen, mentioned the mass suicide of jelly fish that Bill and I witnessed during one of our excursions. We came upon a small isolated beach of pristine sand. There was something strange about the surf line. The weather had been calm for several days with no reports that might account for rough weather further out at sea, but as each wave rolled heavily onto the beach, it disgorged tens of thousands of dark, penny-sized jellyfish. The face of each wave was black, heavy, and dense with their numbers. Soon the beach was littered with small black circles which instantly fried in the sun's heat as if a huge tree had suddenly shed its leaves. Just jellyfish, some might say, but there was something deeply disturbing and contradictory going on. If self-preservation is the driving force of natural selection, here was one species seemingly intent on reducing rather than enhancing their survival strategies by committing mass suicide!

Was it a predator that had herded them to the beach? An annual event? Presumably enough of them survive to do it all again. Since nature usually only culls the weakest or those which are a prey species, it was all very baffling. Were these the Lemmings of the sea? We left the scene of carnage in silence and feeling rather sad.

Grand Cayman had introduced us to the kind of working environment that is only possible in a warm, sunny country. Hardly a difference between work and play, swimming in bath-warm water before dinner, watching the sun disappear from yet another bright blue day. A sun that behaves like a bag of fluid, as if the clear horizon was sucking it in, waiting for the moment when it is shaped like a light bulb before being swallowed by the sea. Yet we knew we would leave.

We could have stayed. Knew we were welcome to do so, even apply for permanent residence, but Ken especially, was still determined to prove that the vessel he had built was well found and seaworthy, capable of taking us across the vast Pacific Ocean and beyond.

Looking back over the many years we spent travelling around the world and despite the fear, desperation, joys, awe, humanity, and inhumanity, it was the right decision. Cayman was too comfortable, too sophisticated for us.

Even then (1991), perhaps more so now, we recognised problems that have changed the world for travellers. Politics, exploitation, unspeakable poverty, and historical outrages have reared up ugly. Despite the economic advantages of being a British protectorate, there was a strong camp that would be rid of us all. Indigenous peoples resent the white-collar jobs held by foreigners. Cayman was also a scaled down example of ecological problems afflicting the whole world. A building programme of banks, churches, condominiums, hotel resorts, and extravagant homes will soon outstrip the island's capacity to deal with it garbage, sewage, and power supplies, added to the more alarming fact that its coral reefs are dying by the acre. Without its reefs and mangroves, the island could revert, in less than ten years, to a mosquito-ravaged wilderness. A community that had learned to adapt to its environment now dependent on an Anglo-American culture which put wealth above centuries of familial and religious values. While it served the more ambitious islanders, older residents mourned the passing of their traditional way of life because it was all happening too quickly to adjust to.

Nevertheless, we think of Grand Cayman with fondness and gratitude and were determined to use the time we had left to make whatever contribution we could as well as making our dream a lot more realistic in terms of equipment.

Re-introducing a telephone counselling service called 'lifeline' was a welcome undertaking. First introduced by Olive, it had been discontinued for want of committed responders despite having proved its value by the frequency of calls. Anonymous pleas for advice or support from the Samaritans and Esther Ransom's Childline in the UK had already demonstrated that every society, however sophisticated, hid an 'underbelly' of personal despair, familial abuse, and a range of situations that cannot be alleviated by either wealth or status.

On an island as small as Grand Cayman, confidentially was a vital but difficult area to navigate. It became a core component of a six-week course which concentrated on an ability to really 'listen' and above all to be non-judgemental, which for most of us is the most challenging of paradigm shifts. Only two of the ten volunteers were men. On might suppose that since many of the calls were about spousal or relationship problems to do with infidelity, alcohol abuse, domestic violence, and attitudes towards servants, a woman might be easier to talk to, although issues of gender stereotyping and prejudice are so much harder to overcome.

There are four essential components to counselling: confidentiality, professional listening, feedback, and empathy. On every course there is a 'Eureka' moment!

In Grenada it had been a discussion about a list of those 'deserving help'. A woman alone with four children to raise was 'deserving', but the son of a wealthy family who had become desperate about his debts was not! In Cayman it was all about a dog!

The telephone was not connected, but the 'lifeline' counsellors were to pretend that it was. I had written out cards which outlined the problems that was being presented... 'You are a twelve year old girl who has just seen her dog run over and killed by a car'. A kind committed lady picked up the phone. The lady with the cue card began… 'My dog (pretending to cry) has been run over.'

'But it's only a dog!'

Oh crikey! I eased the mock telephone from her hand.

'What a terrible thing to happen. Was it your dog? What was its name'?

Replacing the phone gently I looked to the group and waited…

'I guess that was a "how not to"' the otherwise kindly, enthusiastic, caring young woman said sheepishly. Then we all laughed, thus allowing us to joyfully grasp the most important attitude of all. That of acknowledging distress (also anger and despair) even when it contradicts your own value system as to what should matter to others. It may not be an issue that would be upsetting to you or figure large in your own experience, but for the caller it is urgent, classless, and hurting enough to call 'lifeline.'

I told the group about a similar 'Eureka' moment in Grenada which was used in role plays at the end of that course to demonstrate the principles of social work. The event was attended by relatives and officials from Grenada's education department who were to present the certificates. The students were enthusiastic actors. The subject was a tramp!

Even in the UK, a tramp wandering into a probation office, looking for a hand-out was a unwelcome episode. Unkempt, smelling of sweat, leakage, damp cardboard, and with long toenails. All along the corridor, doors would click shut. Audible sounds of relief that they were not the 'on call' officer of the day. In Grenada, the reaction to such an individual would be horror. Dirty, smelly, and no shoes was an unforgivable throwback to colonial abuse.

'Good morning, Sir, can I help you?'

'I'm hungry.'

'Where do you live? Do you have family who will help you?'

'I just wander about – nobody wants to know me.'

'You must have lots of stories to tell.'

'Nobody ever asked me before.'

At the end of the role play, the tramp didn't ask for money or food. Someone had listened to him and respected his choices. The shambling gait, the belligerence which guarded against the usual signs of disapproval were replaced by a cheery farewell. He had received something he needed more, a non-judgemental voice.

What has this to do with cruising? Perhaps it is the difference between being perceived as a tourist or as a visitor. A curious, baleful stare? Or a happy engaging smile. Hastily unzipping the camera case, nudging each other, giggling, pointing, is to treat fellow human beings as if they are 'specimens'. The stare is seen as exactly what it is: rude, patronising. It will be met with envy and resentment and an urgent desire to rip you off! I don't think we ever saw a tourist offer to shake hands or smile a welcome.

Yet a smile is a universal greeting which will lead a traveller into quite remarkable, mutually agreeable, encounters. Indigenous peoples are highly sensitive to breaches of their ancient conventions. To call them 'customs' minimises their importance as a means of social control and group solidarity, especially in places where written laws do not exist.

In matters regarding male and female prohibition, such conventions are very particular indeed. So much so that Western emancipation becomes seriously offensive and destabilising. Many races are beautiful or handsome to Western eyes, especially the women. Dark luminous eyes, shy and coy with one brief gaze, classical features, a swaying 'Hollywood walk' from carrying bundles of laundry or produce on their heads. Perhaps they use Khol to accentuate their eyes; display elaborate oil-sheened hairdos, but life on the islands or in the forests is too arduous, especially for women, to indulge in two-hour makeovers. They are simply, naturally, beautiful. But beware the foreigner who is entranced and shows it! Beware the machete, the punished woman, the angry husband, and disgusted elders.

Yachtsmen, along with most other special-interest groups, tend to wear a uniform: baggy shorts, creased T-shirt, sandals, or flip-flops. Easy to wear, easy to stow, but in many cultures (even ours) it is unseemly to 'visit' without some thought as to appropriate dress. Not meaning to be misogynistic about it, cleavage and bare thighs, however fascinating, can be disturbing, embarrassing, and sometimes insulting. Some years ago an incident occurred in Turkey that made headline news in the British tabloids. It served to highlight cultural sensitivities regarding dress and behaviour. A group of English lads presumably de-sensitised ('wasted' that is) following a bar crawl, exposed themselves in full view of several local women. Turkey may well have a non-secular government, but it is also predominately Muslim.

It was said that the 'elders' in the community supplied the knives to their young men, making them honour-bound to punish such a terrible breach of their religious beliefs. It was an outrage that could only be resolved by attrition. The subsequent death and injury horrified the British, but for the Turks it was honour-restoring justice for such an intolerable insult. In a rural village, young men would have been executed for lesser infringements than occurred that night.

***

Coaxing a stroke victim towards their optimum level of recovery resembles what is now known about child development. In order to re-connect with the world, Ken needed welcoming messages from it: heaped up praise for every small sign of progress, sometimes just for trying. A warmly modulated tone of voice, not the artificial 'poor you' voice so often encountered in care homes and on geriatric wards. Shrill sounds frightened him, as they do a child. Throughout that 'born again' phase, each small achievement was as rewarding as that first smile of recognition, the first word, weaning, crawling to walking, toileting, the first tooth.

However demeaning it may sound to engage with an adult in this way, it worked for us, both at a practical and emotional level. Although the child analogy didn't include tickling, coo-ees, or 'diddums', our relationship during those first two years was indeed that of mother and baby.

Building our boat, sailing her around the world, was a highly unpredictable lifestyle, but from now on until our allotted time in this world, an organised daily routine was essential. This adjustment, above all others would lead to an astounding level of recovery. Not that it was a planned strategy, it simply evolved as the only way to deal with total dependency: mouth care, eye care, twice weekly showers, regular turning to prevent bed sores, shaving, moisturising, nose hairs, ear hairs, nail cutting, hair dressing, mental stimulation, exercises, and incontinence care. Eventually, as with any repetitive task, a flowing rhythm, like a beating drum, like a cuckoo clock on the hour, shaped our days. Ken would slowly learn to anticipate every what, when, and how.

How wonderfully heart-warming it is to see a happy child. One who lives in an environment that feels safe, having a 'presence' to reply on, to be kissed, held, to believe that being able to sit on the edge of their bed counts as nothing less than an Olympic achievement.

It was many months later before Ken could understand what had happened to him. 'I broke my legs', he would say. More than a year later, I could talk him through the fact that he had suffered a catastrophic brain haemorrhage.

For the first few years, we relied on agency care staff. Two at a time, as there must be when sling hoisting is involved. Rolling Ken skilfully onto a slide sheet before wrapping the sling straps around his shoulders and thighs then using the beam hoist to lift him from bed to chair. No matter how smoothly, kindly, or reassuringly done, it was horrible to witness... a limp, helpless, undignified procedure.

Essential though it was, the quality of care was unpredictable, sometimes disturbing. Some of the women seemed too young to be giving intimate care, leaning away, dabbing at Ken's groin rather than wiping. Visits were sometimes forgotten altogether or very much later than agreed in the care plan, leaving me to risk the hoisting myself. Few of the faces became familiar which meant having to show each new person where the washing bowl, linen cupboard, and supplies were kept and to describe Ken's range of abilities. On seeing a tracheostomy and feed peg, they may have thought he was in a vegetative state, leaving them to carry out their tasks mechanically and as quickly as possible, without explaining what they were doing or verbally reassuring him. It was all very stressful and debilitating but also, sadly, totally understandable. Underpaid, undervalued. Sometimes treated like a family servant, chivvied by the agency to take on more visits than they could manage. Some spoke only Basic English and were perhaps more familiar with less compassionate cultures. Those similar problems that have beset our cherished NHS.

Babyhood is fleeting. Any mother will tell you that. And so it was with Ken. Unless a meticulous 'baby diary' is kept, it's hard to remember each small step, other than the thrill of them. There was a first time when Ken rolled over in the hospital bed by grasping the rails, called me by name, laughed at something on TV (babies laugh, almost as if they are primed to practise being happy rather than the surely more sophisticated appreciation of the ridiculous, innuendo, or slapstick).

At that stage, there was no thought of Ken ever walking again, but perhaps as with lower limb amputees or those with spinal injuries, he might one day transfer to his chair on a slide board, using the compensating strength in his arms. But greedy we are not. Living without a breathing tube or being liquid fed through his abdomen were already heaped-up blessings.

CHAPTER 20

DUDLEY MEETS HIS MATCH

Friends and colleagues gathered on the bankside to watch us leave. Olive took my hand. 'I'm scared,' I confided. 'Every time we set sail is like the first time. I'm not even sure we are doing the right thing.'

'I'll pray for you both,' she said.

When I look back now I can only believe that her prayers were answered.

Dudley was shut in the forward cabin until we were half way across North Sound, well beyond leaping or swimming distance from land. He came on deck looking frantic and wide eyed. He was distressed, sea-sick, and frothing at the mouth. We wondered, anxiously, whether we had made a wrong and selfish decision to carry him with us.

Choppy trade wind seas and quick spiteful squalls. A sobering forty-eight hours for us all. The squalls seemed to bear down on the hour, creeping over the horizon like a huge black duvet, deleting the stars one by one. Dark, menacing. Curtains of rain trailing like valences from the lower rim.

Dudley was refusing to eat or drink but found refuge in the bilges where a boat's movement is least felt. Taking a break from the tedious march of squalls, we lay a-hull for six hours, both of us sleeping in the cockpit. Extraordinary! The wind died away, as if suddenly tired of hassling us so.

Instead, the ocean caressed us like a lullaby. Not even a ripple on the surface. This then, was the 'gently billowing sea' of literature and its rhythm rocked us into sleep. A small finch fluttered into the rigging, handsomely dressed in black with brilliant orange bars and chest. He landed on each of our heads before flying into the saloon for a look around. Before resuming his own course to somewhere, he took water from Dudley's dish which pleased us greatly. He left a breeze, as if to thank us. Twin foresails and main now gave us 4knts in the right direction. On the third day, Dudley joined us in the cockpit, much restored, eating and drinking. A curious cat is a happy cat. The swishing sounds against the hull intrigued him. Flat bellying to a scupper, he sits hypnotised by the movement of the water rushing by.

32nm to the first waypoint inside the Gulf of Mexico. A coastguard cutter hove into view, calling us up on channel 16, ordering us to heave to and prepare to be boarded. Four very professional young men came aboard. I think we were surprised to find them so polite and cordial, despite all their shiny emblems of authority and revolvers at their hips. We were advised about safety requirements in USA waters but not searched. They were intrigued by our journey from England and wished us well. They left a warning; two freighters had sunk in the gulf during the last four days of severe storms. 'Suggest you slow down your approach skipper, there will be "leftover seas" to contend with.'

The two-legged and four-legged crew of *Imago* now slipped into a smooth, practised routine. Relieve the 2am watch-keeper before dawn. Cereal and tea for breakfast, during which we discuss sailing tactics for the coming day, and log our twenty-four hour speed and distance. If *Imago* feels nicely balanced, we can relax as we watch the sun rise.

Dudley has become a proper ship's cat, moving easily around deck, his somewhat bossy personality more pronounced than ever. Whenever we were attached to land, he would take us for a stroll along the bankside after dinner. When he felt we were exceeding territorial limits (his), he would sit, yowling a warning until we turned for home. He acknowledged his topsy-turvy world by 'marking' his belongings: rope, rigging screws, sails, and soon established favourite places to snooze, depending on sea conditions and the position of the sun.

After seven days at sea, we have a little less than 200nm to run. In flat calm we are motoring, the dinghy towed astern. A cattle egret has been perching on it for more than twenty-four hours. Dudley spotted it this morning. Should anyone doubt the number or variety of expressions on a feline face, we can attest to the following: shock, indignation, anticipation, logistical planning, an 'other-worldly' joy! The egret, bobbing to the rhythm of the sea, was unperturbed. The game that followed had Ken and I rolling in the side decks. Staggering with mirth, we went below to find the camera. The frantic contest between feathers and fur went the full twelve rounds. Who would have guessed that an egret could be so playful, so taunting, and so humiliating! It flew from the dinghy to the pulpit. Dudley, ears and belly flattened, eyes huge, stalked to within a few feet of his target before launching an attack. With a leisurely flap of its wings, the egret then flew to the pushpit. Dudley assumed an air of indifference, but we heard him growl in frustration before stalking then rushing to the other end of the boat. Bow to stern, over and over. Couldn't concede, couldn't resist. After half an hour the egret, having goaded Dudley further by preening its feathers between rounds (I'm getting bored you little twit), retired to the dinghy, where it and cat glared at each other. Dudley was exhausted. Ken pulled the dinghy close to the hull to get a final picture of them both. Dudley leaning over the side rail panting, the egret only feet away, both eyeing each other, the victor and the vanquished! By next morning, the egret had vanished, taking with it a wonderful after-dinner story to tell.

Channel 16 alerted us to the fact that we had missed two tornados by only twenty-four hours. Storms that had inflicted significant damage just North of Clearwater where we are heading. It hardly seemed feasible as we motored on a barely undulating sea.

Next day, seven miles into the mouth of the bay, we sighted the outer buoy. Further in the depth, sounder records forty feet so we anchored at midnight, not only for respite but also with concern about the aftermath of such violet weather. We slept in the cockpit, waiting for dawn.

Caution may be a strange word to use when volunteering to face such elemental forces as oceans and wind. Edmund Hillary is quoted as saying, 'Well, we knocked that bastard off' after 'conquering' Everest. It seemed such an ungracious comment, lacking in respect for both the mountain and the many who had lost their lives in the trying. Respect for the sea is ingrained in maritime lore; to challenge it as if were a foe is a foolhardy mind set. We are slowly learning our sea lore: cloud formation, 'left over' seas, and the vagaries of current. Our favourite clouds, if only because of their predictability and their portent for wind, were the poetically named 'Mackerel skies' and 'Mares Tails.' Such cloud formations were recognised centuries ago. 'Mackerel skies and Mares Tails make tall ships carry short (shortened) sails.'

Caution and respect now served us. By 3am, winds were gusting to Force 7. Dudley headed for the bilges as all hands hauled anchor and set a reefed main and storm jib. Hundreds of small rays swept past, plainly visible in the smooth sides of each approaching wave. Channel 16 broadcasts regular warnings to all shipping. Several red flares have been sighted. As dusk fell, we reached the far end of the bay where we could anchor safely and watch as the tall buildings lit up one by one as if seeking to join the stars in the night sky. The Skyway Bridge loomed high above our small ship.

Weary but elated. We have reached America! Next morning, with breakfast foremost in our minds, we took the dinghy to shore, only to find ourselves back in England! The transit moorings where we planned to stay for a while, bordered a small park where sparrows, squirrels, doves, and starlings flitted and rummaged between tree-lined pathways. It was only when we sat in a café to order breakfast that we knew for certain that we were in the USA. What a performance! Thank goodness hash browns don't come medium, rare, or blue!

'Full breakfast please.'

'Eggs?'

'Please.'

'Two eggs or three?'

'Two.'

'Fried, Scrambled, Sunny-Side or Over Easy?'

'Fried please.'

'Bacon or Sausage?'

'Both please.'

'Crisp or medium?'

'Medium.'

'Hash browns, Grits, or Home fries?'

'Hash Browns.'

'Bread?'

'Please.'

'White, Wholemeal, or Rye?'

'Just a white roll please.'

'Coffee or Juice?'

'Coffee.'

'Jelly?'

'Pardon?!'

The waitress expected quick snappy answers. While we pondered each choice, her 'Hollywood smile' remained fixed, but when her hand moved to her hip, we knew she was finding us tedious!

Transit moorings (marinas) were expensive but easy access to water and power, which half of our world manages without, had now become luxuries to us also.

We phoned family and friends. There was concern about how long our journey had taken, especially as they knew about the tornados. Those close to us were clearly monitoring our safety. It was reassuring to realise that they were looking out for us, however distant the caring. These are 'mind hugs' and they don't need a postage stamp.

While our experiences in America were fascinating and mostly enjoyable, we soon concluded that it was a society full of contradictions. Succeed spectacularly or fail miserably. Shabby alongside glitz. Policemen weighted down by shiny emblems of authority, carrying enough weaponry to wage war, not that many of them looked fit enough to chase an elderly lady, let alone a thief on the run. Too loud. Too competitive. Too edgy.

Despite an uneasy balance between a monstrous ego and a genuine moral imperative, we also encountered a truly engaging alter-ego full of openness, generosity, and a fascination about the British Islands. Castles, Woodstock, greenness, Stratford, rain, grand houses, Tower Bridge, afternoon tea, pubs, thatched cottages, tweeds, antique shops, driving on the left, manners, Shakespeare, great houses, London buses, palaces, pastoral living, smallness, quaintness, Royalty, and pageant. But everything appeared intense and charged, as if the whole vast country was on the edge of a nervous breakdown.

Guantanamo, Draconian prison sentences, twenty or more years on death row, Abu Ghraib humiliations. It didn't feel at all like the 'land of the free.' Yet they landed on the moon, have made significant breakthroughs in science and technology, possess the means to annihilate the world, assume the moral high ground while yet consuming most of the world's resources.

That wonderful statement in the Bill of Rights (1791) 'the pursuit of happiness' appears to elude today's American citizens.

Dudley is the 'darling' of the pontoons. Wandering up and down the gangways, leaping aboard any boat that took his fancy. No-one had ever met a cat as bold and friendly as he. Then he went missing, causing us terrible grief and heartache. Thirty-six hours passed. We spent hours looking for his body, between the boats, alongside all the quays. We put up notices at the end of every pontoon. Nothing. Sitting silently on our sad, diminished vessel, we began our mourning.

A shout went up. 'Is your cat very big and black and white?' Yes! It couldn't be any other, surely. Well, talk about a mother scolding her adolescent son for staying out late… 'where the hell'… he just gazed out from our neighbour's bilges, eyes huge, ears flattened. The skipper thought he was still hung over when he woke, bleary-eyed to find a furry alien face staring at him! Enough to make you swear off the drink! The reason for midshipman Dudley's AWOL became clear. Our over-imbibing skipper had a girl cat! She and Dudley had gazed at each other for thirty-six hours, the only breaks occurring when Dudley cleared her food bowl and overloaded the litter tray. Sodden with bilge water, a little tottery on his paws, but none the worse for his hopeless assignation. Having assured our still bemused neighbour that his girl cat couldn't be pregnant, we carried Dudley home, to spend a beautiful evening in a mood of celebration, relief, and not a little amusement

Having learned how to order an American breakfast and that castration doesn't diminish a cat's desire, we headed once more into the wide Gulf. After a week of damaging storms, the bay spread smooth and glassy as far as the horizon. Our wake stretching into a long straight line behind us.

Hailed by shouts and frantic waving from a drifting power boat, we altered course to lay alongside. The boat had been rented out by three German lads on holiday. Although they were towing an inflatable and wearing lifejackets, there appeared to be no communication equipment aboard. They had waved at other passing vessels which had only waved back at them!

After reporting the situation to the coastguard on channel 16, we waited with them for more than an hour until the hire company arrived to tow them back to the resort. A night wallowing at sea would have been a very miserable and frightening experience for them.

By then it was early afternoon. Not having any deadlines or strong tidal issues to contend with, we decided to anchor overnight somewhere along the inland waterway just a few yards outside the channel buoys, entering the system via the swing bridge into Longboat Pass.

Perhaps our manoeuvres looked suspicious. Within minutes, a coastguard vessel ploughed to a stop beside us, ordering us to stop immediately, stay on deck, and do not move! Bulked up by military-style uniforms, fingering the holsters at their hips, four men leaped aboard to carry out the most thorough search so far. Despite explaining that flares inevitably run out of their 'flare by dates' during long voyages, we were duly 'cited' for a crime so serious that it took twenty minutes to write up. Why weren't we wearing life jackets? A copy of the citation eventually arrived at our holding address in England. Still, it was an interesting souvenir.

***

The consultant jerked his head back in surprise. I looked down, blushing with embarrassment. Were we being impertinent in asking for more when mere survival had already defied the odds?

He had listened patiently as I described Ken's progress. 'He can push up from his wheelchair with his arms; sit on the edge of the bed without support. His legs are strong from using a floor cycle and elasticated straps several times a day, but his legs are still bent at a preposterous angle (fixed flexion deformity) which has stopped us making further progress. Is there anything that can be done to help him to at least transfer himself from bed to chair, using a slide board?'

The consultant now smiled at us. 'I shall be pleased to do whatever I can, Mrs Gogay. Most patients who suffer severe strokes at Ken's age (sixty-six) just give up.' Ken and I looked at each other. I raised my eyebrows. He shook his head. Give up?!

We were offered a choice between two procedures. Stretch the ligaments by force followed by serial splinting of both legs with plaster casts over a period of several weeks. Alternatively, invasive, infection-risking surgery behind each knee. Since neither procedure carried any guarantee, we opted for the stretching.

CHAPTER 21

AMERICA. DREAMS AND NIGHTMARES

Peaceful evenings at anchor are welcome respite for most sailors. Ken was sorting out charts for safe stopovers while I settled down with a book, thinking how much we felt at home on the boat, that once below deck, we might just as well be bobbing gently on the Thames.

'This looks interesting,' said Ken. 'It's just a small spit of land, called the Dry Tortugas, dominated by a massive fort.'

Having never fired a shot, either defensively or offensively, Fort Jefferson is slowly sinking under its own weight. Although it is now a National Park, much of the military equipment is still in place, together with documentation compiled during its use as a prison. It made for fascinating reading. A list for rations dated 1868 included barrelled pork, cured hams, fresh beef (which was swum ashore), coffee, tea, white and brown sugar, bread, flour, cornmeal, hominy, rice, beans, dried apples, mixed vegetables, ketchup, lard, syrup, vinegar, hops, and tobacco. Canned items listed were oysters, clams, lobster, corn, potatoes, peas, onions, milk, peaches, pears, strawberries, peas, milk, and jellies. We wondered which of these provisions were issued to prisoners!

Even more fascinating were the log entries, one of which was disturbing, the other somewhat farcical.

'1865. Wednesday. March 1st. Corporal Erskine shot a black. He was sent to arrest him and the black showed fight. He let him have what he deserved.'

'Sunday 19th. Dr. Holden and Old Frost had a cat thrown in the breakwater for the sharks. But he did not seem to like cat meat and did not touch her and some of the prisoners hauled her up on an old shirt they had fast to a line. Mrs Devensorf was mighty mad about it.'

A formidable array of munitions lined the ramparts, the most sophisticated weapons of their time. 200-pounder Parrot Cannons with an eight-inch muzzle could launch a 175 pound missile to a distance of 2,000 yards. But the behemoth Rodman smoothbore, weighing twenty-five tons, could fire a 315 pound load as far as three miles. It took a seven-man crew to load this beast, in as little as one minute ten seconds. Below, in the courtyard, stood the hot shot ovens where steel balls were heated into smoking red incendiaries. These deadly weapons were first used by the British against the Romans in 54BC. Their awful consequences guaranteed their use for many centuries. One of the Polish Kings refined their use in cannon and in 1782, when defending Gibraltar, the English destroyed part of Spain's fleet with these hideous incendiaries.

At the time of our visit, the Park Ranger was a bright, enthusiastic, young woman called Caroline

Wiley. She had a fascinating C.V. Twenty years as a Park Ranger, three of them at Jefferson. After starting her career as a law student, she supervised a camping ground in the Smokey Mountains, an experience which changed her direction in life towards that of conservation. Becoming a ranger involves intensive training and covers wide-ranging skills: emergency medical, firefighting, boat operator, customs formalities. The islets are often used as anchorages for drug traffickers so she tours the area most days, gun at the ready. She once intercepted a small boat carrying 1,000 pounds of cocaine and single-handedly arrested the crew of three. What a girl!

In 1836, Horatio began construction of the fort. Its walls were eight feet thick. The records being too numerous to cover in a day, we never learned whether he himself completed the project, or even if he lived to see it, though he was said to have suffered greatly from boredom and loneliness.

By 1864, with not a single gun having been fired with intent, the fort was re-commissioned as a prison. John Wilkes Booth, the assassinator of Lincoln, along with many other, less renowned felons, served his life sentence there, though it is unlikely that clams or oysters were part of his diet. In 1867 a Cuban prisoner was said to have infected both guards and prisoners with yellow fever, resulting in many deaths. Following a second outbreak and two hurricanes, the garrison returned to the mainland in 1874.

In its day, Jefferson was the largest fort in the Western hemisphere. All the construction materials were supplied by cargo boats, including 16,000,000 bricks as well as vast amounts of coal. Pilings and yards, blackened with soot, are still evident.

We ventured inside. Long cool corridors brought welcome relief from the blistering heat. A yellow sun had bleached all traces of blue from the sky, heating the stonework so that the whole building shimmered in it. As our eyes adjusted to the muted colours, so did our minds. The military aspect, with its visions of mutilation, burning, screaming, now utterly eclipsed by what can only be termed the 'art form of bricklaying!' Arched ceilings, swirling patterns, especially in the Chapel. We wondered. Who were these artisans? Where did they come from? Men who could transform a military outpost, a prison, into a Cathedral. Biblical really... a place designed for war now sinking into the sand, bees excavating mortar from its bricks to build their nests. A costly, extravagant, posturing folly! No more useful today than as a five-star staging point for migrating Sooty Terns arriving from Cuba or South America, in their thousands.

We anchored overnight, just a few hundred yards off the atoll, from which vantage point we could admire the magnificent outline of the fort as dusk fell and shine a torch into the brilliantly clear water. A fishing boat was anchored nearby. Even as we killed engine, a crewman rowed over with a fine snapper for our dinner and an invitation to spend Christmas with them in Key West. We hoped such gestures didn't only depend on what flag is flown from the stern, though in country after country, we learned that such cynicism is misplaced within the sailing community. Duly chastened and it didn't hurt a bit!

Carefully planned routes, timetables, and 'must see' destinations no longer concerned us, although right times and wrong times that took account of seasonal weather patterns remained sensible precautions. Our journeys now would be decided by our encounters with other sailors, comments made on Channel 16, and fishermen. We would simply travel. Incidental would replace planning and would enrich our voyage in being guided to our destinations by the people who lived in these places.

A day and night sail brought us to the long channel that leads to Key West. Needing dawn light to eyeball the buoys in those treacherous shallows, we anchored in two fathoms of water, a few metres outside the markers. In four to ten fathom soundings, we started our approach at dawn. Turkey Buzzards alighted on the spreaders likes so many sailor lads on a tall ship. Dudley was beside himself at the audacity of it!

Key West. Brighton of America. A touristy, quaint, self-conscious, and glitzy place where personal freedoms appear to contradict, once again, the 'pursuit of happiness' aspired to in the 'Declaration of Independence.' Convinced that we have stepped into a crazy world of burlesque, we cautiously anchored among brightly painted houseboats, many of which were so rotten and rusted that a mere breeze might sink them.

Our usual greeting: a smile and a quiet 'hello' were received with gleeful amazement.

'Hey! You're British!' The voice boomed, a pumping handshake lasted too long. The only sense of community was the 'uniform' of genuine 'Key Westers', bandanas, hats of all description, and cut-off shorts. Artistic, eccentric, a drop-out haven, and judging by the number of sleeping drunks, a place live to the death. A huge uninhibited party. All day, all night, all year.

Nevertheless much of the quaintness was also fascinating. Colonial and Caribbean architecture, unusually narrow streets lined with artists' studios, gift shops, mini bazaars, cafés, diners, and shabby entrances into bars and clubs. Ken and I looked to each other with raised eyebrows, sharing our disquiet. There would be no evening excursions, and we must lock the boat securely. Tourists, being instantly recognisable, are fair game. Several barely sober youths spent much of their time riding bicycles along the jetty to plunge into the harbour, bike and all. An amusement for visitors that would earn the odd dollar. Best seen later in the day as speed and derring-do accelerate in direct proportion to the intake of Miller Lites, Buds, and shots of rum and whisky.

Drinking coffee, soaking up the atmosphere. Sitting at the next table were Frank and Holly. By the second coffee, we were sharing the same table and being invited to dinner aboard their boat *Rushcutter*. They struck us as a decidedly mismatched pairing. She, a girly, nearly blonde, energetic gal. He, a pot-smoking, older, moody, 'laid back too far' individual.

Did we sense something a bit shady about Frank even then? Could we have foreseen that something as innocuous as a café meeting would lead to the worst and most miserable of our sea journeys?

Their relationship was only a few weeks old but already struggling. Putting our doubts to one side, we spent several evenings with them. Frank was an experienced sailor, teller of a good yarn, but he revealed nothing of his past nor showed any curiosity about ours. Rather unusual for 'cockpit talk', which tends to revolve around 'Where have you been? What inspired you to acquire a boat, sail the oceans?' Topics which in the telling speak of character and personality together with guidelines that can lead to survival.

They were planning a cruise to the Bahamas before spending time in Dominican Republic in the hope of finding charter opportunities.

Despite the contrived atmosphere of Key West, we did enjoy a remarkable show on the dockside. An evening ritual called 'sun downing' (later exported to the UK as 'happy hour'). Each of the entertainments on offer earned a capful of dollars. Cats sitting on pedestals, like lions, jumping through hoops, yowling on command like an out-of-tune choir. Extraordinary. We hoped they were trained kindly. Jugglers, palm readers, stand-up comics, artists, and contortionists.

Twenty minutes before sunset, everyone gathers at the dockside to watch the sun's slow descent towards the horizon. We understood the sense of awe, its predictability, and its timelessness, though to witness the transit on a cloudless evening at sea had more impact.

Having spent an enjoyably different Christmas, if somewhat disenchanted by The Key West interpretation of 'living life to the full', we made our way North to Sugarloaf Key where we had arranged to meet up with Marian and June Bug from Cayman. After a tortuous, meandering passage, we anchored in the bay opposite Marian's two-storey, timber-built house. A nostalgic place for Marian, as she had lived there with her wheelchair-bound husband until he died. During dinner, we watched our first racoon as it nosed amongst the seaweed looking for food. At night, we slept in a huge American-style Emperor sized bed and giggled as we waved goodnight to each other across the expanse that separated us!

Travelling further up the Keys towards Marathon was to follow a serpent's trail. Each small Key emerged like the coils of a lurking monster. Although the channel is well buoyed, it is not an area to safely sail at night. The slightest variation in course risked grounding. Even with *Imago's* long shallow keel, there was often less than a couple of feet showing on the depth sounder.

Tornado watch! The broadcast interrupted the 'traffic' on channel 16 as we set anchor for the night. As the front tore through, we experienced our first 'white out.' Visibility nil and anchor light dim as a candle in a cave. Vicious squalls rolled in like marching squadrons. The anchor lifted as if we'd dropped a mere fishing hook from the bow. Fortunately, just a few metres outside a channel marker, we grounded softly and remained stuck fast for the next two days. There were no large boats to tow us off, but as the weather calmed, several powerful inflatables came to our aid. Manoeuvring like tugs, they swivelled us back into the channel. Clearly they had 'seen it all before'.

Being one of the largest of the serpent's coils, Marathon Key was a good place to stock up on provisions. Ken bought an alternator/controller to boost the batteries with thirty amps, doubling our capacity. He was always looking to the future.

Florida Keys are a great place for day sailing. Some are too small for development and barely accessible by land. Several times we squeezed out from the designated channel to spend a few hours walking round them. Some are protected parks where deer, racoons, and birds live in comparative safety... those which stray onto the highway end up as road kill.

Rodriguez Key proved to be a thrilling example of these small backwaters. Looking through binoculars to assess its safety for a dinghy approach, we nearly passed it by. Littering the small beach we saw what looked like dozens of discarded plastic plates! We thought there might be a natural eddy where debris from fast food outlets had fetched up onto the beach. Prepared in our minds to feel disgusted, we stepped ashore, only to stand rigid with amazement. The 'plates' had tails! Ken turned one over with his foot. The remnants of a jointed leg ending in pincers broke away. Crabs! Horseshoe Crabs. The beach was littered with them. Having neither seen nor heard of them before, we were entranced. Most of them had been dismembered and crushed by wind and surf, but above the tide line we found several flawless specimens, though none with their delicate claws intact. For some reason, they had chosen this particular Key to moult, as all crabs do. Whether it was part of a mating ritual remains a mystery, but the spiny carapace and the horseshoe shape, looked as prehistoric as we later learned it was. This particular work of nature apparently required very little evolutionary improvement beyond its inspired prototype of some 400 million years ago. Protected by a hard, convex, sand-coloured shell, having built in contact lenses and able to draw its ten legs under its body, it was hard to imagine anything less than the horny, beak-like mouth of a fully-grown turtle getting the better of it. The tapering triangular-shaped rear spine was attached by a double ball and socket joint, allowing for shallow water propulsion. When semi-submerged in soft sand, it would look ominously like the poisonous barb of a stingray (if you can scare off human predators, you've cracked it)! Whether resting on the sea bed or the beach they pass as large pebbles… or plates! Whether biologist, engineer, military strategist, inventor, or artist, a horseshoe crab is a marvel.

Collecting several of the best-preserved specimens, ranging in size from juveniles three inches in width to foot-wide adults, we carried them back to *Imago*. At some time in the future, when we had walls instead of bulkheads, we would hang a 'flight' of these extraordinary crabs, instead of ducks (and so we did).

On arrival in Miami we met a scene of devastation. Approaching 'No Name Harbour,' close to Biscayne Bay, we passed by swathes of damage caused by hurricane Andrew. Remaining tree stumps from trees that were broken in half were now being bulldozed from the ground. None of the boats in this tiny harbour had survived. A coastguard auxiliary boat was soon alongside to carry out the usual checks, which we again failed. But it was a friendly, more casual encounter than the armed boarding out at sea. Brian and Davis welcomed us to the US of A and wanted to hear what it had been like to travel from the 'British Islands' in a boat. Apparently they had seen a short piece of film of our departure from Cayman! We know nothing about it nor ever got to see it, but it seemed enough to make us 'cause celebre.' After an amiable chat, they arranged to meet us at the Miami International Boat Show. They then insisted on escorting *Imago* to the main port area off Watson Island where we could anchor safely in quiet water. This side to the American character only served to exaggerate its contradictions: friendly, helpful, gregarious, racist still, gun-toting, top dogs. Something like a collective bi-polar disorder. We would experience both personalities of this vast, complicated continent during the next few months.

Brian and Davis invited us to their homes, always a huge privilege for a traveller. Both families were chaotic and troubled. Achingly sad. Brian lived with his mother, she addicted to Tetris games, he to pornography. Both passions took priority over homemaking. Their houses were clapboard bungalows, each having a substantial 'backyard.' Not a flower or a bush to be seen. The remains of short-lived interests lay everywhere: weathered kayaks, camping paraphernalia, de-laminating surfboards, and wrecks of cars. Davis was clearly estranged from his wife and children and deeply unhappy. All rather distressing for us. Yet both men were so kind and helpful towards us. Where to shop, good advice, but warnings too, about pretty much everything! As they drove us to the supermarket, the guard at the door with his pump-action shotgun, they wound up the windows at every set of traffic lights, eyes darting left and right, tensed for trouble. We realised then that we must padlock the companionway doors from the inside before we went to bed.

Brian invited us to a meeting of the Coastguard Auxiliary Association and give a short talk on 'safety at sea.' We! Who had out–of-date flares, no safety harnesses, and no life raft! I chatted away a bit; using words like 'awareness,' keeping deck areas clear of lines, not getting your foot caught in a jam cleat, preparing in advance for the gybe, the tack, and the falling barometer. It all sounded rather lame to me, but we were politely applauded before being presented with a personalised plaque which we treasure still. Two days later we attended the AGM where almost everyone won an award. There was a militaristic feel to the event. It ended with a liturgy to 'the flag.'

The night before the AGM our dinghy was stolen, despite being chained to the stern. Brian found us one to borrow, but we were about to earn enough to replace it. A boat without a dinghy is to abandon all hope of survival. During the general chatting as the meeting ended, we were introduced to Assad Mahmood, the Egyptian owner of a thirty-six-foot sailing boat. Having been holed and sunk during the hurricane, it was raised and transported to a yard in a very sorry state. All of its inner woodwork lay in heaps. A yawning hole was still visible below the waterline. He was desperate for his vessel to be repaired, after what he described as 'cowboy rip-offs.' He struck us as a very emotional man. Tears welled in his eyes, but knowing that boats can do that to a man, we really wanted to help him.

Over the next four months, we spent every day working on his boat, though soon realised that Assad's expectations were hopelessly unrealistic. Every piece of timber had become mouldy from salt water and exposure, requiring weeks of sorting and sanding. No fitting plan, nothing labelled. All the electronics needed replacing, a new engine installed. The propeller tube and housing, being larger than the original, involved redesigning the stern opening for the shaft. In effect he was asking us to build another boat in sixteen weeks! Having completed the otherwise most expensive and skilled of the jobs, we left the labouring to others.

Davis had found us another mooring within walking distance of Assad's boat. It lay next to a truck depot on the Miami River. 'La Cabana' was a Cuban family business. Not sure what they thought about having British neighbours, but a cat that lined up dead rats for morning inspection was a foreign relations coup! They warned us to be careful. Of what?

It was only a short distance to a small shop, just outside the yard gates. Leaving a stew pot on simmer, we popped out to get a loaf of bread. As we strolled back to *Imago*, we heard noises aboard but just thought it was Dudley making mischief. I was first to board. A man was rifling through the galley cupboards. What a shock! Behind me I heard Ken bellow in anger. He practically abseiled down the companionway steps before grappling with the intruder, bundling him up into the cockpit. The fellow shook from Ken's grasp and ran off down the towpath.

I was trembling with fear. 'What if?' Questions filled my mind. He could have been armed with a knife or a gun! He might have kicked Dudley to death!

The young man, living on a small boat a few yards from us heard the commotion, watched the thief scale a fence and disappear, before coming to check if we were OK. His name was Terry. We invited him aboard. During his eight months at the mooring he himself had been robbed four times! Terry was planning to set sail on his own adventure, working locally in order to fully equip his boat before setting off.

I was alone on board when the next intruder came aboard. He was half way into the front hatch when I confronted him. Terry was home that day and saw the man board us. Running over with a machete in his hand, he 'arrested' the thief and marched him to the coach yard office where the villain was pushed and shoved a bit when they realised he was a fellow-Cuban. While waiting for the police to arrive, they shouted at him. 'These people are British! What will they think of us?' It seemed a rather old-fashioned view of British integrity, but it was wonderful to hear! The police came to see us a couple of days later. 'We had to release him as there was no physical or material damage.' Within days we fitted four new bolts to the hatches and bought a siren alarm system.

***

For six weeks Ken wore Plaster of Paris 'leggings' split along the shin line so that they could be prised open and removed for washing and creaming his legs.

'What should I do with these?' I asked the bin men, 'Can you take them?'

'Have you got an old pair of socks?' I found an old pair that needed darning. Did they realise that disposing of the 'legs' warranted a celebration? Perhaps limbs were just unusual items of rubbish! After putting the socks on the casts, they drove away with them sticking out from the rear of the dumpster. British humour at its best!

We were now referred for physiotherapy. Parallel bars were over-subscribed at the Rehab. Unit, so after arranging for bars to be fixed along the corridor in the flat and a hand rail on the wall next to Ken's bed they came to us twice a week. After pushing up from the wheelchair with his arms, Ken grasped the rail and stood. One step to the left, one step to the right. These simple movements became more smooth and confident as the weeks passed. At the end of the allotted period of their engagement, we were left with a rigid walking frame and the promise that they would re-engage if Ken made further progress.

The diary entry for April 3rd 2006 is written in red. Large letters, underlined, an exclamation mark and an asterisk for emphasis. From a sitting position on the edge of his hospital bed Ken fitted his forearms into the sleeves of the walking frame, raised himself up and took two steps. Immediately I sat him back on the bed. I just couldn't bear for him to do more. It overwhelmed me.

He hadn't had to think about it. One foot followed the other. Proper steps. Mind to muscles. Instinctively. He's going to walk again!

Student introduction to social work course –Grenada

Dudley meets his match

Communal Living – Kuna Indians – San Blas Islands

Imago heading towards the Channel

Ken reaches optimum level of recovery

Imago passing under Tower Bridge, 1988

Pelican visits – Venezuela

*National Dress – San
Blas Islands – Panama*

*Having fun with Ken
– Darien River
Panama*

Tropical blossom trees – Grand Cayman

Setting out on islands trip with lads from Grenada

Hoopoe visits

Imago

Tar footed kitten – Greece

Child's dugout

Foster parenting – Grand Cayman

Ship's cat – Dudley

CHAPTER 22

TRAVELS IN THE BAHAMAS WITH THE AUXILIARY COASTGUARD AND A CON MAN

We would enjoy several cockpit chats with Terry during the weeks that followed the attempted robbery, mostly about the acceptance of violence in America. Muggings and tourist attacks seemed commonplace. Only recently, a woman tourist had been beaten to death at the roadside after being 'bumped' in her rental car, her licence plates and the company's logo having given her away. That particular incident made International headlines in being so brutal, even by American standards.

Brian wanted us to buy a gun. According to the statistics, that would mean one more added to the two hundred million already owned by the population in America. We declined. He was shocked. Every night sharp crackles of gunfire echoed from the suburbs. Some were celebration shots fired into the air: births, engagements, weddings, others probably more sinister. Watching USA news programmes on our battery-operated television was far from reassuring. Hyped up. Graphic. Bloodied bodies on the sidewalk. Fast talking, breathless, screaming newsreaders dwelling on every gory detail.

Oh for a quiet anchorage in a calm lagoon!

The Rodney King beating trial was being held in L.A. The Waco cult siege would soon turn into an indiscriminate fireball of horror.

Food. Be it snacks or the challenge of 'all you can eat.' If Americans ate grass the whole world would have to be a meadow! Diners, road stalls, all the brand named fast food outlets, many of which were poised to join McDonalds and Kentucky Fried Chicken in other countries of the world, rich or poor. Constant grazing or chewing as they walk, pavements carpeted with gum. We ventured into a supermarket. A worthwhile visit, as are all ethnic experiences! A bowl of cornflakes with evaporated milk had proved a satisfying snack during night watches, so we headed for the cereals isle. New and improved, enriched with vitamins, reduced sugar, fruited. Bunny-shaped for children, hoops, loops. No cornflakes! There may have been, but half way along a fifty-yard aisle I felt so overwhelmed that I suggested we leave. On the way out we had to pass the ice-cream, section. We who were so satisfied with vanilla, strawberry, or chocolate, were now close to panic. We made for the exit and immediately stopped by security and the gun.

'You didn't buy anything!'

'We only wanted cornflakes.'

'Well, where are they?'

'We couldn't find them.'

The security guard didn't say anything else so it was hard to know what he was really thinking, but we had spoken so he knew we were British. His look softened a little, like it does when addressing ninety year-old 'cupcakes' or those who are intellectually 'challenged.' He let us go. I forced myself to make for the exit with a calm stroll, bravely conquering an urge to run!

The last straw was probably the sandwich!

'Two ham sandwiches please.' They were delivered to our table on a dinner plate (and in America even the dinner plates are big as serving platters). Our sandwiches were two and a half inches thick. A sliver of ham cowered under a duvet of salad. Oozing with 'Mayo,' crisps scattered around the edges. Hinged jaws, evolutionary marvels though they are, may be handy for singing high notes or cleaning your teeth, but a gaping mouth in a restaurant? Tasteless? Ken has a large mouth. It makes his smile electric; even so, his first bite released a lava flow of 'Mayo' into his lap. 'We need a flower press,' he mumbled. But boat builders are so ingenious! We asked for a knife, cut the sandwich into slices, squeezed out the excess 'Mayo,' 'passed' on the crisps, and discovered the ham. Designed by industrial psychologists, supermarkets and fast food outlets are surely intended to raise matters of choice to a stress level that can only be relieved by buying furiously just to get out. If the whole world consumed and discarded at such a rate, we would all share the fate of the buffalo... and soon.

To be fair, frugal living for the average cruising boat is the norm. Limited storage space means that most provisions, beyond the first few days are non-perishables carefully chosen to last at least a month at sea. Before setting out, we toasted slices of bread (al a Melba), storing them in vacuum packs. Vegetables bought unripe might last two weeks, especially, cabbage, swede, carrots, potatoes. Lemons and limes lasted throughout the longest of our ocean passages. During really foul weather, hard boiled eggs and a tin of rice pudding each, sufficed. Conserving fuel for navigation lights and instruments was far more important during those first few years than running a fridge or freezer. Twelve years into our travels, we acquired a small counter fridge. Our excitement at such sophistication was ridiculous! But it was another tip from a cruising wife that would change our whole approach and provide us with properly sustaining meals for the next nine years. We bought a restaurant-sized pressure cooker, dozens of preserving jars, chicken, beef and lamb. Before we left America, we had stowed some fifty jars of nourishing stew. Minutes to heat, whatever the weather.

Where next? A return visit to Grand Cayman? Are we ready for the Panama Canal? Or shall we island hop in the Bahamas? The matter was soon decided for us. We travelled up the Keys without stopping. The ever-vigilant US Coastguard stopped us twice but didn't board us. Back at Watson Island we met up again with coast guard auxiliary Brian. He had lost his job and asked to join us for a spell to see if he liked the way of life and to experience a deep sea passage. Frank also reappeared. His trip with Holly had ended in acrimony. His boat was stranded in Dominican Republic where a lien had been placed on his vessel because of court proceedings over a failed business. We agreed to have them aboard.

While they set about making arrangements, we went to a meeting of the Sierra Club with Assad. Being the largest conservation group in the States, we expected cutting edge solutions and post-buffalo enlightenment. But this was no 'grass roots' organisation, more a 'Masonic' opportunity for social and business introductions. The brief agenda concerned bolder signs along the inland waterways, urging speed boats to slow down in order to reduce crippling and often fatal injuries to those few Manatees that survive. The parking area was full of six door cars, sporty gas guzzlers, drinks and refreshments all served up in polystyrene containers! Like consuming a banquet then ordering a diet Coke!

Americans seem rarely to ask or seek advice but do presume that if there is stuff 'they' cannot live without, neither can anyone else! Brian insisted that if we were all going on a boat 'trip', we 'must have' a barbecue on the stern deck, an air compressor, four dive tanks and his three bags of personal gear. He was mortified to realise that we didn't possess an IPERB distress beacon.

Frank had the same mind set, but whereas Brian was genuinely looking for ways that weren't money to show his appreciation, Frank's motives were not only self-serving but also shady at best and downright illegal at worst!

It just didn't feel right.

'It's what they want,' said Frank as he passed up TVs, tools, radios, and batteries from his dinghy.

'Won't they be confiscated?' I tried.

'Trust me. I know them all; they'll swap with us for fuel and stuff.'

He proceeded to load up *Imago* until every conceivable space was filled, turning her into a container ship. Our boat was never so heavy in the water and the force of Frank's personality, his garrulous confidence, and his instant camaraderie stood testament to the skills required of a successful con-man. And we, foolishly stood testament to victimhood.

All aboard. No worries about checking the charts for a compass guided route or marked hazards, we have our own 'pilot' aboard who has 'done this trip several times.'

As we passed 'Government Cut', where the cruise ships docked and entered the bay, Brian spotted a raft which appeared to be just bobbing about with no sign of propulsion. Neither an outboard nor oars. The thought that the occupants might be sleeping in such a heavily trafficked area triggered Brian's training as a coast guard auxiliary, and he suggested that Ken draw alongside to investigate. Giving the first signs of the personality clash he would have with Brian, Frank, with some petulance said, 'It's none of our business, let's get on with it.'

It was a 'Marie Celeste' raft. A flimsy construction made from a tractor inner tube tied to large polystyrene blocks. Inside a small canvas-covered cuddy were packing cases marked 'Cuba.' We eased the craft alongside with the boathook. Floating in the water-logged bilge were a couple of full water containers, clothes, recently caught fish, and a makeshift mast.

'Just leave it,' Frank shouted. 'Cubans, they try it all the time.'

Silence. We three must each have thought it prudent to ignore such callous indifference. We were barely three miles into the journey yet there was already enough tension aboard that you could smell it, taste it.

'Use the VHF,' advised Brian, 'call up the coast guard.'

Frank snorted and went below. Brian gave a very professional report: GPS position, status of the vessel. Within minutes, a military jet screamed above our heads.

We should have turned back, deposited Frank, his contraband and opted instead to take Brian on a Bahamian cruise. Oh that we had!

That first evening we anchored between two islets, having nearly collided with them in pitch blackness. He who 'knew the route like the back of his hand,' shrugged his shoulders before retiring to his bunk, followed shortly thereafter by Brian. Ken and I took our usual turns at anchor watch. Even so, we did the following twenty-four hour sail without the help of either man.

It was a huge relief to spend two days in Nassau, especially for me. Frank was a misogynist, Brian was never able to sustain a relationship with a woman. Both behaved as if I were the hired help, as if I had abseiled from the moon! Only Dudley looked to me, though even his expression was reproachful! Ken was distant too. But I know him. He was 'hanging tight,' as they say. Sooner or later Frank would be 'trouble' and on a small boat at sea, 'trouble' is a large, inescapable threat.

After booking in, we spent most of a day in town and like all ex-pats, temporary or permanent, enjoyed a bit of British nostalgia: 'yellow perils,' English cops in tropical uniform, pads and tickets at the ready, reliable transport, tarmac roads. The museum focused on Bahamian slave history, though by doing so described little about at people who have inhabited the archipelago for millennia.

Having anchored among lobster-fishing boats and small freighters, we noticed the first shocking clue as to why the world's reefs are 'bleaching.' Did researchers realise at the time what a sadly accurate description that was? Tons of the stuff were being shipped aboard. Barrels of it sat in specially constructed cradles on their decks.

We asked a fisherman, 'Why all that bleach?'

'To flush lobsters and big grouper from crevices!'

Nassau is steeped in history. Although sharing the same slaving past as so many other Caribbean communities, Bahamians appear to have emerged from a totally understandable and justifiable resentment to one of confidence and pride. Relaxed, welcoming, not a scowl to be seen. The only other island to have reconciled such dreadful grievance had been the French protectorate of Martinique. The benefits of unloading the heavy weight of historical resentment seemed as adult and wise as is an amicable divorce from a domineering marriage, where the children are not burdened by the notion that half of them is bad! Concessions to tourism appear neither overstated nor grasping. It was such a pleasure to wander through the straw market, a floating bazaar operated from Guatemala, without the 'carpet seller' pounce! English newspapers too! Ridiculous, unconcealed joy! Headline news, 'Cat for the House of Commons.' How British was that?!

We spent the next day aboard, pottering about. 'The lads,' as I now thought of them, including my own unfaithful skipper come life companion, sat in the cockpit as twilight turned to black. Chatting away with the lights from cruise ships as a backdrop. Hollywood lighting, me in the wings offering snacks. I sat below reading, Dudley purring in my lap. 'You and me mate,' I told him.

Feeling much restored and hoping that at some time in the future we would visit Nassau again, we plotted a day-sailing route through the rest of the Bahamian islands, overnight sailing being far too dangerous in these shallow, reef strewn waters. That night we anchored off the sinisterly named 'Shroud Key.' A barren but pretty outlook. Conch were so abundant that Brian skin-dived for them. Not knowing the Caribbean way of cooking them, we cut the meat into strips and fried them. Despite each having our own teeth, trying to chew leather was clearly beyond their design tolerance! Interesting and revealing too, Ken, Brian, and I giggled as we drooled. Frank snorted. As made our way out from the anchorage next morning, we passed huge caches of beer bottles and empty shells, rising up in hazardous mounds like small islets.

Frank's behaviour was becoming increasingly bizarre. Despite having sailed through the area just a month previously, his advice (only when asked) was vague and far too casual for such a shallow and hazardous area as the Bahamian Banks where depths are often less than two metres. Great Exuma was very nearly a leg too far. Negotiating a winding entrance channel in twilight, *Imago* grounded twice. By anchor down, Ken and I were bone-weary and dearly wishing we had never met Frank. He had presented himself as a fellow sailor in need, yet persisted in abusing our instinct to help him. It was all about to get much worse!

Ken and I, Dudley too, needed time together. A taste of 'life before Frank', so we took our passengers to the beach where there was a small pier from which they could enjoy a walk. Brian stepped ashore and asked Ken to throw him the 'rope' to pull up the dinghy.

'It's a painter,' sneered Frank.

'Rope' will do,' Ken shot back.

Brian was a coastguard auxiliary, a brave man, not just checking craft for contraband or to comply with USA rules about safety equipment, but prepared to go out in the rough stuff to preserve lives, the equivalent of our own RNL1 volunteers. Frank's remark was patronising, pompous, and unnecessary. Brian had also earned a silver star in the Vietnam War, for crawling into a cave occupied by the enemy to rescue a comrade.

Back on board, we seemed to breathe differently, we three and *Imago* belonged to each other again.

Gt. Exuma is a peaceful anchorage for most of the year. It relies on an annual cruising regatta which is said to net two million dollars. Otherwise, its people depend on small scale farming and fishing. Brian came across a deserted, overgrown orchard and brought back forty pounds of huge ripe grapefruit wrapped in his anorak. A new and welcome addition to the larder. While Frank spent the day in his bunk, the rest of us peeled and segmented the fruit, packing it into quart jars before preserving them in the pressure cooker. It was pleasant work, having something of a pioneering approach to foraging and self-sufficiency, such tasks fitted the life style we had chosen.

Frank had totally disassociated from us all. It was patently obvious that he himself was suffering. But why? He surely realised that in the Bahamas, day-sailing is the only safe option, that however much he was fretting about his own vessel, the safety of *Imago* and her passengers was a skipper's obligation. For whatever reasons, a 'bad dream' was soon to become a nightmare. The next leg to Long Island was the beginning of that awful transition.

CHAPTER 23

FOUR MEN, SEVEN LADS, A WOMAN, A CAT AND A BRIGHT FULL MOON

Imago appeared to be of the same mind...let us be done with this! She hurried along in fine style averaging six to seven knots in a brisk following wind. We rarely consulted the speed log. It was the 'voice' of the wind and 'weight' of it that guided us. As the sound increased to a low moan, Ken reduced sail.

'Why the hell are you doing that?' shouted Frank. I wondered how soon the situation would explode into a full-scale row. It was a huge relief when Ken passed the wheel to me before going to sit on the stern coaming where he could growl and cuss for a bit. Quite a blow threatened as the wind topped forty knots, but as we entered the lovely, almost enclosed harbour, the sea became tranquil, leaving the wind to vent its irritation elsewhere.

It was Halloween night. A big red moon entered stage left, bathing the anchorage with a pink glow, as if she had passed the sun on her way in and was blushing from her encounter with him. One of those nights when

Ken and I would have stretched out on the cockpit seats, feeling deeply content, stilled, in love with our surroundings.

Right girl! No better way to sooth a savage man's breast than food. A jar of chicken, home-made roux sauce, rice, slices of melon, chocolate biscuits. 'Voila! Chicken fricassée! I announced as I rang the cockpit bell. Frank accepted his tray with listless indifference. Ken caught my eye with his 'somebody's heading for trouble' look. Frowning first, I shook my head, before winking my approval of his self-control. Confrontation on land can generally be managed, especially if it is not fuelled by alcohol: remove your wretched person from my sight, you Varlet. Run. Walk away. Spit on the ground. Or that wonderfully precise invective 'Sod off!' However, in a six-foot cockpit or a fourteen-foot saloon, 'walking off in a huff' doesn't have that same 'Hollywood sweep' effect.

By late evening huge rollers were crashing into the harbour entrance, transforming the tranquil harbour into open sea conditions, the beginning of a dreaded 'Norther.' Brian the brave swam over to help another yacht re-anchor. A fifty-five-foot racing yacht was forced to leave the small dock or risk catastrophic hull damage. Mosquitos gathered, sensing a deluge. Ken and I spent the night on anchor watch, wrapped in foul weather gear, clutching wetted rags to our faces as protection from those clamouring blood suckers.

Dudley found his usual storm berth in the bilges. At 7am a 'whiteout' obliterated the land the boats, the heavens. With it came the rain. Rain that stings your face, finds its way into wet gear, bows you down. We were a miserable ship.

During a lull in what was to be a forty-eight-hour weather front, we could see what would have been a delightful meandering walk to the higher ground at the rear of the bay. Two small churches stood side by side. An improbable couple. A failed marriage of sorts. Each stood testament to the schisms that dilute both the power and the wisdom of all major religious. Each had been commissioned by a Bishop who changed his religion from Catholic to Protestant! Christians both, yet no accommodation towards each other. Was it impossible to hold services in the same church at different times?

Frank was becoming increasingly agitated by the delay caused by the weather. Massive breakers beat against the outer Cays and reefs, but so far the anchor held firm. It was only when Frank rolled up his sleeves to release the sweat pouring from his body, when the tremors in his arms caused him to clasp his mug with both hands, that the penny dropped. He was suffering withdrawal symptoms! Whether from alcohol or drug abuse, we wouldn't know until we made landfall, but it was abundantly clear that we had a very sick man aboard.

I spoke to Ken, 'He's a rogue, love. He could be putting us all in jeopardy. Some addicts can become violent. There are sores breaking out around his mouth and on his knuckles. What do you think we should do?' Ken was angry at having to weigh such risks, but the urge to reclaim our home and lifestyle, his faith in the strength of *Imago* and perhaps a smidgeon of respect for a fellow sailor who had a least tried to resist carrying his drugs on our vessel. The thought of *Imago* being impounded and all of us being hauled off to prison was visibly shocking to him.

'We'll break out and make a run for it.'

It was a decision that would lead to one of the most heart-warming encounters of our travels.

After checking the charts for Crooked Island and a nearby atoll, we lifted anchor at 4pm. An escape from the lagoon was a desperate gamble. Huge rollers crashed over the bows. White water, high as a house, swept along the coamings. At times we 'disappeared' into the maelstrom of boiling water until finally, we met those huge swells that marked the abating of the weather front.

By 7pm, stiff with tension, we dropped anchor in the calm waters of the atoll. Shining our powerful deck light from the bows, zigzagging between the 'bommies' (coral heads) we headed towards a small fishing boat, presuming that they had anchored in good holding ground. There were signs of agitation aboard as we approached. A man running to the bows, bending over the anchor winch, hand lines hastily drawn in by those who were fishing from the side decks. Two small dinghies bobbed at the stern.

Waving a greeting to them, we set about the usual harbour routines: laying out the anchor, switching on the mooring light, and tightening sail ties on the boom. The crew of the fishing boat watched, silent and unmoving. Finally one of them waved back at us. We responded so enthusiastically that they all began to wave, smiling broadly, hollering out their greetings like a chorus of seagulls.

What then followed was an evening of such joy and camaraderie, such a 'night of nights' as to rank as one of the most vividly remembered encounters of our fifteen-year journey around the world.

Illegal fishing explained their earlier consternation as they thought we were a patrol boat. Though barely thirty feet long, their vessel accommodated eight young men, including the thirty-year-old Captain. All hailed from Dominican Republic, some twelve hours distant. The lads were stocky, well built, and happy seamen. Other than cook and Captain, they were divers. Strapped onto the deck were two powerful compressors attached to 100 feet lengths of hose. Theirs was a risky way to fish.

'The foreigners took all our fish... we have to feed our families.' Yes, we thought. Three of the lads rowed over to *Imago* to gift us with a twelve pound grouper, sea biscuits, milk fudge (!), and sweets. Ken gifted them back with engine oil, boiled sweets, a bottle of wine, and coffee (which they craved).

'Share with us,' said Ken. We had plenty of potatoes aboard, so while the lads filleted the fish, I cooked a mound of chips. We didn't have twelve plates aboard, so Brian made up the shortfall with double thickness cooking foil. When all was ready, the Captain signalled for the remainder of his crew to row over to us. Ken rang the cockpit bell, 'dinner is served!' Sound the dinner gong, the Dowager *Imago* looking regal, fish and chips. All rather British!

Five men, seven lads, one woman, and one cat, all topsides, tucking into one of the best tasting fish in the sea, accompanied by the crispiest of properly chunky chips and not one mention of oozing puddles of tomato sauce or 'Mayo.' A little salt, a sprinkle of vinegar, just enough to enhance the flavour of a fish that makes cod taste bland.

'Needs a squeeze of lemon,' Frank remarked.

'Never mind, eh?' Ken shot back. Once again, a 'Frankish,' unnecessary remark. I could only laugh and shake my head.

After the meal I made a large saucepan of strong coffee – the lads seemed to have an insatiable appetite for it. A dollop of evaporated milk added a gourmet touch to round off the banquet.

The risen moon seemed to hover above us, bathing the lagoon in silver. Full and replete, we all lay on deck looking at the stars. Our young Captain could speak some English. He warned us to avoid Gt. Inagua where a yacht skipper had been robbed and shot in both arms. A blockade of Haiti was being enforced by gunships and even here we could see helicopter lights, circling, high in the sky.

The atoll surrounded two tiny Cays and areas of sand bars, submerged or exposed, according to the tide. Two large vessels had foundered here. The largest was a freighter 'Lady Eagle,' now home to a pair of nesting Ospreys, the smaller, a Liberty Ship from WW2. Both ships had been picked clean of anything not welded down. The lagoon itself was a vast tropical aquarium of spectacular coral and fish.

We had a small combination television below. Ken brought it up into the cockpit and slipped 'Raiders of the Lost Ark' into the DVD slot. The lads were jubilant! Squeezing into a close huddle, they never took their eyes from the twelve-inch screen, laughing and cheering at the action scenes, the expressions on the face of Harrison Ford. We wondered how they could laugh in the right places without understanding what was being said, but as we watched with them we realised that Action Movies, along with Westerns, can be understood in any language. How's that for 'actions speak louder than words?'

Perhaps it was the fact that Ken and I were of parental age (indeed how proud we would have been to have them as sons) that made their attitude towards us a delightful combination of teasing familiarity and deference. For the first time during this otherwise ghastly cruise, I was given both a face and a voice! In return, there was nothing I wouldn't have done to give them joy. Dudley's bold friendliness and his insistence in joining their huddle astonished them. But for the life of me, I couldn't remember whether they still ate cats in the Dominican Republic!

Close to midnight, as the moon neared its zenith, the lads disembarked, shaking each of our hands as they lined up to leave. They would be selling their catch at their home dock come late morning. Half an hour later, dinghies stowed, they motored out of the pass, waving, their small boat fading to a charcoal-coloured shape before finally being swallowed by the night, leaving us alone again in an empty lagoon.

After setting the GPS to anchor watch, Ken and I slept in the cockpit to prolong the experience, not wanting anything or anyone to spoil it.

'We'll remember this and the rest of it will soon be over,' I said to Ken. Dudley wrapped himself around my head; the lovely moon began her descent. I couldn't help but gaze up at her once more. 'Thank you,' I whispered.

At 9am we carefully made our way out through the pass. We should have charted another overnight anchorage, but the urge to get to Dominican Republic overruled our usual caution. Frank was breaking out in sores. He smelled dreadful, having not washed since we set out. Before reaching open water and the final run into Puerto Plata, we must negotiate a three mile gap between two last islands. Pitch black, only the GPS and precise way points keeping us on course, not a single light showing from the land. As the only spare 'hand', Brian was called from his bunk. He and I stood together at the pulpit for two hours, scanning the water for debris, or if we got it wrong, overhanging trees! We both sank to the deck with relief when Ken announced that we were through.

During the following day both wind and seas increased. By nightfall, conditions deteriorated to such an extent that we became silent, tense, and afraid. A wind that moaned now began to scream as *Imago* battled into a ferocious headwind. Strong currents bounced off the islands, creating breaking waves that rolled us scupper to scupper. Huge white-water rollers exploded over the bows, soaking us. Under assault from every quarter, it was almost impossible for me to steer and nearly too much for Ken and Brian. They took turns of fifteen minutes each, collapsing with exhaustion between stints. Frank remained below. The coffee canister discharged its contents over the cooker top and was soon joined by an open can of evaporated milk that had been wedged hard between lines of plastic storage jars. Frank made no move to pick them up, even grinding them into the carpet when he came up to relieve himself. *Imago* heeled over as never before. Dudley hurled himself into my lap, claws out, holding himself fast in my skin. Twelve foot seas from every direction. Both Brian and Ken were heroes that night. With the wind now exceeding forty knots and simply no 'set' to a sea that now mauled and shook us. We were helpless prey, as is the mouse to the cat.

It was Brian who earned the medal that night. 'Mentioned in dispatches' would not have done proper justice to his bravery and stoicism during his first experience of storm conditions. We learned later that a fifty footer had foundered, her five South African crew surviving to tell their tale after spending eight days in a life raft. After a long hard haul and as the storm abated, the town lights of Puerto Plata could be seen twinkling through the dawn haze. Ken and I looked at each other, sighing deeply, no less relieved than if we ourselves had been shipwrecked and now nearing salvation.

Three aboard *Imago* are nursing severe headaches and sore muscles. The fourth leaped ashore, fresh as a daisy and made for the nearest bar. We remained anxious about our cargo, but customs were cordial and soon wheeling and dealing with a suddenly affable Frank. But he never spoke to us again, never thanked us for his free charter. As soon as he had bartered the items stowed aboard *Imago*, he was done with us. The only times we saw him after that were at the bar.

Although it was a two mile walk to the nearest restaurant, Brian joined us for our traditional landfall celebration. We all felt hungry, but ate little. After so many days of tension and anxiety, we were all severely dehydrated. Back on board, we slept for ten hours, the longest rest we'd had in more than three weeks. Brian had developed a weeping sore on his thumb similar to those on my knuckles. Adding injury to insult. Frank had passed on his highly contagious impetigo!

Over the next two days we spent hours disinfecting every handhold or surface that Frank may have touched. The cooker top emitted a putrid smell from the spilled milk and had to be unscrewed from its fixing plates to be cleaned. We scrubbed the carpet on the dockside. Ken and I added several new curses to our repertoire. Although Puerto Plata is small port, there was a village atmosphere. Small scattered housing, unmade roads, and a single dilapidated shed served as the only municipal building. Most homes comprised a single room with one bed or partitioned areas for sleeping.

Doors stood open, showing interiors that looked homely and prettily decorated. Apart from the odd working vehicles standing ready to offload the small freighters and a few scooters and bicycles, most journeys were undertaken on foot. Dozens of apparently communal goats wandered about amongst the pedestrians. No dogs. No cats. Once again I tried to remember: Do they eat them? Fortunately Dudley remained on board, cowed by the unrelenting din of music that was by turn, loud, louder, louder still!

Brian and Ken helped one of the fishermen haul his boat. 'Come my house,' he said. Such invitations are a rare honour and more than enough to set aside the tribulation and fear of the last three weeks. A small generator throbbed in the background to provide a candle's worth of light and a very fuzzy black and white picture from the TV. The fisherman's wife and four children crushed together on the sofa, the rest of us sat cross-legged on the floor. Our host held the rabbit ear in his hand, constantly adjusting it to catch a signal. Frank had been right about that at least, to own a TV was a wondrous novelty. We were never made so welcome nor felt as safe as we did in this small community that nestled among mangroves, overlooked by grand mountain ranges and close to the river that separated it from Haiti, their beleaguered, impoverished, strife-ridden neighbour.

Farewell then to what we remember as the 'town of scooters.' Small 50cc Honda's roared along every footpath, carrying impossible loads; a man, his wife and a child, two enormous cages full of live geese, three gas cylinders, enough palm leaves to roof a house!

We now decided on an open sea route for an uninterrupted journey north of the Bahamas back to Miami. Brian had stories to tell, Bill had booked his holiday with us, and Marian was going to drive Ken to Fort Lauderdale to buy a solar panel. If we did decide to take on the Pacific Ocean, we knew we must also invest in a powerful auto-pilot. We were novices still and the Pacific is one of the most formidable, mysterious, and hazardous places on the planet. Pimpled with islands, most named, others that appear and disappear as volcanos erupt from the deeps, sea mounts agitate the surface of the sea, powerful underwater currents. A place where monsters might yet lurk.

Ken returned with a story to tell. 'I was agog. You would have been aghast.' He smirked. Dotted along the freeway. Hot dog stalls. Young women dressed in two sequins and a G-string! 'Hot' dogs indeed!

When Brian told us that a space shuttle would blast off in ten days' time from Cape Canaveral we were thrilled. Everything about the Universe, galaxies, the origins of life, held us in thrall. At sea, gazing up at the swirling density of the Milky Way, we would lie in the cockpit trying the grasp the enormity of one light year, ten trillion kilometres, always failing. But we loved the figures: the Earth is 4.5 billion years old, the most distant galaxies are 16 billion light years distant, approximately 100 billion galaxies in the known universe!

Before leaving for Canaveral, we took Bill to Sea World. The tubular glass construction was as remarkable as the inhabitants. Sharks, turtles, shoals of psychedelic reef fish, squid, lobster guarding their rock crevices, realistic turbulence, waving fronds of coral, and grouper nosing the glass. To left and right, above our heads. Almost authentic except that divers fed the carnivores. A nautical zoo of wonders that left us even more determined to journey on and meet many more of our forebears, our cousins, our ancestors, in an amazing world that would be such a diminished planet without them.

Photographs, videos, and TV coverage. None of which can fully capture the thrill and drama of witnessing a rocket launch. The scale of it, the tension. We anchored in the sheltered bay opposite the launch pad the night before the scheduled launch. Even from a mile distant the structures looked immense. Eiffel towers piercing the sky. Throughout the evening the scaffold was bathed in powerful beams of light as vehicles and personnel swarmed around its base. We had been warned that the noise and vibration would be equivalent to that of 1,000 large motorcycles revving up!

8.50 a.m. Camera ready. Check watches. Turn on the radio to listen to the countdown. 7.6.5.4.3.2…abort! This was the ultimate in dud fireworks, a couple of puffs of blue vapour leaked out from the engines only to drift away and quickly evaporate. However disappointing, we readily agreed that to shut down at such a late stage of the countdown was never a lightly considered action nor the safety of astronauts a lightly considered responsibility.

We consoled ourselves by visiting the Space Museum. Imagining the pioneers strapped in like Formula 1 drivers in just as small a space. Those first tin-thin rockets flown by men as brave as the first sailors and explorers.

Still tired and perhaps a little disillusioned by the exhausting predations of Frank, we decided to return to Grand Cayman and there consider our future.

***

Our carers spoke of bed-bound clients left alone for hours, developing pressure sores. Depressed, resigned, and fading away. Yet unless a stroke victim is paralysed or unresponsive, exercise is the key that leads to whatever optimum level of recovery a person is capable of in terms of physical and emotional health.

Circulation, digestion, muscle tone, and continence control all depend on movement and for the receiver it communicates optimism, achievement, and personal engagement. For Ken, twice daily exercise periods would lead to an astounding level of physical and mental improvement as well as more subtle effects that would suddenly emerge to surprise and delight me.

Even before Ken took those first two steps, he had willingly engaged in bed and chair exercises. 'Swimming' with his arms, pulling on elasticated straps, bending and straightening his legs on a slide sheet, lifting them up with weights attached. We acquired a foam football. It was weeks before he could catch and throw it when it landed in his lap, but gradually his co-ordination improved to a point where he could catch it even if he couldn't throw it back. The first time he bounced it back, he laughed out loud.

Within a month, two steps became a bed length, the width of the nursing room and soon after that he was pushing the shower chair up and down the fourteen metre corridor in the flat. When the physiotherapists returned, they hugged us both.

We were asked to attend a meeting of medical professionals who were all familiar with Ken's records and the severity of his stroke. When Ken raised himself out of the wheelchair and walked across the room, both physiotherapists and I cried as the room erupted in applause.

One of the Doctors approached us as we were leaving. 'What led you to believe your husband might walk again Mrs Gogay?' He may have thought my answer strange. 'Because towards the end of his time in hospital, Ken recalled his signature and kept writing it down. That was when I knew that his mind was mending.'

CHAPTER 24

WRONG TIME. WRONG PLACE. WRONG MIND SET

Throughout an uneventful sail back to Grand Cayman we talked about our experiences of America. Without having seen anything of its magnificent landscape; The Grand Canyon, prairies, or the Rocky Mountains, our impressions were neither fair nor balanced, though we knew for certain that we could never feel comfortable in such an insatiable environment.

The statistics may be no more alarming than for other countries, but for us they still spoke loudly. One person shot or stabbed every three minutes sixteen seconds. Sounds of sirens and the screech of ambulance were as ordinary as the constant drone of aircraft taking off from Miami Airport at a rate of seventy per hour. Some of the 'downtown' areas are quite literally and liberally scattered with drunk and hopeless bodies. Recycling and conservation are fashionable but no amount of separating glass and beer cans will alter the muddy colour of Biscayne Bay or reduce the millions of tons of daily garbage that pours out from three-fridge homes or the takeaway arcades that line each thoroughfare. We thought about the sad fate of urban wildlife. Miniature deer living on Big Pine and Sugarloaf Keys. Delightful, shy, standing just twelve inches at the shoulder, found nowhere else in the world. At the last count just thirty remain. During the six days we were there, seven had been killed by cars which had blatantly refused to slow down as they passed the well signposted sites.

Manatee (also called dugong). Prehistoric link to the great sea mammals. Less than 2,000 left, yet within a month a dozen more have succumbed to lacerations caused by twin 150HP outboard engines attached to speedboats, their owners refusing to grant 'constitutional rights' to anyone except themselves.

It's true! You can walk into any pawn shop (a multi-mega business) or arms supplier and buy a pistol or rifle. Another Constitutional Right and the killing and maiming goes on. As in Jamaica, every business must have an armed guard, razor-tipped fence, guard dogs, and barred windows.

It all suggested a fragile dependence on 'wants' over needs. The recent hurricane had provided a shocking example that was widely broadcast. In all the mayhem, disaster, and shattered dreams, many of those being interviewed were crying out for ice! A truck driver delivering this seemingly priceless commodity was even forced to leave his cab as it was being looted by an angry scuffling crowd!

We were never so glad to see the low-lying lights of Cayman.

Having been logged as 'persona grata' by customs, we were cordially invited back to our 'second home.'

Within two weeks we were offered several 'job and finish' tasks with NCVO. Painting the walls, ceilings and doors at the retirement home, re-furbishing a building and painting all the cots for use in a baby unit, and converting the largely unused porch at the rear of 'The Pines' into a craft room for the Pink Ladies.

My change of role from that of manager to labourer caused some bemusement among the caring staff, though they seemed to find it even more curious that a married couple worked so harmoniously with each other. I overheard them sometimes, 'They good together. She done tellin' him what to do.' I should add that, 'telling Ken what to do' was a long played banter between us. Ken being the senior partner in all things practical, it was as ludicrous as it was fun!

Within a few short weeks, the unrelenting emotional fatigue melted away, leaving us feeling younger, coaxing us into the future, hopefully a little wiser. The urge to travel onwards reasserted itself. We felt that we had weathered the worst, though whether our change of heart would have come about without that full moon night and 'Raiders of the Lost Ark' would always remain one of those 'floating' questions.

Dudley was delighted to be back on home turf. Back to lining up dead rats on the bankside for morning inspection, terrorising the three guard dogs in the boatyard, growling in frustration at the parrots gossiping in the coconut palms, taking us for a walk, and doing his toilet down the crab holes.

Ken and Marian flew to Fort Lauderdale to buy stainless steel rigging and a top-of-the-range self-steering unit, an Autohelm 7000. Galvanised rigging had been the cheapest option when we were building *Imago*, but as surface rust, caused by a salt water environment began to fall like dandruff onto the deck, it pitted the paintwork.

Our friend Bill joined us for his second holiday in Cayman and in time to join us on our last voluntary contribution to the work of NCVO, which was to renovate a roundabout for the children's playground. Bending over, bottom in the air, face as red as a house brick, he spent hours with a spanner tightening the nuts onto the threaded bolts. What a team! Ken drilled the holes, I inserted the bolts, and Bill finished the job.

'Not much of a bloody holiday,' he grumbled.

'No less tedious than de-heading annuals or thinning out seedlings mate,' we answered. Banter being an affectionate expression for our friendship, it snapped and cracked between us like a sitcom. In truth, Bill was nothing less than delighted to be making a contribution on an island he loved as much as we did, especially as we were saving NCVO the $8,000 cost of a replacement.

With our 'shipwreck fund' topped up, new rigging and a powerful autopilot, we bade farewell to Cayman for the last time, taking with us the best of memories. A few days before leaving, we went to the NCVO charity shop and several garage sales. We were now heading for some of the most isolated islands in the world where clothes, eyeglasses, screw top containers, fishing hooks, saucepans, pencils, paper, plasters, and colouring books, would be welcome gifts.

Once again Dudley stayed in the bilges for two days, which was about the same time as it takes both Ken and me to get our 'sea legs' back. He emerged as his mischievous, flying fish predator self.

The auto pilot proved a heaped-up blessing. We would never again be brought to our knees by fatigue. It didn't eliminate the 'hairy, scary' times altogether, but for the most part it introduced us to the ''joy of sailing' and the time to fully appreciate our surroundings. We could now leave the wheel when the dolphins joined us, lean over the bow and almost touch them.

The course we charted to Panama involved some tight navigation around shoals and cays but also avoided the big ship routes. 'We'll have to lay over for a while in Panama,' said Ken. 'We've used eleven pints of engine oil in fifteen hours!' That sounded like having to find piston liners and rings for an elderly Ford. If we couldn't find spares in Panama, we might have to consider a new engine and sacrifice most of our 'shipwreck fund'.

At 8am on the 2nd of May 1996, 23nms from the canal holding area, we were on sharp lookout for converging ships. At 1pm Ken decided to motor-sail to be sure of making the breakwater in daylight. This was no place to spend a night lying a-hull!

Closer in, we passed through a gauntlet of anchored ships lying on both sides of the approach channel. Vessels from Norway, Asia, Japan, and the Philippines. Some looked as though they had waited years for a commission. Finally, the marker buoys emerged from the city haze to guide us into the inner bay. As we skirted another breakwater at tick-over speed, there were the yachts! Anchored down at 5pm, feeling exhilarated at having reached this long-awaited destination.

Just before reaching the inner harbour we were hailed by a beautiful 'Oyster' yacht named *Deusa* who followed our line and wanted conformation about the yacht anchorage. Robert and Rosemary would become life-long friends, cross the Pacific with us, and share many of the island destinations.

As well as arranging the transit, finding engine parts, and beginning our anti-malarial medication, we needed to find out from boats coming through the canal from the Pacific side, what Australian and New Zealand rules were current about having animals aboard. We knew of several cruising yachts with pets: dogs, cats, parrots, hamsters. Even a gerbil or two that the children couldn't bear to be parted from. Opinions varied. Some thought that an animal could be taken ashore in a cage while the boat was being searched and cleared. A much more alarming opinion was that there were no quarantine facilities so they would simply destroy the pets! We would have to wait and see and can now declare that Dudley not only arrived with us in 'Aussie', but also left those shores alive and well.

Clearance procedures were surprisingly complicated, considering the history and importance of the canal. A whole day to-ing and fro-ing between different buildings, each with their own departments. We soon realised that each page of a mountain of paperwork exacted a charge which eventually totalled $62.50! The most we had ever paid for clearance to enter a country. Of course there were agencies that would do it all for you at exorbitant rates. Having at last been 'officialised', we took the dinghy over to the yacht club. It was an exciting place to be. Cruising the Pacific generated the same enthusiasm as preparations to cross the Atlantic. A hubbub of noise enveloped us, drinks littered the tables, and sounds of laughter and the telling of yarns rose and fell like a background symphony. From table to table went the 'professional friends,' taxi drivers, and line handlers.

'I'll take you to the best nightclub, the cheapest supermarket, the fuel depot.'

The line handlers were the most persistent. The fifty dollars they charged was big money, the competition fierce. We paid one guy five dollars to go away (nicely). He was a reeling drunk, but his desperate entreaties were heart-breaking. He was eventually evicted by a barman, using what we thought, was an excessive amount of 'persuasion.' Even the immigration officer asked us to hire his two sons.

Yacht Clubs and marina bars have evolved over time to meet the needs of cruising sailors. Many have showers (nobody washes in foul weather), book swaps, weather information, equipment exchanges, laundry facilities, and spare charts. After a particularly gruelling passage they are an oasis in the desert.

Panama must rank as one of the most cosmopolitan cities in the world, though English, being the international maritime language, is widely spoken. Merchant seaman and cruising sailors assemble here from all quarters of the globe, yet it would seem that historical enmity and ethnic prejudice can be set aside simply though shared encounters with implacable, apolitical, ocean waves! Even so, the unease we had felt in Jamaica and America was also present. Fear, tension, that one degree below boiling point. We took heed of warnings not to walk alone at night, avoid downtown bar districts, not wear jewellery, and dress casually. But during the day, the City became lighter and brighter, more Caribbean. Buses are privately owned, distinctively decorated with beautifully painted works of popular art and lettering. Some of the pictures were 'Carnival decadent' – full frontal females, even genitalia. One particularly voluptuous image made me feel naked! Amongst the hordes of jostling people were black-haired Spaniards, Chinese, and indigenous Indians. Many had red streaks in their hair from some ethnic mix of genes. Skin colour ranged, as wood does, through Pine, Teak, Ebony, and Mahogany. Buildings reminded me of Cuba: dilapidated, crumbling, open sewers and culverts with very strong smells.

The offices that supplied the paperwork for transit formalities were bare unpainted rooms lined with ancient office equipment, the computer age had yet to have an impact. Christmas decorations, sagging under a weight of dust, and dead geckos, had not been taken down for years. For some the living is easy. An office job confers huge status, if that can be judged by the complacent, patronising attitude of those who sat at the desk issuing curt orders to their bowing minions. He who wields the stamp was clearly a man of lofty distinction.

We tried to do as much business as we could afford with the multitude of street vendors. Strong, black, 'stand your spoon up in it' coffee came in small, plastic cups. Most customers downed it in one swift gulp like a whiskey chaser. We preferred to sip rather than risk its effects course through our veins like a shot of adrenaline. But we did become somewhat addicted to slices of pineapple! Tied up in small plastic bags, ready to eat, tender and succulent, oozing juice. Long before multi-culturalism was being touted in Europe, Panama had embraced it. Turbans, bandannas, skull caps, berets and all manner of religious and national garb. The strongest impression of all was that this was a 'buccaneer' city. Tenement block poverty, police who look like soldiers, armed guards in the well-stocked supermarkets (some with automatic rifles), and the seemingly inevitable vulgar disparity between rich and desperately poor, the sick, the disabled.

And yet, rising above this fascinating and uninviting city were forests and mountains. Humid. Lush. We gazed at them with longing. We took a walk to the outskirts. On one of the paths that led towards the mountains, we came across a line of marching troops! Soldier ants. We tried to locate their starting point, but after battling through the jungle for thirty yards the vegetation became too dense. The antenna to tail column was flanked by formidable guard ants, all 'front end' and ¾ of an inch long. Carried aloft, some still struggling, were captured insects: spiders, crickets, moths, beetles. Something about that voracious horde mirrored the city.

Rather than risk venturing out after dark, we spent our evening at the yacht club or visiting other boats. One such was to a vessel named *Palu*. The boat was a sponsored self-built catamaran. The whole of the superstructure was covered with names. Intriguing. Aboard were several charming French lads who were nearing the end of a project linking Pacific island school children to similarly aged students in French schools. The names were those of youngsters they had met and been invited to write on the boat. It seemed to us a delightful way to link them with their counterparts in Europe, leading to pen-friendships and sobering lifestyle comparisons.

The transit rules insist on having two professional line handlers on board, though it had become traditional for cruising boat crews to offer added assistance. Being such a singular and special experience, some relished the chance to do it all again. For cruise ship passengers, too, it was one of the highlights of their voyage. For small boats it is a truly incomparable experience. Our own transit was an international event. Two Brits, one Frenchman, three Panamanians, and one Cayman cat!

The construction of the Panama Canal must rank as the most ambitious engineering feat of the modern era. It may not offer the aesthetic appeal as, say, the Sydney Opera House, or an Olympic Stadium, but its colossal dimensions that bisect such a glorious setting (all of it now a National Park) stands as a monumental statement about enterprise and ambition. In another respect, it is also a memorial. A burial place, that serves to remind the world of the huge number of workers who died in accidents or from diseases such as Malaria and Yellow Fever. Yet none were 'wasted' lives if account is taken of those hundreds of other lives saved when ships foundered, as they so often did, in the vicious seas of the South Atlantic. Although we gasped when learning that the average cost of transit for a merchant ship was 78,000 dollars, it has to be weighed against lives and millions lost when a container ship goes down.

A wonderful day. Our pilot arrived at 5.20am to be welcomed by a jolly gang aboard *Imago*, who were as excited as adolescent 'groupies' waiting to greet our pop star in the flesh...the Pacific Ocean!

Leading us through the massive 1,000 foot locks was a medium-sized freighter – a Labrador leading a Chihuahua! On-shore line handlers throw 'monkeys' from the top of the high walls down to the vessels (long ropes with a leather-bound knot at the end) to which we fixed our own 125 foot lines. These are then taken in or paid out with the rise and fall of the water. The rate at which the locks are filled and drained is staggering. Some 250,000 gallons are pumped in or out. On this first day of a forty-eight-hour journey, we passed through two sets of triple locks before a meandering route through the lake system, passing beautiful forested islands, mountains in the background, lush with jungle, fading from view into a blue mist. And from all directions the discordant notes of birds and chattering monkeys and other stranger sounds throbbed around us in ceaseless clamour.

Having never been a good thrower of a ball, I was happy to let the men relieve me of the chucking and reeling in of ropes. Not that I felt 'girly' or redundant. Every woman knows that 'sustaining the troops' confers equal status! Scrambled eggs on toast, sandwiches, grapes, raisins, and juice for seven men being no mean feat, especially as it had to be prepared when tied up in the locks. I am always the helmswoman in tight quarters, Ken being the more impetuous with the throttle than I. Ken is an unusual skipper in that regard, there is no 'rightful' position between us though the Panamanian pilot was visibly shocked!

By early afternoon of the second day we reached the last lock. The Pacific Ocean lies thirty feet below us. To transit the canal in which a small boat has less significance in the landscape than a floating leaf is to experience the full magnitude of this engineering marvel.

As we entered the huge bay, we were alarmed to find it littered with debris. Whole trees floated by, bulk timbers, all manner of crates, fishing buoys, something that looked like half the roof of a house barged into our hull. Whether this was a normal 'fetching up' eddy or the remnants of a storm, we couldn't tell. Whatever the cause, it was unnerving and potentially very dangerous. Being a steel boat, *Imago* could take a thump or two but hitting whole trees would be as disastrous as colliding with a reef.

Proceeding very slowly, we set out a fishing line. Within seconds, a sailfish took the lure. It released itself with a characteristic leap, then leaped again as if in triumph. A magnificent sight. We were glad not to have caught it. The next hit was a Dorado weighing about fifteen pounds. We managed to bring it close to the hull only to lose it at the last minute – gone was a magnificent feast!

Late morning on the second day, a US helicopter 'buzzed' us, hovering barely a mast height above, cowering us onto the cockpit floor with its downdraft. Switching to channel 16, we gave them our particulars before asking for a weather forecast.

'Stand by *Imago*, we'll go up and have a look for you.'

At the height of our own superstructure, the horizon lay some ten miles distant. From 1,000 feet a plane could spot conditions that were hours away. Within minutes the helicopter was circling above us again to warn that a twenty-five mile front was approaching, barely two hours ahead of us. Time at least to check below, re-stow anything that might work loose. No need to tell Dudley, as he would find his usual 'storm berth' in the bilges. As the front loomed towards us, black and threatening, our spirits dropped along with the barometer. We haven't got our sea-legs yet and are heading into the largest ocean on the planet and already battling a ferocious current. Ken angry and frustrated that we are hardly able to make two knots. The rain began as spitting drops, as if from a leaky bucket. Not nearly enough to suit Poseidon's plans so he proceeded to tip the whole bucket over us – a bloody big bucket! A sustained wind of twenty-five knots, gusting thirty-five, battered us for the next six hours. We are only able to maintain a southerly heading with the rudder hard over to resist a sweep to the east. The mainsail rips in two with a noise like a rifle shot. We hank on our second best and only spare.

On the fourth day we have barely covered twenty-two nautical miles towards our waypoint North of Galapagos. A US navy ship flashes beams of light on us at 11pm. They ask for our ETA! I reply, 'it might be fifty to sixty days at our current speed.' I realise the implications then, indeed a quick calculation of our progress revised that figure to three months! I was appalled and scared.

After spending all of my night watch worrying, I waited for Ken to take over at 6am to suggest that we call a halt. We are pressing too hard and I no longer believe that we will get away with it. We are struggling.

As soon as we turned, heading north, back to Panama, *Imago* settled into five knots and easy sailing.

Every sailor we have ever met has experienced the 'slough of despond'.

Over the next three days, we plot and plan for a life back in England, *Imago* moored in some quiet backwater as we wait for the seasons to unfold, perhaps believing that we had tried as hard as we could.

CHAPTER 25

IF IT NEVER RAINED HOW COULD YOU APPRECIATE THE SUNSHINE?

The canal authorities were very suspicious of us wanting to transit again so soon. Perhaps they thought we had stocked up on marijuana from the Perlas Islands lying out in the bay.

Ken and I have a special relationship with fate. However spiteful, teasing, secretive, and interfering an influence, it would also bestow great benevolence upon us. We were to transit again but under very different and reassuring circumstances.

We now set out to explore more of Panama. Three miles out from the Colon side of the canal, we turned starboard, having decided to spend a few days at José Pobre. Although named on the chart, suggesting a settlement, there was just a single beachfront bar! Listening out on channel 16 is a sensible habit near coastlines or in shipping lanes, but we were shocked to hear a message that seemed directed at us!

'Sailing vessel approaching José Pobre.'

'Twin-masted vessel approaching José Pobre.'

We gazed about but could see no other vessel in sight. It must be us! We called back.

'Sailing vessel *Imago*...over.'

'A fishing boat has capsized ahead of you. Can you assist?'

'Message understood, we are heading that way.' A mile or so further up the coast, we encountered huge wallowing seas. From the crest of each wave we managed a brief glance around before a breakneck slide into a deep trough. We ourselves were now in danger but the call had come... a call that no sailor can ignore. An outcrop of fractured rocks to starboard. Two figures standing upright. A sturdy-looking dinghy careering toward them. There was nothing we could do to assist unless there was someone in the water. We closed in as much as we dared.

The VHF blared out again.

'The boat is lost but the fishermen are safe.'

Now we had to turn, but the timing would be crucial. Although the waves were smooth, they reared up higher than anything we had ever seen before. To meet them side-on would roll us over and likely dismast us. Ken took the wheel, grabbing a few degrees to port off each wave before rotating at the bottom of a trough to bring the waves astern to us. I blew him a kiss.

As we tied up to the pontoon leading to the bar, the owner came out to take our lines and thank us.

'We couldn't have got to the rocks, we could only look for anyone in the water.'

'How many were aboard?'

'Three, but they all got ashore. You went for them, they'll come and thank you for that.'

The bar itself might qualify as one of the strangest in the world! Our Swiss proprietor is a genial alcoholic, his partner a young Grenadian woman. Their two young children played with boisterous energy. Uninhibited by clothes or supervision, they climbed, tussled, chased land crabs, and paddled in the stream that ran down from the high ground, while their mother spent much of her day washing clothes in huge plastic bowls.

'We serve the village men, they come to the bar for two days, drink themselves senseless... and dance.' Indeed they do and as 'fate' would have it, we were there to see it. There was something Gaelic about the way they danced: jogging, hopping, bouncing on their toes with quick small steps. A 'lads only' outing, a two-day Carnival, and an uninhibited celebration (or was it?)

The drinking matched the rhythm of their dance. The ground beneath them soon flooded from spills as pint after pint poured down their throats. An almost ferocious determination to cast themselves off from reality.

Eyes glazed over, men staggered into the undergrowth to vomit and urinate. Some began to cry. The bar owner turned up the volume of the music. 'It's what they want,' he said.

Still they danced, hanging on to each other for support until one by one they slumped to their knees before finally keeling over, lying as they fell, into the darkness of their minds and the darkness of the night. Heaped up, as if from some calamity or dreadful mishap.

What made them do it? If all behaviour has meaning, what was this? We could only surmise. Perhaps the harshness of their lives, family responsibilities, the controls expected of women, and the male bonding evident the world over (in pubs, at sporting events). Was it an antidote to violence, a substitute for war? Whatever it was and for whatever reason, it didn't look like fun… more a scream, more a desperate urge to 'let go.'

'Most of them pay for their drinks and snacks,' explained the bar owner. 'But they sometimes pay in livestock. I've got four beef cattle out on the meadow behind the hills.' His name was Marcus. He had chosen a 'Gauguin' lifestyle for himself. A choice we could readily understand. The village proper lay a couple of miles inland. Bananas and fishing provided for the small population of seventy-five (swelling to 200 when children were home from school). Pigs, tethered by waistbands, nosed in the mud and tree roots at the edge of the water. Magnificent pet parrots, wings clipped, occupy a dead tree. Holes bubble in the dark sand. The children pounce with flattened sticks to gather up a pail of whelks.

Several European sailors have journeyed to this region and chosen to stay.

Beyond the reef, below a blanket of slate-grey clouds, white-capped waves stretched to the horizon. Yet it was in places such as this that we learned, along with all other living things, to bow to the wind and that humanity, for all its arrogance is powerless against the forces of nature: hurricane, flood, fire, and avalanche.

We felt no sense of urgency or impatience to move on, were quite content to 'wait on the weather', and immerse ourselves in the present. A new and rewarding way to be.

Early one morning, we packed a lunch of bread, cheese, raisins, and fruit and rambled along the beach for three hours at the edges of the jungle. Ken photographed a huge red flower, a frog with blue and black stripes, and a butterfly wearing pearl spots on its electric blue wings. Colourful rocks and pebbles lay scattered on the foreshore like the daubs on a well-used artist's palette: red, blue, and green. A hummingbird came to the red flower and posed. Huge trees, lianas, bromeliads. Wet, humid, lush, and vigorous. A man passes us along the track. A paraplegic on horseback. He cannot wave or turn his head, but he smiles.

Small patches of jungle had been cleared to grow bananas, maize, and fruit trees. Just enough to serve the village. Just enough. Above the tide-line dugout, canoes lay waiting for calmer weather. A 'family' of canoes, some over twenty feet long, designed for serious fishing, others adolescent sized. But nothing could stress the importance of a fishing community than the 'baby' canoes. I sat in one that was barely five feet long!

A couple of miles into our walk, we came across the village and waited on the outskirts to see if we were welcome. A Mr McKenzie, the accepted 'elder' of the village, strode out to greet us. As well as running the only shop, he was 'paterfamilias' and happy to talk with us. He was deeply concerned about how outside influences are affecting his village, about the USA and drug interdiction.

'We've always used cannabis,' he told us. 'No-one gets violent with it. A party here is more like a church social, but lately the young girls have started drinking, taken to wearing sequin tops and hot pants. Some of them are being paid to visit the yachts!'

What to say? He was an educated man who was deeply concerned about the erosion of traditional values. We swapped 'National Geographic' for a couple of books from his small library and gave him some children's clothes for distribution. He gifted back a bowl of limes. How thankful we were that our gifts were not viewed as largesse or benevolence. Charity implies need and had no place here.

Just as we were thinking of 'going native' somewhere near this charming stop-over, we experienced an encounter which put us firmly back in forward gear. The stormy conditions had forced more yachts than usual to seek shelter in this small anchorage. Returning from our explorations, we were delighted to find that Rosemary and Robert on *Deusa* had anchored close by. That evening we joined them in the bar. The usual 'small boat' talk was in full flow until an American skipper sauntered into the bar. Rangy, tall, loud, and garrulous.

'Whisky sour, man.'

Marcus shook his head.

'What kind of goddamn bar is this?' The American sneered. The atmosphere cooled and stilled.

'Suits us.' Shrugged Ken.

'British huh? Not much space on the map there. Where would you be anyway if we hadn't won the war for you?'

Ken had spent two years in post-war Germany as a serving soldier in the REME and had seen men still dying from efforts to dig out and haul away the shells and munitions of war. I saw his lips tighten and his body go tense.

'The US of A is the finest place on Earth –do you hear?' Yep, we all heard.

'Aa'am sick of all this jungle shit, goin' back to Panama, get me some decent red meat.' If he was that belligerent without his T-bone steak, what was he like after one!

Later that evening, a silver line appeared along the horizon below the back end of the front, like the chink of light under a closed door. We would wait another day to avoid 'left-over' seas.

On our last night, Marcus and Valerie took us up into the hills where the streams ran, to catch crayfish. Shining a torch onto the surface of eddies and shallow pools pin-pointed their eyes like those of rabbits caught in the glare of car headlights. Bigger hands were better at scooping them up so Ken and Marcus paired up while Valerie and I exalted over our few successes, squealing with excitement and frustration when they scuttled from our grasp. Before leaving for the San Blas islands next morning, in company with *Deusa* and new friends on *Zazen*, Valerie called us over to a breakfast of succulent crayfish. In Panama they would have sold for seventy dollars a pound!

Whenever we recall to mind our time in the San Blas islands, we think of Magi and Begonia. Magi the Brazilian, Hollywood handsome, ringlets of hair, pothead, and probably the most uninhibited person we would ever meet. If there is such a personality as a 'free spirit' (without the angst that usually accompanies such a claim) then he was undoubtedly it. Invariably dressed in a tank top and colourful cotton pantaloons, I cannot imagine any woman being unmoved by his sensuality!

His companion of a few weeks was also a beauty. She had interrupted her law studies in Spain to seek adventure. Although they were a 'visual' match, their relationship was as chimeric as a cloud of smoke – she could never hold him to her. He was a fawn, a satyr. Not only were they 'sunshine people', they were linguists, which confers a huge advantage when travelling. In addition to their native tongues, they were also fluent in French, Portuguese, and English.

By the time we said goodbye to Magi and Begonia, having spent several delightful weeks among the 300 island in this unique archipelago, they had gifted us with their optimistic, immerse yourself in the present, attitude to life.

As we approached the main island, El Porvenir, to book in, we passed several small launches carrying compressors attached to long coils of hose. According to our depth sounder, the young men aboard appeared to be skin diving to depths of seventy feet! We learned later that it was a life-limiting, sometimes fatal way to earn a living. Decompression sickness would blight their lives well before middle-age. Even as we set our anchors, dugouts were disgorging from the shore-line. Kuna Indians quickly surrounded each boat, hassling loudly to sell us Molas, holding them up for us to see. As part of their national dress, these oblong panels are made up of finely stitched layers of 'trading cotton.' Each layer of brightly coloured cloth is slashed and hemmed in turn until the colours become traditional depictions of fish or warlike faces. They form the back and front of blouses worn by married women. Those fashioned for tourists were of birds, flowers, or geometric patterns. Intricate, painstaking works of art, the stitching so fine as to be almost invisible.

We knew that we would buy some but wanted more time and choice in the matter!

'Mola, Mola…buy, buy!'

'Later,' we replied.

More and more dugouts arrived and banged against our hulls. Pointedly and not without some irritation, we draped all the fenders we possessed, even coils of rope. They simply pushed them aside or used them to tie up hard against our sides. The clamour increased to the point where it sounded aggressive and intimidating. We couldn't even leave the boats to book in! Some of the women stood up, held there as the canoe rocked dangerously, by the women around them, hands grabbing at the guard rails as if intent on boarding us. Some of the women held up babies and infants. Perhaps they thought that it would increase their bargaining power! Short stocky attractive women, with flattened rectangular features. Coils of coloured beads decorated their legs from ankle to knee. Wrap-around cotton skirts in vivid patterns completed an ensemble that would grace the catwalk of any fashion show.

But it all became disagreeable. Nothing we said could dissuade them. Finally, we went below and locked the companionway doors. Still they banged on the hull, shouting, 'Mola! Mola!' An hour and a half later just as we had decided to haul anchor, they finally paddled away.

The San Blas islands are extraordinary. Hundreds of islands, many supporting a small self-contained community. Some so tiny as to look like the classic cartoon depiction of a castaway on a desert island, sitting under a single palm tree. Shallows and sandbars make it a treacherous area to navigate. Charts are incomplete and mostly date from the 1800s. Ken would stand on the end of the bowsprit, gesturing with his arms as we wound our way past bommies and sandbars; making sure that the sun was high enough in the sky to spot them.

Kuna Indians are fiercely protective of their culture (national dress isn't worn just to satisfy tourist curiosity). They are even said to have repelled Panamanian troops during a brief skirmish some years before. But however much they resist, change is already evident. There are schools on the larger islands. Mainland plots have been allocated for growing crops. Portable generators provide lighting and outboard engines have increased fishing ranges. Inevitably perhaps, there was also evidence of social competition. A child's plastic pedal car, garishly pink and red, lying disregarded in the bushes, a grotesque anomaly in such a place.

Generations of isolation has inflicted genetic consequences on these proudly independent communities: albinos, disabilities, and stunted growth. One of the fishermen confided that in the past, albino babies were taken out to sea and drowned, that elders decided on male and female pairings. Once a decision was made, the woman was taken to the 'bridegroom's' hut and thrown into a double hammock!

Many of the young folk are now leaving to work in Panama City. The first attempt by a foreigner to build tourist lodges was burned to the ground, though he was certain it would happen in the future. The speed at which change evolves will be crucial to these people, as it is to all native societies who encounter the modern world of competition and avarice. We could only hope that the benefits will be distinguished from the ills. If we were to judge by the onslaught of a flotilla of dugouts... the dollar reigns already.

We talked about it later as we watched the young men in their dugouts returning in the twilight from their fishing trips. Was so-called 'progress' such a bad thing? Would travelling be such an exciting experience without the differences between peoples and customs? Do we want the whole world to be covered in concrete?

I thought we would be passionate protectionists, advocates of indigenous peoples and non-interference in their way of life. We supposed instead that it was more about freedom to choose while still encouraged to maintain their cultural identity and avoid exploitation. Perhaps our notions were as naïve as our sailing experience, but if the Scots can choose to wear the kilt and the Welsh retain their language, surely differences in dress, foods, and most traditions should be encouraged and admired? Neither the Dhoti nor the sari should be obstacles to a professional, artistic, or political life. Very few Kuna Indians are 'free' in that sense. They are utterly constrained. Unless they embrace at least some compromise, they will remain fishermen and mola makers whether it suits them or not.

Yet we admired the simplicity of their lives. Eco-friendly dwellings made from woven bamboo sections, roofed with layered palm leaves, the ground between each hut kept swept and cleared of garbage. Tiny gardens and plants were cultivated in cut down polythene water jugs, birds in pretty wicker cages. Small extensions from each hut hung out over the sea to serve as toilets. Some of the huts were large enough to house several women and a dozen or more children. Not a grown man to be seen. Perhaps they were out fishing or perhaps it was a matriarchal society... but then again, if you are thrown into a double hammock, you might well prefer to live as a sisterhood!

We commented on the macramé style artistry of rope patterns used to lash together the support structure. But the reaction towards our admiration was as strange as it was revealing – they seemed offended! Did they think such praise patronising, false flattery? Or was it simply, 'how can you, who build in steel and concrete admire rope lashings?

But the Kuna Indians already knew that exploitation would come sooner than medical facilities or schools.

A bright red twin engine plane circled the main island before making a bumpy landing onto the narrow airstrip. Lettering on the fuselage spelled out 'Red Lobster.' A rangy, gum-chewing American disembarked, spat on the ground, and leaned against a wing looking bored and insolent. A line of villagers made their way towards him, carrying sacks of lobster and crabs (kept alive in foreshore pools). The pilot opened each one, smelled it, felt the bottom of the sack in case rocks or coconuts had been included, weighed them, peeled a few dollars from a wad then threw the sacks into the plane. It was then that we realised why young men were having to dive to dangerous depths and further away from shore, risking their lives to supply 'Red Lobster' diners in America.

Some of the islets are separated by only a few hundred metres which create dozens of natural eddies. Vast amounts of driftwood, including whole trees, became trapped, some of it boat-shaped and too new, grim reminders of catastrophe at sea. The largest of the debris is towed ashore to be fabricated into dugouts, furniture, paddles, toys, firewood, and surprisingly comfortable seats and stools.

No matter which island the good ships *Imago*, *Zazen*, and *Deusa* anchored off, the begging never stopped. We passed over fishing hooks, magazines, children's clothes, reading glasses for 'Papa' fishing line, and pencils. But it was never enough. Children were sent out in their tiny dugouts to beg cigarettes, dried milk, and chocolate. All done with great guile and lots of smirking. Although the begging was less aggressive from the smaller islands, the atmosphere was still unfriendly. When one woman held out her baby, saying 'Take, Take.' I waved her away. Angrily, I do confess. It all felt horribly undignified. Never a greeting, no hint of gratitude, just whatever could be conned out of the 'Gringos.'

'Give us a coconut?' I suggested.

Once it was realised what I meant, one of the dugouts returned to shore and came back with a breadfruit from one house, a coconut, a crudely carved Kuna doll from another. This felt better. Just one coconut altered the meaning from that of simply distributing largesse to one of mutual exchange, irrespective of value. And they understood, clapped and laughed. Phew!

As always, we talked about what we saw and felt during our travels. Do a people who have the basics in abundance, an ordered family-centred life 'need' the flippancies of modern life? Toys that need batteries every month to operate? Is a manufactured doll a more loving gift than one painstakingly carved by a father and dressed by a mother?

All these magnificently attired women wear gold chains, elaborate earrings, nose piercings, and colourful strands of beads. Perhaps the many hours and patient skill required to make a Mola is better rewarded by yachts than from trading them in Panama, where intermediate profits reduce their value to that of slave labour. Red Lobster diners, coconut traders... thieves.

Despite our efforts to understand the context behind the daily begging ritual, it was irritating as a cloud of hornets.

We would entertain a family on board, with coffee, biscuits, and juice for the kids. Before leaving they asked to take coffee for Grandma... and she wants cigarettes too! A fisherman cut our line to steal a fishing lure. We heard of a couple whose boat had foundered on a reef. While they were still aboard, Kuna Indians had come out to them and stripped their boat clean!

Had we not been in the company of Magi, Begonia, Rosemary, and Robert, I doubt if we would have stayed for long. Consummate sailors, seasoned travellers, wonderful stories, and wonderful characters. Magi was an advanced sailor who had earned the money to buy his boat from being a delivery skipper. He has sailed to India and climbed in the Himalayas. Robert and Rosemary had been adventurers for all of their married life, canoeing, kayaking, and road trips. Robert had grown up on a tobacco farm in Rhodesia and had a safari business in Salisbury. With the advent of terrorism and tourists being killed they sold the company, bought a camping land rover and shipped themselves to South America, ending up in Brazil.

Magi was a 'Jack Russell' character. Inexhaustible energy, smoker of ten joints a day. He would catch fish enough for all the boats, organise a barbecue on the beach, skinny dip, and snorkel with us.

Ken caught a five-foot shark on twenty-pound line. After a long struggle, he brought it close enough to the side of *Imago's* hull for us all to admire before releasing it. Served it right! It was the same shark that bit my nice three-pound pan fish in half! Normally we would snorkel everywhere we anchored, but in these murky waters once was enough. We spotted a twenty footer resting in a rock crevice. Some chaps wake up in a grumpy mood. Quietly as possible we swam in the opposite direction.

We were surprised when a middle-aged man paddled out to us without a portable shop of shells, beads, molas, and green coconuts. *Deusa*, having moved on through the islands missed out on this unusual encounter.

'Come eat with my family.'

We readily accepted such an unexpected invitation. Magi passed down a bag of onions and a newly caught fish weighing some eight pounds. A friendly encounter with these people had seemed so unlikely that any notion of subterfuge or pretext would not only have been ungracious, but also never entered our minds.

But it was insincere to the point of farce. Our host wasn't saying 'come eat with my family.' His real message was, 'Look, see how desperately poor we are.'

Our 'dinner' was an embarrassing stage-managed affair, an ingeniously different form of begging. A low table had been set with four chipped and stained enamel bowls and four plastic forks. A serving bowl sat ready in the middle, containing several pieces of marinated onion rings mixed with a few flakes of cold fish! Two mouthfuls each and a serious risk of food poisoning.

Although our conniving host sat with us, he did not eat. His wife and several children peeked over the half door leading to the sleeping area. He ignored our attempts to engage him in 'dinner talk.'

'How many children do you have?' Did you build your own house?' Then came the well-rehearsed speech to elicit our sympathy.

'Yachtsmen have given us lots of presents: T shirts, plenty rope, tins of food… they very good people. Me have plenty children.' He sighed. 'Very hard.'

After an hour of listening to him describe how miserable and wretched his life was, we took our leave. 'A pleasure to meet you, Sir, thank you very much.' The remains of our huge fish and bag of onions wafted through the hut. Back to *Imago* for egg, chips, and baked beans!

Our time in the San Blas Islands stretches into weeks. The relationship between our three boats was close and mutually rewarding. As we each run out of basics, such as flour, potatoes, and onions of course! We supplement each other. When Magi ran out if gas, we gave them the small canisters from our soldering kit. He in turn would catch us fish. We would shine torches on the water when darkness fell, which was when the larger predators were hunting and sighted huge spotted eagle rays, even the rarer cow nose ray, six feet long, a dancer with wings. We all revelled in our self-sufficiency, tapping into those most ancient of life challenges which had coaxed mankind towards awareness and survival skills. Serving only our needs, wanting for nothing. We really could 'do as we liked' day after day with no-one to criticize, judge, or take offence, neither helping nor hindering. The word 'freedom' had meaning. We simply took our space amid the landscape, as entitled as trees, rocks, and grains of sand to our place in it. We are only in touch with the outside world through the BBC news. We hear, with shock, about Manchester, the TWA airplane atrocity in Scotland. All the more disturbing to imagine as we spent idyllic evenings in the cockpit gazing at a backdrop of mountains on the mainland and the palm fringed outlines of a dozen small islands.

Despite the irritating clamour to buy Molas, there were two encounters that earned our respect and admiration. We met the artists. The first was a woodcarver who transformed driftwood and mangrove roots into exotic beasts and figures. A sculptor who could gaze at a contorted piece of wood in the way that a sculptor 'sees' into a lump of granite or marble to reveal whatever subject comes to mind. Wonderful. Too expensive for us to buy, though the artist clearly understood our appreciation. The second was said to be the most famous Mola artist in the islands. Although the finest Molas are intricate, colourful, and involve many hours of patient stitching, they are generally made by women, but the specimen pieces are done by a few men. We were fortunate to meet one such master craftsman. His creations, for which he could earn hundreds of

274

dollars, took several months to complete. Diego, the famed mola artist, was a shy, slim, young man with long slender fingers and the poise of a dancer. Decidedly 'camp', small delicate features. There are many societies in the world where boy children are gender directed to appear female. They are not 'lady boys' in the modern disparaging sense of the words and may not even be homosexual, but for whatever reasons they assume a respected place in the community. As well as being delicate of figure, Diego was also modest and charming. There was something wistful and wise about him. We felt honoured to meet such a man.

Although we would never run out of basic sustenance (fish and rice), our boats need fuel, and our families would be wondering what had happened to us! Yet not once did we miss telephones, traffic, throngs of bustling people, or the din of civilisation.

A day sail later *Zazen* and *Imago* were back in Colon. We arranged for money to be sent out from our 'shipwreck fund' in England to stock up with provisions and fuel. Anchored close by was a pretty yacht named *InI* with Scott and Debbie aboard. Scott was an American who changed our somewhat jaundiced view of the USA. A learned, thoughtful man, interested in comparative religions, as inspired and fascinated as we are by all the creatures who share our planet, deeply concerned about morality, ethics, and the human condition. Such imponderables made him a troubled man, a seeking man. Debbie had met Scott during her own hiking adventure and despite having never sailed before, agreed to cross the Pacific with him.

We met, we talked. We liked each other. And so it was that *Deusa*, *InI*, and *Imago* formed our Pacific Convoy. Our three boats would set out together for the Galapagos Islands and Marquesas.

Having spent Christmas at José Pobre, we all had several weeks to wait for the optimum time (February to June) to transit the canal again. *Deusa* and *InI* would return to the San Blas islands, and *Imago* would visit Colombia before rendezvousing again in Colon.

***

Two and a half years on from those first few steps, Ken was walking confidently, up and down the corridor using his rollator. A year after that, he could manage two lengths with only a walking stick. Finally, he was able to walk a length unaided, sit and swivel onto the passenger seat of a car, and negotiate a short flight of stairs.

Although his physical skills emerged first, it would take much longer for his memory and social competence to keep pace: remembering names, building a boat, sailing round the world, days of the week, and mastering a sentence.

Brains. Complex, fragile, and mendable. The only organ with which we can recognise the three 'worlds' we inhabit. A personal internal world, our day by day world, and the world at large. For several years Ken inhabited only a 'day by day' world that centred round our daily routine. It would lead him gently back to himself.

And as it did so, not a day passed when he didn't surprise and delight me. Monday didn't register to Ken as the beginning of the week, rather as 'shower day' as was Thursday. Wednesdays and Saturdays were bacon and egg sandwich mornings, Friday was boiled egg.

By 2009, six years after his stroke, Ken had reached his 'optimum level' of recovery. Everyone involved in his care and rehabilitation knew that they had witnessed a remarkable and prognosis-defying regeneration.

Ken could now read a daily paper and a large print book, play Scrabble and Rummy, engage in banter, drive a mobility scooter, laugh, and smile. He would always need dependent care: washing, toileting, dressing, padding by day, a sheath and bag at night, but such trivial needs now felt normal and ordinary.

Courage and bravery however, is not recognised or rewarded by either an implacable sea or by its cousin… inexorable fate… Ken suffered a heart attack.

CHAPTER 26

JUNGLE MEDICINE, DINNER DATE
WITH AN ARMED GUARD AND
THREE ROTTWEILERS.

SECOND PANAMA CANAL TRANSIT,
A NEAR DISASTER, HUNTING FOR
GOLD.

After booking in once more at Porvenir, we quickly
moved on to Tiger Island before the Mola fleet had time
to gather their forces. Locking up the boats securely, we
took our tenders to the mainland where the Panamanian
government had allocated an area of land for an
agronomy project. Rice, tomatoes, peppers beans, yucca,
and corn were grown and tended by Kuna women. The
significance was explained by a Kuna Doctor who had
converted a large hut into a clinic alongside the
allotments. He cared for his patients with traditional
herbal remedies as well as with modern medication. It
was an enlightened approach. He genuinely didn't mind
if a cure was attributed to the traditional ways or the
new. He was also willing to accept that many herbal
remedies had a sound scientific base and that by using
them he was able to allay suspicion about 'new-fangled
treatments.'

'The main health issues for the Kuna people are malnutrition and TB', he told us. 'They lack vitamins from vegetables. They tell me no-one has AIDS, but I'm not convinced.'

There was also a small school catering for about three dozen children. They were taught during the hours that the women tended the crops. At the end of the day, they would return to their respective villages by dugout.

We had each brought notepads, pencils, sharpeners, crayons, and two large bags of boiled sweets. We thought they might be useful as merit awards for attendance, good behaviour, or top marks.

The children were enjoying playtime. A teacher took one of the bags and scattered the sweets on the ground. Screaming, shouting, pushing, and shoving, the kids behaved like fish in a feeding frenzy. There was something embarrassingly colonial about children scrabbling in the dust as if to 'entertain' the 'Gringos.' As we walked down the steep path towards the shoreline, three of the older women followed us. Rosemary was holding the remaining bag of sweets, having decided to gift them elsewhere. As she turned to speak to them, one of the women punched the bottom of the bag, spilling most of the sweets onto the path. Turning away, we left them with their booty, not even able to comprehend how we might have caused offence. Perhaps we should have asked for a coconut!

We had noticed burial sites near each village which revealed a strong belief in an afterlife. Graves are covered with bamboo or tin-roofed structures. Items of daily use: pots, mugs, utensils, were arranged on a small table near the grave. The area is cleared and tidy, decorated with small plants. Seats are situated under the nearest shade tree so that relatives can visit, sit quietly, or rest there. Whether this practise was introduced by missionaries (some graves marked with crosses) or from an ancient tradition is uncertain, but whether from belief or hope we would see many versions of ancestor worship during our travels.

Marian, our friend from Cayman Islands had asked to join us again for a holiday. It was the reason we chose to sail the comparatively short distance to Cartagena. We felt that Colombia might be a more unusual destination for someone so well-travelled. And so it proved. With a week to wait before her arrival, there was time to absorb the atmosphere of the city and seek out places of interest.

'It feels Victorian,' remarked Ken. What a perceptive statement that proved to be. Not just the obvious disparity between rich and poor, but the vindication and rightness of it. Dozens of street venders held small trays slung from their shoulders. None pressed us to buy, perhaps that would be seen as impertinent. A few boxes of matches, five cigarettes tied in a bundle, a few dog leads, combs, balloons, shoe polish, shoelaces, and small bars of soap. Hardly enough to buy a modest meal for a day of labour.

We were sitting in a dockside café. A middle-aged man at the next table left his seat and stood over us. 'Ah! You're English.' He offered his card. 'Trauma Doctor' (at a prestigious New York Hospital). M.D. followed by a long line of other qualifications.

Affable, charming. He arranged for a taxi to pick us up next morning to meet his son and daughter-in-law who had recently married.

Several miles beyond the city the land stretched out towards a range of hills in the far distance. 'I own all the land you can see,' he said. His son strode out from their newly built mansion, kissed his father on the forehead as if he were a 'Mafia' Godfather. Our Doctor was quite unabashed about telling us that his was one of a few dozen families in Colombia who 'own the lot,' including the odd gold and emerald mine! The signet ring he wore would have bought a mega-yacht!

'The nurses at the hospital shake my hand and try to pull it off,' he joked. His daughter-in-law appeared at the doorway of the house, as did three exceptionally large Rottweilers. She didn't quite curtsey, but held back, accepting a slight bow from her father-in-law.

We wondered for a moment whether our coffee had been 'spiked', surely we were hundreds of years adrift, in a pre-Victorian time warp. As guests, it seemed inappropriate to engage in a social or political discussion, though the casual conviction of superiority, privilege, the perceived right and due of their status was astonishing.

Unsurprisingly, the families are now under siege by guerrilla groups such as FARC, though it will be a long and bloodied road towards dismantling such a system, and in the short term, just as problematic for the peasants as the existing structure.

Several incidents bore further testimony to this landlord/serf dichotomy.

We were offered tea. As the maid served us we thanked her. When she had left the room, the Doctor leaned towards us to say quietly but firmly, 'don't speak to the servants.' Later in the day, we all lay in hammocks while they smoked a few 'joints' and we enjoyed the magnificent landscape. One of the servants was ordered to call a taxi as they were running low on cigarette papers! The hire car was sent on a ten mile round trip to get some!

Earlier in the day, as we walked from the hired car towards the mansion we had passed the ground floor window of the newly married couple's bedroom. The bed linen had been turned back to show the Patriarch that son and daughter-in-law were doing their duty to provide a son and heir!

Nevertheless, they were charming and generous hosts. They insisted on driving us out to a rural restaurant for an early dinner. The Rottweilers came too. Pre-arranged bodyguards carrying assault rifles hovered round the table. A truck stopped outside. Several soldiers approached the Doctor to warn of a skirmish with FARC less than a mile further along the road. We wondered if this might be an adventure too far!

Later in the day, we were taken to the outskirts of the estate village where the workers' shacks were situated. Hanging below a stout metal tripod was a huge cauldron bubbling away on an open fire. A vessel big enough to boil a body!

'Look' said the Doctor, 'they are happy. We let them build their houses, we feed them.' He then demonstrated his largesse by throwing a whole chicken into the cauldron. This last gesture seemed to acknowledge our discomfort. Although we had tried hard to control it, we found it increasing difficult to think, let alone talk. The daughter-in-law was even more perceptive. I had started to take a photograph of the cauldron.

'What do you want to do that for!'

I don't think it either placated or fooled her by saying, 'it's the biggest one we have ever seen'! Not only did she have wind of us, but she also had three Rottweilers practically 'glued' to her person!

An extraordinary, complicated day. As travellers, we are neither qualified nor inclined to criticise or pass judgement, though in this case, 'they are happy...we feed them,' sounded as though they were looking after chickens! (I was once invited by a neighbour to stand inside his newly built hen-house. 'Tell me', he said, 'if you were a chicken, would you be happy in here?')

The two cities of Cartagena, old and new, are steeped in history. Centuries-old monasteries serve as unpretentious sanctuaries. Surrounded by dark stone walls, that block out the sounds of the city, they are cool, shaded, flower-bedecked places that invite contemplation. We sat quietly in the courtyard. An hour passed. Perhaps we were thinking, though it felt more like an immersion into some peaceful other-worldly realm. It wasn't an unfamiliar feeling; night watches on a calm moonlit sea induced a similar state of meditation. Perhaps it is the silence.

The museum housed some of the oldest manuscripts in existence. A single silent monk painstakingly writing his immaculate calligraphy, decorating each page with exquisitely beautiful illustrations in red, blue, and gold. Each a lifetime of work.

Marian, as was Bill, were enthusiastic, easy-going friends to have aboard, able to adapt happily to bunks, buckets, and a cat in their lap as they ate. We showed her the manuscripts, visited the gold museum, and spent several evenings at the yacht club. On her last night, we all went to a fancy dress party. She and I dressed as pirate girls, Ken in drag! Having mentioned the event before her arrival, she brought with her a long XXL dress for him to wear and two balloons. We ruffled his hair with gel, applied several layers of bright red lipstick. Couldn't do much about his beard or plimsolls, but he was 'man enough' to play along with us. The judging was made by hand raising from the revellers. Although more 'Pantomime Dame' than Diva, Ken won second prize! The bar owner's girlfriend, dressed as herself, came first, (no-one dared to vote otherwise)! A couple on a visiting yacht should have won hands down for a brilliant idea: dressed in green and red crepe paper, they bobbed from side to side down the room as port and starboard buoys!

Another eventful transit of the Panama Canal. This time towing a thirty-foot boat called *Raroia*. On board were a brave young couple from the old East Germany (said to be the first to sail the world from that communist country). Their vessel was an elderly steel boat, having such a low freeboard that its deck was barely eighteen inches above sea level! Even more remarkable was its electric engine powered entirely by solar panels. The canal authorities had denied them passage on the grounds that the engine could not develop the five knot minimum requirement for transit. Having clearly engaged a benevolent fate in much the same way as we had done, it was one of those mysterious predictions that they should meet *Imago* on that day. We managed to negotiate on their behalf though we had first to demonstrate feasibility by towing little *Raroia* to and fro across the holding bay in front of the administrative offices.

Still with *Raroia* alongside, our four boats exited the final lock only to meet with near disaster! Our convoy had been headed into every lock by a multi-storey cruise liner. As we entered the narrow channel leading into the Pacific Ocean, it revved its engines. A tsunami of agitated water almost tipped *Raroia* over. All but one of the rafting lines securing her to *Imago* snapped like cotton threads. I turned hard to starboard to take the waves stern on, dragging *Raroia* around with us. Our pilot screamed into his hand-held radio at his colleague on the cruise ship, but it was too late. As the tiny boat pivoted round to our stern on the remaining rope, she rose high and smashed into our dinghy up on the davits.

With the help of our fellow sailors, we repaired the dinghy over the next two days. Still we rejoiced. We refused to let what might have been a tragedy to spoil our champagne celebration.

Having been inspired by Thor Heyerdahl's account of the 'Kon-Tiki' adventure, their tiny solar-powered boat continued on towards Galapagos, 'see you in *Raroia*' they shouted and so they did!

Robert left *Deusa* for 'business' reasons while *InI* and *Imago* stayed at Balboa and prepared for a 'shake down' cruise to the Perlas Islands and the Darien River. He returned with a gift for his wife Rosemary. A tiny Jack Russell terrier puppy which they named 'Tara'. As if to re-enforce the extraordinary relationship we would all enjoy until we reached the Solomon Islands, we each now had four-legged sailing companions who would not only adapt to life at sea but also delight us with their

285

personalities. Mo'bay the cat aboard *InI*, Dudley on *Imago*, Tara on *Deusa*.

Having agreed on twice daily radio contact, we bought a single-side-band radio and a large-scale chart to mark our routes. Our three-boat convoy would cover a two hundred mile swathe of ocean, with *Deusa* to the North, *Imago* in the middle, *InI* to the South. Quite close in such a vast ocean, though we would each encounter very different conditions with *InI* having the worst of it, but all of us struggling with a 'moderate' El Nino event. Unpredictable currents, torrential rain near the convergence zone, and rolling from scupper to scupper in waves that had no 'set' to them.

Being well within the optimum time to set out for the 850nm run from Balboa to Wreck Bay in the Galapagos Islands, it was decided that we would have 'shake-down' cruise to the Isla Pedro Gonzales islands which lie in the middle of the great Bay of Panama and into the Darien River on the way back. We had been warned that the inhabitants in the islands did not welcome visitors, especially those who might stumble upon a marijuana farm. So we swam, caught fish for dinner, admired the unusual slate-grey rocks eroded over millennia into ornaments that would have graced the grounds of a great country house. Basins, troughs, pedestals, and seats. Many of the pebbles were uniquely strange, their softer components eroded into so many holes that they looked like lumps of Emmental cheese. During two nights at anchor we saw no living soul. They were the most secretive and lovely islands we had seen.

We would never have dared to enter the Darien River on our own, especially as none of us had charts for the area, but both Robert and Scott could handle their boats with exquisite skill. *Deusa* led the way with her fin keel. If she could negotiate the depth, we all could. Our experiences in the misty river delta rewarded our temerity in such a way that the challenges we faced on the greatest ocean in the world no longer filled our minds with anxiety but with anticipation and excitement. What better way to live in this world. What better way to die. The currents flowing in and out of the river were fierce, but the holding was good. Above the tide line we could see several dugout canoes, some of them under construction. After pulling the dinghy up on the beach, we strolled over to look at them. With thumb and index finger, we stroked along their length, following the smooth precise thickness of the hull. Curls of wood, from adze and chisel littered the sand.

'Is good, yes?'

José was standing a few yards off, watching, pleased that we were admiring his work. It was the best of introductions. He and Ken, fellow artisans, appreciating each other's skills. The craft at anchor made with modern tools, the other with axe and adze, both worthy as each other.

José arranged for all six of us to take a long journey in his largest dugout to a tribal settlement which he told us had only been 'discovered' twenty years previously. The people were genuinely happy to meet us and show their crafts. They are famed for two remarkable traditional skills; some of the finest woven bowls and plates we were ever likely to see again, and carved Tagua (ivory nuts). The bowls were so tightly woven that they could hold water. Each piece depicted

287

traditional motifs: insects, whorls, and geometric patterns, using lengths of thin wicker dyed in local soil and river deposits (red, black, and ochre).

Tagua nuts, brought back from trees only found in the high forest looked like non-descript tomato-sized pebbles. Once the woody skin had been scraped away, the interior was indistinguishable from the tusks of elephant or walrus. Using the crudest of tools, each nut was carved into wonderful miniature sculptures: leaping fish, toucans, crabs, sting rays, and frogs. We all bought several of them as well as an uncarved nut to remind us of their origin and transformation.

The palm-clad wooden framed huts were raised on stilts, high enough to need a ladder of notched planks to reach the doorway. If the notches faced down, the occupants were 'not at home' to visitors. Young boys strutted around on tall stilts. Ken and Scott were soon surrounded by happy smiling children who squealed with delight when Ken allowed them to finger his beard. As well as the ivory nut carvings and some of the woven items, we each bought a palm fibre hat for one dollar. We didn't need objects to remind us of such a joyful encounter, but for all of us they would treasured for the rest of our lives.

José invited Ken and me to visit his parents who lived in a valley not far from the river. On the way he told us that he had found enough gold coins to fill a jar and a fabulous gold eagle which had fallen from laden saddle packs along old Inca trails when the interior was looted by the Spanish. 'Maybe we find you some.' The universal lure of gold. We felt it with a nudge of shame.

José paddled over with his ten-year-old son next morning and lashed his dugout astern. 'Not far to see my family.' 'Not far' was a nine mile trek, deep into and 'up, up, up' the mountains! Without sustaining coconut milk every half a mile or so, we felt we might die. The sweat from our faces travelled down to our feet. When our panting became audible, José would send his son to shin up a palm for green coconuts. Finally we could look down into a huge and lovely valley of pasture where horses, ducks, and chickens surrounded a sprawling wooden house, close by a river way down below us. An Elysium field. Going down was as strenuous as climbing up. By the time we reached the homestead we both wanted to lie down and expire. It was early afternoon by now and we realised with a thud of dismay that we were in no condition to walk back through the mountains. I feared for Ken who was visibly melting away, soaked with sweat and looking ten years older. *Imago* meanwhile, lay anchored in the middle of a river that had a tidal rip of five to six knots!

We couldn't disguise our distress. José's mother chided him for it. We smiled but could hardly speak.

After meal of plantain chips, rice, onion, and a tin of sardines which, in our weakened state tasted like a roast with all the trimmings, José led us to two saddled horses for the trek back – salvation! My horse had only one eye! Each time it crossed a narrow ditch, it bent its head so low to look that I nearly slid down its neck. Several times it collided with the rear of Ken's horse. Wimpy Gringos on horseback while a sinewy middle-aged man and his son walked and ran all the way back!

But that household, hidden in the valley, was an Eden. Vegetables and fruit just 'there' and everywhere and roundabout and inside and out were the dogs, pigs, chickens, and geese. As we were leaving, a whole iguana was thrown onto the cooking fire for their evening meal.

José's son took the helm for the journey back to the anchorage. Ken took a photograph of the proudly grinning lad. At times like these, we wished we had a Polaroid camera with which to gift a photo. They would hang it in their homes as a cherished possession. Hopefully he received it through the post despite the very short address: José. Darien. Panama. 'No problem,' said José, 'everyone knows me.'

After such a heart-warming encounter, the Pacific challenge felt less daunting. Our boats set about the usual preparations. Stocking provisions, acquiring the permit to visit the Galapagos, sequencing the charts, and filling up with fuel. Ken decided to carry a deck cargo of four barrels of diesel which earned us the nickname of 'Exon *Imago*.' In large part, it was about the low cost though we reminded the 'jokers' that our boat had the greater carrying capacity and that they might have cause to rendezvous with our 'oil terminal' if they ran short!

The 850nms from Balboa to Galapagos took only eight days though we had to motor-sail much of the time. Without the genius of Charles Darwin, we wondered if this somewhat barren archipelago would have become such a 'must see' destination, though for us it had always been that.

There are few other destinations on the planet that demonstrate so clearly that successful conservation relies on animals having economic value rather than from the kind of moral awakening that ended bear baiting or slavery. Safaris protect many species in parts of Africa though sadly, elephant and rhino remain victim to notions of status, wealth and medical quackery.

To be able to walk among sea lions suckling their pups, huge tortoises, iguanas a metre long, and albatross gliding high in the sky, was a magnificent experience. Local people are less impressed, especially as they have to construct barricades on the bulwarks of their fishing boats to keep the sea-lions at bay. They would otherwise be weighted down to sinking level by three metre blubber boys who find small boats an ideal basking platform and toilet!

Sea-lions are burlesque entertainers in the wild as well as in captivity: clowns, buffoons, and slapstick artists. Hauling themselves out of the sea, using their immensely strong flippers, they crowd onto floating pontoons or any undefended vessel until the final body tips them all back into the sea at which they proceed to start re-loading once more to reach tipping point as if it was a fun thing to do! Perhaps it was?

Geologically, the Galapagos Islands had a violent past. The six of us hired a Jeep to view lava tunnels and massive sink holes caused by the collapse of ancient volcanoes, some several acres across and too deep to peer into. On one of the outer islands, herds of feral horses have learned to negotiate the steep volcanic buttresses as surefootedly as goats.

We now faced our longest uninterrupted passage. Galapagos to the Marquesas, some 350 nautical miles further than the Atlantic crossing.

Our skippers seemed to relish this ultimate testing of their boats and their skills, but while sharing coffee and 'girl talk' on the day before we set out, we lady bosons shared our fears about basking whales, jettisoned containers lying just below the surface, sea mounts, and rogue waves. We hugged each other in case it was goodbye.

***

July 31st 2009

It was strangely un-dramatic. Ken wasn't gasping for breath or clutching his chest, but was clearly in distress. I wiped the clammy sweat from his face and body before calling for an ambulance. The pain was in his back, on the left side. The ECG was alarming. I could tell by the way the paramedics glanced at each other.

Blue lights, a pill placed under his tongue, and oxygen at the ready. We were met by the trauma team at the local hospital who looked at the ECG graph and immediately diverted the ambulance to the specialised cardiac unit at Bart's Hospital in London.

Tests revealed ischaemic heart disease, pre-cursor to a potentially fatal cardiac arrest. Ken was treated conservatively for several days while waiting for more urgent cases also needing by-pass surgery.

A long scalpel incision, veins stripped from his legs, ribs dislocated and prised apart, heart stopped, blood re-routed though a machine, age-related risks. My own heart was bleeding.

Eleven days later, Ken underwent a double by-pass operation. I had visited as usual to shave him, cream his legs and feet, sometimes needing to give him personal care and deal with his incontinence. But on that morning, his bed was empty! No-one had telephoned to let me know! For one ghastly moment I wondered if he had died.

The staff room was full of people. I stood by the open door. No-one caught my eye other than to glance in my direction with that 'look through you' gaze that makes you feel invisible.

I sat on the floor. Looking down improved their eyesight.

'Your husband has had his operation, he's in the ICU unit.'

'His bed was empty I didn't know, no-one told me,' I said lamely.

A monitoring nurse sat at the end of his bed. Ken looked more like a specimen than a living person. Machines hummed, tubes vibrated, a ventilator hissed, and a bloody stain seeped through a dressing on his chest.

Incredibly he was able to return home on the 7th Day.

'You've done well, Ken,' the surgeon said.

CHAPTER 27

A COSMIC VISITOR, AN END TO OCEAN FISHING, SPOOKY WATER. DESECRATION. ONE OF 'OURS' GOES MISSING.

The Pacific Ocean. One of the most capricious and mysterious destinations on planet Earth. A vast lonely place where all notions of human dominance are humbled. Between Galapagos and French Polynesia, the chart is barren. No-where to run. No retreat. We would be rolling in the deep for more than thirty days. So many reasons to be fearful: sea mounts, underwater volcanos, basking whales, islands that are said to rise up suddenly then just as quickly disappear, and conditions that can be unpredictable even at what are considered optimum times for the passage.

Before setting out, I read Ken an entry from *World Cruising Routes* by Jimmy Cornell. 'Almost any well found modern sailing boat is able to travel from point A to point B under most conditions.' And by now we knew that *Imago* was both well found and tested, as were we.

With a powerful auto-pilot, radar, GPS, and single side band radio, we felt confident about all matters practical. Travelling in convoy with friends provided emotional reassurance – a priceless piece of equipment.

At 0800 and 2000 the call went out: '*Deusa, Deusa…Imago, Imago.*' A short report about the day's run: co-ordinates, weather, and compass bearings. Sometimes a little banter, 'Tara ate our last tomato!' Then *InI* would come up and we would all mark our charts.

The Pacific crossing proved to be an uncomfortable passage for us all. Changeable winds, calms, squalls, and unpredictable currents. An ocean that rolled us and rocked us all the way across. But a long ocean journey is rarely without incident. Four indelible events will forever come to mind.

We thought at first that we were seeing a contrail from an aircraft lying just above the starboard horizon, but next evening and every night thereafter it appeared again. Comet KOHOUTEK, guiding our way, keeping us on course, adding even more wonder to the night sky.

Now and again we would trail a fishing lure from the stern. A mackerel-sized fish provided a gourmet meal for three, once we had prised it from Dudley's jaws! With larger fish, we followed tips from other sailors, pegging strips onto the guard rails to dry in the sun or marinating them between layers of salt and sugar to preserve them. Several times the reel screamed and stripped the line to breaking point. Perhaps a tuna, perhaps a shark. One afternoon Ken was relaxing on the side deck, close enough to arrest the run of whatever had taken the lure. It took him twenty minutes, inch by inch to bring the Dorado alongside, a weightlifter's effort to bring it on board. It had swallowed the lure. We could not release it.

A huge, gilded, handsome fish. Silver bright, with iridescent blue and green dorsal colouring. Ken lifted it up onto the cockpit seating. One and a half metres long. Eyes as large as teacups. Eyes that looked out at us: accusing and slowly clouding over. Even Dudley backed away. And as it died, the colours faded to grey.

We had taken more than we needed, contradicted our beliefs, felt like murderous thugs, and never fished the open sea again.

Daylight. My watch. Ken was reading in the cockpit. A glassy surface on a barely undulating sea. Fifty yards ahead the ocean is boiling. There are no birds circling above it.

'This doesn't look right,' I called to Ken. We knew about bait fish balls, that birds could spot them from miles away as predators forced the fish to the surface before launching an attack. This was different. Not hot. No steam. Not the eruption of an underwater volcano, just softly exploding bubbles.

'Veer away!' Ken shouted. We had no idea whether an air and water mix would affect our buoyancy, but it looked sinister enough for us to back away for a nautical mile and keep a sharp lookout for the rest of that day. Nightmare thoughts about such an encounter during moonless nights. Could this be an explanation for sudden disappearances at sea? Not then or since, have we ever read an account that would explain what we had seen

The detritus of twentieth century consumerism laid out on the surface of the ocean like a grubby stain. Polystyrene, pulverised plastic, fishing nets, fenders, clothing, flip-flops, dead birds trapped by their feet, snorkels, masks, and vegetables thrown overboard from yachts and cruise ships. Not only as far as we could see but also way beyond the horizon. Barely a catspaw of wind, but forced to sail at half a knot, carving a way through this depressing rubbish tip rather than risk sucking the odorous morass into the engine water inlet port. Ten hours later we reached open water. Five nautical miles of wading through stinking garbage. Ten hours of shame and pathos.

Aboard *InI*, Scott and Debbi were having a hard time of it all. Vicious squalls and torrential rain. Debbi was sick, anxious, and fearful. We who had served our sailing apprenticeship in a more gradual way from Force 3 to Force 7 felt for her distress. Sailing is not an easy way to travel. Two thirds of the way into the passage, their predicament suddenly seemed dire. Scott missed his morning radio check. *Deusa* and *Imago* tried calling them on the hour for most of the day without success. Finally it was decided that we would try to track their co-ordinates from the evening before by making allowance for the weather Scott had described, their rate of knots, and adding the ten nautical miles a day gained from the ocean current. *Imago*, being the boat closest to them, would head SE to intercept their line.

Day after day we gazed steadfastly along the horizon, looking for a small yacht with tan sails, the glimmer of a masthead light during the night watches. Nothing.

Finally, reluctantly, we set a new course for Nuku Hiva in the Marquesas. From a mile off the coast we spotted two dinghies powering out from the harbour entrance. Robert, Rosemary, Scott and Debbi! Coming out to guide us in. Tying their tenders to our stern, they

297

climbed aboard to celebrate the safe arrival of our convoy before escorting us safely into the harbour. Scott knew we had looked for him. He had served in Vietnam, thanked us with his 'buddy' look. 'Mo'bay chewed through the single sideband cable,' he explained.

Although the islands looked spectacular, most of the anchorages are very exposed, often dangerously so. Hundreds of abandoned anchors litter the seabed beneath the murky waters, but any thought of salvage risks a grisly death from a hammerhead shark! Having sailed well over 6,000nautical miles since leaving Panama, we were all looking to some quiet anchorages from where we could explore the islands.

Mindful of the fact that we must reach a well-protected anchorage before the onset of tropical storms, we spent a week at the neighbouring island of Hiva Oa before marking our charts for Raroia and Tahiti. Our route would take us through the reef-strewn mass of islets that are known as the Tuamotus, the largest group of coral atolls in the world.

CHAPTER 20

ENCHANTED ISLANDS. MEMORABLE ENCOUNTERS.

The Tuamotus comprise a mass of small islands and atolls which interrupt the passage to Tahiti. Largely uncharted, they were avoided for many years as too dangerous to negotiate. Those who dared sailed only in daylight, relying on eyeball navigation with the sun high in the sky to spot tell-tale alterations to the colour of the water, those dark shapes of reefs and shoals that would spell disaster. In 1987, when we set out, there were only six satellites circling the Earth, providing updates every six hours through a Loran receiver. But by 1997, co-ordinates were continuous and accurate to within a few metres. This would make some of the most isolated areas of the Pacific available to cruising yachts.

An overnight sail on a south easterly course took our happily re-united convoy to find safer shelter at Hiva Oa, from where we might make a more direct heading for Raroia and Tahiti. This time we kept closer order, *Deusa* and *InI* slowing from time to time to allow our more ponderous vessel to catch up. Even so, by the time we entered the pass into the lagoon at Raroia, the tide had turned. Huge, turbulent, and agitated rapids were now exiting a mile-wide lagoon through the only gap, barely thirty metres wide! Only a full engine-smoking throttle prevented us being thrust back out by a colossal water cannon! Turning starboard, we sighted the main settlement. A distinctively Japanese man waved us away from a large area of stakes and netting before pointing towards the far end of the lagoon where we could just make out a group of yachts. Realising that he was protecting oyster beds, we acknowledged his warning before heading out across what was a pristine wonderland of sea-life. Ken climbed up onto spreaders, to point our weaving way around the 'bommies' (dense patches of coral growth lying just below the surface). And there, amongst the small group of yachts was *Raroia*!

Within minutes of securing the anchor, some 100 metres inside the outer reef, we were both snorkelling, leaving Dudley with his nose sticking out from a scupper, his tail no doubt swishing behind him as he gazed at the feast below. Gangs of small rays, giant clams welded into rocks, displaying mantles of blue, purple, green. Flying gurnards, their pectoral fins spread like wings, nosed along the bottom. A fashion show of fishes, a ball, a gala, a pageant, and the wavering beams of sunlight through the water a film director's tour-de-force. Walks along the small ribbons of beach were a delight. They might also have been deadly. One of the more experienced sailors advised us to wear flip-flop sandals or better still, short rubber 'wellies' to protect against poisonous cone shells buried in the sand. 'Wellies' might be the last thing to consider packing for the tropics, but monsoon rains, fire ants, scorpions, barbed fishes, sting rays, and sea snakes jogs the mind somewhat!

Black pearl farming is the main industry and mostly owned and operated by ex-patriot Japanese. It was unclear what the arrangement was as far as the islanders were concerned, though there were pearls for sale in a few of the shops despite the scarcity of visitors. Exceptional specimens fetch hundreds of dollars (dependent on roundness and colour as for all pearls), though to us they looked like stainless steel ball-bearings. Rosemary bought two that were deemed imperfect, but their kidney shape made them affordable and more 'interesting,' as earrings. In sharing the island's name, *Raroia* had been fêted by the villagers. A name which will always be remembered as the place where Thor Heyerdahl's raft 'Kon-Tiki.' fetched up, close to where we were all anchored. They were gifted with a pearl each and made very welcome.

An early tropical storm made its stealthy approach as we slept. Anchor alarms sounded, hatches slammed open, and deck lights were switched on. Wild water was slamming into and over the reef. All but one of the boats backed away and reset anchor successfully, but soon after, one small vessel drifted onto a hard sand bar, causing her to bounce on her hull. Being a wooden vessel, she would soon crack her seams from the stress.

Every boat in the anchorage switched on their VHF and tuned in to channel 16, which for all vessels, large or small, serves as an emergency frequency or to establish contact before agreeing another channel for general conversation. Blocking channel 16 is highly irresponsible. As we all switched to an agreed frequency, we heard sounds of distress from the grounded boat.

'We are bouncing on hard ground...we can feel the hull flexing...we are going to break up.'

As well as the agitated voice of the woman, there were sounds of locker doors slamming open and shut, contents crashing onto the saloon floor. 'My husband has tried to power us off but we are stuck fast.'

Karsten, skipper of *Jaisila*, and the most experienced sailor in the group, launched his tender and powered his way over to the stricken vessel. Grabbing the longest rope he could see, he climbed their mast without using a boson's chair or life line and attached it to the top of the mast. Securing the line to the stern of his inflatable, he proceeded to power away from the stricken vessel, leaning her on her side so that she slewed across the sandbar into deeper water. We cannot speak for the rest of our convoy, but even Ken would not have known what action to take and so promptly. We all admired Karsten's bravery and seamanship. He chose to join us for the meandering route through the Tuamotus to Tahiti. Knowing of our lack of experience and having the same sail configuration as that of *Imago*, he kept close order with us so that we might copy his sail plan. We became better sailors because of him.

We reached Tahiti in June 1997, nine years after setting out on our journey. Time had lost its usual meaning. We called it 'earth-time' because we were only bound by our planet's spin, its orbit of the sun, and its effect on weather, currents, and seasons.

Tahiti was expensive, extremely so, though as in Martinique, the people have readily taken on a French identity. The infrastructure was in better shape than on many of the other islands. Solar panels are much in evidence and most of the fishing boats are equipped with imported outboard engines. Perhaps the French government felt more obliged to placate the islanders after more than 200 nuclear tests were carried out on smaller atolls in the archipelago. (National Geographic. April 2015). Local fishermen still attested to strange deformities among their catches.

The French painter Gauguin lived in Tahiti for long periods from 1891, where he found inspiration for his post-impressionist style. He captured the brightness and beauty of both the island and its people. The very sun seems to cast a special light. Girls still wear flowers in their hair and move with confident grace.

The outstanding highlight of our stay in Tahiti was a 'Bastille Day' concert of dance, music, and chanting. It took three men to carry some of the drums onto the huge grass arena. A slim, long-haired, outrageously beautiful young man stepped up to the stage in front of the seated dignitaries. A pure tenor voice floated into the air. Even as the first note sounded, the arena was stilled. Language became irrelevant. It was a love song: pathos, longing, and nostalgia. Perhaps it was a lament about loss: the erosion of traditional values, a requiem for long past irretrievable times. We wondered how he had not been 'discovered' to grace the whole world with his talent. We all tried to smooth away the goose bumps from our arms. As the sun slipped into the sea, floodlights illuminated the arena in preparation for the most eagerly anticipated event of them all. Groups of dancers entered the arena wearing 'faux' grass skirts. As each 'set' of dancers made their entrance to take up their positions, they were wildly applauded by their supporters. This was a serious competition with both costumes and dance routines awarded scores. Each group had chosen a theme colour: red, green, blue, and yellow. Both men and women sported elaborate headdresses. The green group wore pandanus leaves, earning our vote hands down for authenticity and eco-friendliness.

Floodlights. The dark night sky wearing its own costume of sequins exaggerated the colours, so that the arena became a magical setting for what was to come. Waving a feathered baton, urging on his own group of performers, was the dance-master, acting like a cox in a rowing race, a conductor with an orchestra, weaving between his group as they swayed and shimmied, regulating the pace to match the beating drums. More than a hundred performers, distinguished only by their chosen colours moved in rippling, undulating lines like wind over water, compact as soldiers on parade.

After a dazzling four hours came the finale. The dancers had left. The arena was empty. A single drumbeat echoed across the green field, leaving a throb that seemed to float over the stands into the heavens. A beautiful young girl flanked by two bare-chested youths walked gracefully to the centre of the stadium. She began to dance. The young tenor who had moved us so when the celebrations began: his voice, his youthful beauty, his modesty, his manly pride, and now a young woman, matching his grace, expressing womanhood with the same pride, purity, and confidence as he had done. At times she would lift her arms to the sky as if in supplication, sway with sorrow, and stretch up her neck in defiance. Then, with sudden abruptness she stopped. Looking towards the dignitaries, she removed her brassiere, flinging it to the ground as the floodlights were extinguished. One of her escorts draped a shawl around her shoulders before the three now ghostly-looking figures strode gracefully out from the arena.

What a statement! How eloquently delivered. 'You came to our islands and were disgusted by our bare breasts – I defy you!' I think we were the first to stand up from our seats and applaud such a gracious, meaningful, rebuke. Four hours of dazzling spectacle and for all of us a strange sense of loss. Whether in tune with their own message of loss or because we would never see the like again? We couldn't tell.

For thousands of years the Pacific islanders had believed that they were the only people in the world, their land all that existed. Yet much about their evolved culture mirrored the hierarchies of modern societies in having an elite: hereditary chiefs, elected elders, and those who prescribed social mores and prohibitions. Then came Captain Cook, imported diseases, and missionaries. The affects were devastating. On Tahiti alone, early explorers estimated the population to be 50,000 to 60,000. By 1800, these numbers were reduced to 7000. Banning bare breasts was the least of the depredations inflicted and yet, as we had just witnessed, perhaps the most symbolic.

Nevertheless many aspects of this ancient culture are steadfastly maintained. For the traveller, ethnic experiences are a fascinating excursion into human history and adaptability. If the whole world became a 'little Europe' or a 'little America', the perils of ocean sailing would surely have less thrall.

Nowhere else in the world would a clash of cultures become more disturbing than those encountered at our next destination, Eastern Samoa, also known as American Samoa. Both Samoans and Tongans are big people. Historically speaking, a large person had 'weight' in the community as someone who was well fed, successful, and superior. In Eastern Samoa, this distinction was blurred. Every man, woman, and child appeared morbidly obese, irrespective of their social status. American restaurants such as, 'McDonalds and 'Kentucky Fried Chicken' were congested with diners from early morning until late at night. An atmosphere of dejection and lethargy hung in the air. Many of the ex-patriots were veterans of the Vietnam War, still suffering from their experiences, blanking out the horror with drugs and alcohol. The first of these men we spoke with said, 'I own this island.' The second was a talented architect addicted to Kava, a traditional narcotic drink made from the roots of that plant, its use previously restricted to ceremonial occasions. The consequences of his dependency were catastrophic. His mental deterioration was a sad thing to witness and knowing that he was wasting his talent only added to his pain. Over and over he would tell us, 'I let my father down, I let my father down.'

It seemed to us that the culture of these people had been eroded beyond repair. Until now, we had witnessed a more comfortable compromise between traditional and first-world values. A seemingly insatiable appetite for war, conquest, and humiliation has affected most of the peoples of the world, but the consequences for this small island reminded us of the fate of Bison, Aboriginals, Whales, and Amazonian tribes.

The smell was so strong, so pervasive. It spread across the anchorage, seeping into every cabin, clinging to clothes and skin. Putrid, suffocating, foul. One of the largest Tuna processing plants in the Pacific was in twenty-four-hour production mode. Every day the boats unloaded dozens of Pacific tuna, hauling them ashore with derricks. Those dark, three-metre-long, streamlined bodies, swinging slowly in the air, as if hanging from a gibbet. Industrial processes can be interesting, so we took our tenders over to the wharf where we were granted permission to witness the transition of 'fish to tin', so to speak. Long lines of white-coated and hatted workers skinned and filleted the fish, discarding the tendons and offal into pits below the tables. Before the meat was cut to shape according to tin size, it was smelled by a presumably, 'nasally-enhanced' worker to check for freshness. Once packed into tins with lids sealed pneumatically, they were autoclaved in vast pressure cookers, cooled, and labelled. Packed by size into huge cardboard boxes, they were finally hauled by forklifts to a warehouse ready for export. Between shifts, the fish waste we saw below the benches was collected in large containers before eventually being dumped at sea! Hence the smell.

Since that experience, interesting though it was, we cannot look at a tin of tuna without visualising those beautiful creatures swaying in the air. Later into our travels, there would be many more disturbing examples of moral confusion with regard to humanity's exploitation of all creatures, including each other. And yet every living thing is a genetic forebear, a cousin, family, whether a protozoa, a monkey, or a tree.

Before leaving Apia, we all donned our stoutest sandals for the customary five-hundred-foot trek to the top of Mount Vaea, where lies the tomb of Robert Louis Stevenson. The path wound a way through dense thicket, but the ground itself had been smoothed by the many thousands of footsteps since his death.

It was while we were in a supermarket, stocking up for the long sail to Fiji, that we heard news that shocked the world. As the Tannoy blared out a short statement about a car crash in a French tunnel, causing the death of two men and severe injuries to Diana, Princess of Wales, every trolley halted as shoppers looked to each other in disbelief. A few hours later came the sad and shocking news that she, her companion, and the driver were killed.

Several days later, we set sail for the Western Islands of Samoa, where we sat with a large group of islanders in a hut which had a small black and white television powered by a generator, to watch the funeral. Everyone was deeply moved by her tragic death, the muffled hooves of the horses and the quiet. And how proud we were at such a 'British' display of grief, dignity, and restraint.

***

The wounds healed. Our daily routine was resumed, though morning 'bed exercise' and what we called the 'main session' (walking with the rollator, ball throwing, arm and leg stretching, and deep breathing/exhalation) was now less intensive, becoming instead a level of maintenance, though walking every two hours would continue for as long as Ken was able. Six years have now passed since Ken's stroke and he has reached his optimum level of recovery. Each one of these gifted years has been a heaped-up blessing.

CHAPTER 29

*'There are no foreign lands. It is the traveller only who
is foreign'*

Robert Louis Stevenson

Western Samoa proved to be one of our best
remembered places. Welcoming, authentic, and probably
the most eco-friendly destination we would encounter.
Even as we entered the bay, groups of children waved
from the shoreline and watched us laying out our
anchors.

'Tomorrow,' we shouted, leaning our heads on our
hands to show that we were tired. The sun would soon
pour its mother lode of gold into the sea, so as well as
seeming impertinent to disturb their evening, we needed
a night to test the hold of our anchors.

The children were waiting for us as we untied our
tenders in the morning, clustering round to help us haul
them up the beach. There were palm-thatched huts, tiny
gardens with potted flowers prettying the doorways,
spaces between each house swept clean, and coconut
palms offering shade and separation for each family.

Samoans are deeply committed Christians. Later that
day we would learn how much it influenced their daily
life. After a delightful walk along the beach and sitting

with some of the families, we were walking along a path leading to the anchorage when we noticed the quiet. A group of young men, wearing white shirts and pink lava lavas (skirts) were 'policing' the paths and ushering people indoors. The couple we had been talking with opened the door of their house and waved us inside. It was time for sunset prayers. Not a single person was permitted to be outside of their house.

Husband and wife sat on woven mats, facing each other. We followed suit to one side of them where we would not obscure their line of sight. They spoke to each other in turn, bowing slightly to acknowledge each statement. Despite not understanding the language, the words, delivered as they were, eye to eye, were strong and passionate. It was delivered like an aria sung in Italian to a British audience who immediately know it is a love song. The exchange lasted for several minutes, ending when they each stood up and bowed to each other. It seemed impertinent to ask them what was being said, but the husband spoke to us as we thanked him warmly for his hospitality. 'It is Sunday,' he said (we hadn't realised that). 'The youths you saw were "untitled men" who act as ushers. When we speak, it is to thank each other for our lives, our food, our children and our faith. Sometimes we confess our faults also and ask forgiveness.'

A people who truly live according to their beliefs. It was we who were left feeling unworthy, somewhat chastened, but above all deeply privileged. Imagine if so-called 'first-world' couples did the same: surely marriage counsellors would become redundant. Ken and

I tried to do the same. Shameful to confess that we got the giggles, though even that was cathartic!

Many of the Pacific islanders express their individuality through art and personal decoration. Foremost of these is tattooing. Colour is rarely used as is lettering or portraiture. To our eyes, bold geometric patterns were more aesthetic and striking. Both men and women were often tattooed from head to foot in black swirls, bars, and circles. The edges of each shape were sharply defined, representing many hours of painstaking work with sharpened slithers of sticks or shells. Personal items such as utensils, wooden combs, and shell necklaces are also intricately carved. The most precious possession, to these sea-faring folk is their fishing boat, which is also beautifully decorated and brightly painted. They appear to be designed specifically for local sea conditions on each island, a fact that we would begin to take notice of. A marine architect would better understand why some had high prows, rounded bulwarks, flat bottoms, or outriggers. The ocean might slide past one island and crash into another. Sometimes the tides would roll over the reef, agitating the water into short sharp waves.

Mindful that we should reach Fiji before the hurricane season (December to March) we sailed South, stopping only at Niue, a tiny island claimed by New Zealand, though how that came about seemed curious given the 2,000 mile distance from each other! We stayed a couple of days to rest and prepare ourselves for the 650 mile passage to Suva. Every island we saw begged to be explored, but here we stayed at anchor, swam, repaired any chafed sails, changed engine oil, and generally made sure that our boats were in sound shape to weather any early storms.

CHAPTER 30

CLOSE ENCOUNTER WITH A HURRICANE.

Leaving from one of the outer islands in the Tongan archipelago our convoy set sail on a direct course for Fiji. Conditions were blustery with choppy seas and sudden changes in wind direction. Not unusual close to small islands, except that it continued well into open water. A ghastly trip. Big rolling breakers, spiteful winds. *Imago* logged a record run of 137 miles, but for the first and only time I felt seasick. Dudley had cystitis which added to our feelings of anxiety. The lentils and rice, so cheaply bought from open sacks had bred a colony of weevils so that 'rough weather soup' as we called it, was a nose crinkling thought. We ate the fruit we'd brought from Samoa, boiled a few vegetables, and raided the 'treats locker', subsisting for the most part on hard boiled eggs, vacuum-packed bread, and cereals with long life milk.

The meandering, reef-strewn entrance into Suva harbour is almost a mile long. The thought of land and rest is so seductive that once again we broke our rule about closing with land at night. We only learned later that some of the port and starboard lights marking the approach towards the harbour were not working. We watched a freighter make its way out to sea, hoping we might follow a reverse course safely, but several times we saw the dark edges of the reef just inches from our hull. The tension was almost unbearable. After passing on the wrong side of a marker buoy, then reversing back into the main channel from a depth of less than two metres, we had touched the edges of despair. But it was the last buoy. The dark outline of an anchored yacht appeared in front of us. Another harsh lesson in seamanship and two chastened, exhausted students.

Cosmopolitan Fiji. Crossroads of the Pacific Ocean. With a population that is almost half Asian, as well as smaller numbers of Chinese and those of other Pacific nations. Most Fijian men wear the Lava (skirt), policemen too. As 'manly' a garment as the Roman Toga. Indian women wear beautifully bright and patterned saris. A thriving, busy destination in which to wait out the hurricane season.

For all the 'pursers' aboard visiting yachts, it was a richly rewarding stopover. Acres of vegetable markets, small stores offering fascinating items that are stacked from floor to ceiling like long established antique shops. The cinema complex is a six-screen affair with plush seating and deep pile carpet. I hoped we would see an organ rise up from the orchestra pit...but alas, not as nostalgic as that!

According to the charming English veterinarian, Dudley's renal problems were not unusual for castrated cats when they get older. We wrapped his pills into a fish sandwich and then, while he was happily distracted, gave him his injections. My own malaise was probably brought on by exhaustion during what had been such a violent passage. Both cat and purser recovered within a week.

Although it was now officially Cyclone Season, both Bill and Marian flew out to stay with us. Weather permitting, we made short excursions to some of the outlying islands to enjoy enchanting walks and beach barbecues, sharing with them the special joys of small isolated anchorages. Alone. Listening to the sound of surf, the occasional splash of a feeding fish, nocturnal stirrings from unknown creatures. Above us, the stars.

The museum in Suva seems to have benefitted from International experts and donors. As with all great museums, a single visit was not enough to take it all in. It was large enough to house a full replica of a Tongan war canoe, forty feet long, bristling with massive oars, and with fabulous carving decorating the high prows. Enormous glass cabinets, containing weapons of war told of vicious inter-island raids. Wooden spears, warrior masks, serrated swords, also carved from wood, many having a hooked end designed to carry decapitated heads, some still stained with the blood of victims. Similar artefacts, made for tourists, are sold in the huge central market. Amongst the displays of costume and footwear are the shoes said to be worn by the ill-fated Rev. Baker whose mission to the island ended in his death at the hands of his prospective flock. We bought one of the carved swords for its artistic appeal. Its heft and toothed edges would break a leg or arm as in a knife to butter!

Fascinated also, as we always are, by the non-human inhabitants of the countries we visited, we would wander off for a day, with our bread and cheese lunch pack, to see what may. One of these excursions has to be named 'Ant and Lizard Day.' Ants seem to thrive in every temperate or warm climate. They range from those that bite and would like to drag you below ground, to those tiny sugar ants that plague most homes. Some build covered corridors (tubes of dried mud, spread like veins, up the trunk of trees, ending in vast nests which can reach a metre wide, embroidered into the top branches.

Lizard pouches: bronze, bright blue, lime green, speckled, and spotted. How does a lady lizard choose which heroic effort to reward? Distending throat pouches, puffed out after much head nodding and leg bracing. Red, orange, and blue. Butterfly ties. Fascinating. Worth every minute of the day in our lives 'lost' as we crossed the date line from West to East.

We would never deliberately send our friends home with a 'fright' story to tell and the only comfort we took from it was that the experience frightened us too! Mbengga Island, one of the 840 that make up the archipelago, lay only a day sail away. For us, a less metropolitan taste of Fiji and for them, the chance to experience a night anchored in a quiet isolated lagoon. The view was majestic. Mountains and thick vegetation surrounded us on three sides like the curve of a crescent moon. The lagoon itself looked as smooth as a pale blue tablecloth. We now realise that what we experienced was probably a daily event. Late in the afternoon, a catabolic wind began to preen the palms then suddenly burst down from the mountains into the lagoon. *Imago* lurched round on her anchor and broke free. Within seconds, gusts of twenty-five knots heeled the boat onto her scuppers, throwing us all into the side decks. *Imago* scampered around the lagoon as if the wind was a Labrador and she the ball. An hour later the water was once again as calm as when we had entered. The vote next morning was unanimous...back to Suva!

The El Nino event for 1997 was described as 'moderate.' Even so, the risk of cyclones was increased. The daily weather report issued by the yacht club was relayed to all the yachts in the harbour. Numerous small rivers and swamps afforded emergency shelter where boats could tie off on either side of the banks or hold fast to the fibrous roots of the mangroves.

We were all choosing books from the yacht club library when the hurricane alert sounded. Seven hours to reach Suva on its current course but capable of veering away. Some boats took evasive action immediately, but the holding in the bay had been very solid so we waited. The sky darkened. The hurricane held its course. Two hours before what looked like a direct hit, it veered to the North though the outer margins would certainly be felt. The effect of the wind could be seen on the lumpy horizon. The harbour began to agitate as the gusts bore down. The boats strained against their anchors. The surf line, white with breaking rollers, stretched out towards the anchored boats, rocking them fore and aft and the wind had both weight and voice.

A glancing blow, yet the prospect of a direct hit on the open ocean filled us all with dread. There is nothing more chilling than the full power of the wind in its most capricious mood.

318

Before leaving Fiji, we all hired a vehicle to take us to see an industrial process for which the island is renowned. As we witnessed at the tuna factory in American Samoa, end products are so far removed from their origins that the living and dead proof is hard to reconcile with a respect for living creatures.

The cattle were bunched together in holding pens. Mooing, huddled, and restless. All of them showing the whites of their eyes in fear. One by one, goaded with sticks, they were funnelled into the abattoir to become meat and leather. After skinning, the hides were put into huge centrifuges which stripped the hair. Each hide was then laid out onto cutting tables to be trimmed and graded. The best would become chrome leather for handbags, sofas, and other high-value products while others were run through an industrial microtome to produce soft leather goods and suede. Another bank of centrifuges dyed the hides into a multitude of colours. Fish, meat, skins, all of them necessary throughout human history, but tuna hanging from gibbets, the white eyed fear of ruminants, the business-like detachment of the workers, are the least welcome of our visual memories.

Having spent three months in such a sophisticated environment, we all longed to return to more remote islands where we might walk an empty beach, subsist only according to our needs, gaze once more at the jewels in the night sky. As we sailed towards Vanuatu, formally New Hebrides, a hoopoe perched on the pushpit. As with all birds encountered at sea, it showed no fear. With its black bars and orange topknot, it was quite the dandy. Dudley was having a siesta in the saloon, so we never learned whether a hoopoe could be as taunting and playful as a cattle egret.

After booking in at Port Vila, we sailed between the many islands in the archipelago, anchoring off the lee of them or in the small lagoons. Sometimes we would be beckoned ashore by villagers waving from the shoreline. We might then spend an afternoon sitting with a family while the women and girls made woven mats. Some were rush mats for use in their homes, while others, made from the paper mulberry tree, would become highly valued wedding gifts. Vanuatu, with its history of French and British possession, has developed a strange cultural mix since gaining independence in 1980. Despite having their own language called Bislama, there are separate schools for French and English students. It was hard to imagine that one of these small islands, with less than 2,000 inhabitants was a Second World War base for a quarter of a million U.S. troops.

A toothless, old-too-early sort of man appeared from the bush as I was strolling round one of the smallest islands on my own. He seemed to find talking to a stranger cathartic and kept uncomfortably close as we walked. He spoke at length and in derogatory terms about his wife before intimating that I would be favourably considered because he would, he assured me, 'chuck the other one out.' I cannot now recall how I declined his graceless proposal.

I told Ken that I was only put off by his betel nut habit! This moderately narcotic drug is chewed from a very tender age, turning the tongue and lips a bloody red and causing teeth to rot and fall out by middle age... apart from that...!

But it was a place to see blue striped frogs, technicolour pythons, and sacred red shrimp... much better!

Leaving Vanuatu, we suffered our first serious rig failure when the main boom fractured. Night-time, of course, and far too dangerous to navigate between the islands in darkness. Yet another of those frightful nights, with two humans and a cat huddled in the cockpit, wondering all the time about what to do next if the anchor fails to hold. Oh well, there have been a few of those (the worst of them yet to come).

Within five days of returning to the island, Ken had located a saw mill, fabricated a new boom, and acquired a length of bamboo to convert into a spinnaker pole. With a circumference of thirty-five centimetres and having enormous tensile strength, we blocked both ends with solid cores of wood into which we screwed shackles. Our 'artisan pole' lasted throughout the rest of our journey, indeed, if bamboo attained a girth of seventy centimetres, we would have chosen it for both masts!

Had it not been for that fractured boom, we might not have visited the island of Ngouna before leaving for the Solomon Islands. It seemed sensible to test both boom and spinnaker pole before setting out. Robert and Rosemary on *Deusa* had rendezvoused with us for the 750nm journey to Honiara, and when we were invited to attend the local church, they agreed with us that such a welcoming invitation was well worth waiting an extra day.

The church was small but packed with worshippers. Openings on either side admitted a cooling breeze, birdsong, and animal calls, giving an open-air feel to the proceedings. Although it was a Catholic church, it was devoid of gilt and embellishment. A cross fashioned from driftwood stood at the altar together with arrangements of palm fronds. It was when the congregation sang that we felt the passion, the intensity, and the purity of their faith. The voices of men created a ground bass for the contralto cadences offered up by the women. A sound so exalting that we were almost moved to tears. So genuine, so right. If religion was simply an expression of awe then we too felt it. Robert was Catholic. Although he expressed his faith through his caring and conscience, he would not describe himself as devout. Nevertheless, he felt the service in such a visceral way that he took communion at the altar. The congregation looked to each other, smiling.

The bamboo spinnaker pole held our mainsail at such a better angle to the wind that we gained a knot per hour, making the passage to Honiara in the Solomon Islands one of the fastest and most enjoyable. This long archipelago, stretching as far north east as Papua New Guinea, retains much of its ancient culture, (including chewing betel nut). Island children proved to be the most delightful company. Words like, glum, sullen, tantrums, belonged to some urban dictionary rather than here in the islands. The words we needed here were joyful ones: bright, sunny, smiling, and curious. While we rarely recall the moments of fear and desperation, we vividly remember every time that was joyful, especially those which we shared with other cultures. There is something about humour that is common to all communities. Pretending to fall over, pulling a face, and being utterly inept about opening a coconut, all had both adults and children squealing with delight, instantly dispelling any notion of superiority and instead transferring it to them. And rightly so.

A special afternoon. Lots of children aboard. Ken brought out a small tape recorder. The youngsters giggled, sang, and made important speeches. When we played it back to them, they were open-mouthed at the sound of their voices. A lemonade and biscuit afternoon. As they left, we gave them each a sweet from our 'night watch' jar. There were two left over. We put them on the cockpit shelf so that I could wash the jar. None of the children, who returned at various times, even asked about them and we absolutely knew they would not steal them, even though they were in plain view. How many places in the world are there where that would be the case?

Several days later, we were all invited to a pan pipe rehearsal (there is regular inter-island competition). It was held in a clearing close to the village. We had always thought of bamboo pipes as small instruments played like a mouth organ, but some of them are huge lengths of bamboo supported by trestles. The sound from them is an achingly resonant ground bass for the soprano and alto pipes. As the musicians play, they march and dance. In past times, the ends of each huge pipe were struck with a coconut fibre mat, but more recently they have discovered that the rubber sole of a flip-flop sandal works just as well. Washed ashore from yachts and distant countries, they are also cut into fish shapes and stars to amuse the children or hung as mobiles above their cots.

The sound of massed pipes are as deeply moving as the slow movement of a piano concerto. One of the soprano pipers did a swap of his second best instrument for my wooden recorder. Betel nut stains provided indisputable provenance!

Although the children were such delightful company, it was conversations with teachers and older members of the community that gave us a better understanding of how culture and values have been eroded too much and too quickly to adjust to without causing intergenerational conflict, especially between elders and the young. Many of the young men either leave or resent having to stay. Those who remain actively resist many aspects of traditional ways, viewing them as restrictive or overly controlling. Late in the evening, a few newly privileged families could be seen sitting together on rush mats, in palm woven huts that were larger than most, watching television, a throbbing generator overwhelming the buzz of insects, the sounds of the forest. It looked surreal. Apart from traditional feast days, food is no longer served on bio-degradable palm leaves because the polystyrene plate has arrived. The 'new and improved' plates now join batteries and plastic dolls that litter the jungle and the village surroundings. So sad to think that a polystyrene plate could be a status symbol.

There is no going back, of course, but whoever so patronised these people, who had sung in tune with their environment into believing that plastic was more sophisticated, elegant, and modern, should be drummed out of the universe! As envy, social stratification and greed erode confidence, devalue centuries of acquired skills, and when words like, indigenous, primitive, native, and savage, are used to demean them, both group and individual will surely suffer the inevitable symptoms of abuse: anger, resentment, distrust, and inferiority. While there can be little dispute that some aspects of improved welfare will make life more comfortable, it will be a difficult transition for islanders. How these inevitable changes will combine with older traditions and values will be a bumpy journey along an unmade road.

CHAPTER 31

RELICS OF WAR. A HORRIFIC EVENT. A NIGHT OF TERROR.

Snorkelling was one of the most rewarding pleasures of our travels. Endlessly fascinating. We swam through canyons and forests, over meadows of sea grass, and deserts of sand. Elkhorn, black coral and staghorn growing large and sturdy as oak trees. Orchards of sea fans waving in the current, their delicate feathers and fronds quivering like birch trees. Brain coral crouched low like mushrooms on a forest floor.

Guadalcanal, scene of the first major US offensive against the Japanese in 1942, was a very different experience. Here we gazed down at tanks, armoured cars, airplanes, crockery spilled from ship's galleys, and acres of beer and Coca Cola bottles (many of these fused to the rocks on the shore-line). Local people call it 'iron bottom sound.' Stores, munitions, vehicles, and equipment were dumped into the sea when the Americans evacuated the island at the end of the war. As well as the detritus of war, there was ample evidence that US soldiers cannot manage without beer and Coca Cola. The composition of several beaches is entirely made up of green and brown glass fragments. Roadside vendors still sell the bottles as souvenirs. Provenance being guaranteed by their shape and the names of States which produced them.

Further up the island chain, we heard of a terrible event. A couple on a cruising boat had dropped their anchor in a small bay. Whenever a holding ground is in doubt, especially in murky water, it is not unusual for a skipper to dive down to check the set. This particular skipper surfaced within a few seconds, thrashing at the surface near to where his wife waited at the bow. 'Crocodiles!' he shouted, before disappearing again into a bloodstained sea. She never saw him again.

It was deeply shocking to hear of such a tragic event, especially as saltwater crocodiles were very rarely heard of in these waters. We were all aware of the more obvious risks: freakish weather, uncharted reefs, ocean debris, equipment failure, sleeping whales, but never something as dreadful as this. A creature that might even attack a dinghy on the way to shore, had never been considered.

Having heard such distressing news through SSB radio, a nearby cruising boat diverted to escort the traumatised woman and her boat to a larger harbour, where fellow sailors helped her make arrangements to salvage her life.

Soon after that terrible event, a yacht was destroyed on a reef in the same area. Having met the skipper in the lower islands, the implications thudded home – it could happen to any of us. Thankfully, both he and his lady companion survived, eventually acquiring another boat to continue their travels. A brave couple.

After travelling thousands of miles as a convoy of small boats, the time had come to go our separate ways. Just as for any members of a group which form their attachment to each other from sharing like experiences, especially those that involve danger or adversity, the relationship did not end because of parting. Although we now chose different routes, *Imago*, *Deusa*, and *InI* would always remain as closely bonded as veterans of war, trusted colleagues, and survivors.

Nevertheless, Ken and I felt bereft and anxious. Although our friends had taught us so many sailing skills and shared the delights of our many destinations, we felt that our progress from novice to apprenticeship was still a long way from any claim that we were fully competent sailors!

Still, everyone has to leave home sometime, so we upped anchor and headed NW towards the 'Three Mile Channel' marked on the chart, to begin our passage inside the Great Barrier Reef towards Northern Australia. Later we would round the top corner, cross the Gulf of Carpentaria, and anchor off Darwin. For the first few days we felt lonely and exposed, wondering if we would ever again experience the familiar joy and reassurance of sharing each anchorage with such wonderful friends. Skirting the reef, a mile off shore, we looked out onto a barren coast of sand and rocky escarpments. Imprinted in the sand were the unmistakeable indentations left by saltwater crocodiles, including the cleft from their tails...from clawed feet to tail, fifteen to eighteen feet of deadly menace!

Three Mile Channel is a misnomer, since all it describes is an area where long stretches of impenetrable rocks are interrupted by several navigable channels which are only evidenced by smoother water between otherwise agitated surf lines that smash audibly against rocks and coral. The absence of lights, marker buoys, or poles makes it a derring-do, all-or nothing judgement call. Although we made it safely through, we had made a terrible error of judgement, which to cover an agony of hours short, would lead to our worst experience since Plymouth. It was slack water and the tide was soon to turn.

Phenomenal movements of water surged out of the reef openings. Not only is the tidal range one of the highest in the world, it is also the fastest where it funnels out from the reef in white-water torrents. Earlier in the day, we had heard Karsten on *Jaisila* calling up another yacht. We called him back on SSB to ask if he had found a safe anchorage. Having met him in Panama and Raroia, and knowing him to be a highly proficient sailor, we felt sure he would have found an overnight shelter in which we could find safety before night fell. He gave us his co-ordinates from his position inside the outer reef, but our speed, now reduced to less than a knot at full throttle, would not be enough.

As twilight darkened into night, we realised that we were in terrible peril.

Rigid at the helm, eyes fixed to the depth sounder, I shouted out the figures, 'Eighty feet. Now!' Too deep for our anchor scope of one hundred and thirty feet, but we held.

Despite being a couple of miles inside the outer reef, the sheer volume of water, cascading through the openings, together with a brisk wind, buried the scuppers with every roll of the hull. The anchor rope looked as stiff as a metal rod. Dudley leapt into the cockpit, clung to my chest, paws outstretched and claws embedded. Rearing and straining like a chained dog, *Imago* rode the rapids.

A passing shrimp boat called us up on channel 16 to ask if we were stationary, adding, in a laconic Australian drawl, that the position we were in was, 'a bad place to be.' An hour later the first anchor rope parted as the bow lifted high in the air. I heard Ken moaning in terror as he dropped the last and only anchor we had aboard.

Ken and I had long believed that we were blessed with a benign fate, that the elements themselves sometimes make allowance for woefully obstinate perseverance…never more so than during that endless, petrifying night. Surely it was for that indulgence alone that our last anchor held until the early light of dawn. This time, a warp with a two-ton breaking strain didn't just shred, it exploded.

Slack tide. Soon and with the same awesome power, the opposite force would drive us forward. We called Karsten. He too had endured a perilous night. Huge waves had crashed over the reef, threatening to engulf his small boat in a maelstrom of white water. Needing enough daylight to eyeball islets of coral, we motored in a circle until the sun rose. We would need a tow until we could tie up somewhere or hang on to a larger boat.

Two hours later, Karsten rendezvoused with us to pass on his own second anchor before keeping station with us. Our course towards Cairns lay parallel to a desolate coastline of rugged beauty. Cliff and rock formations looked like great helpings of flaky pastry, topped by a pastel-coloured coating of your choice. Where there had been erosion and landslides, it was as if giants had taken out a huge bite. The beaches and caves in this eerily barren Northern Territory begged to be explored, but a quick scan through binoculars also showed up deep trenches left by large heavy tails! Still dazed by our battles with the tide, both boats anchored off Cairns. None of us had slept or eaten for thirty hours and the thought of another night of terror lay on our chests like a heavy weight. Our newly acquired confidence had been shattered. Cockpit talk that evening was about selling the boat here in Australia and flying home. But there is something about 'halfway' that is like the day after the Summer Equinox – nearer the end of the year and, if we reached Darwin, nearer England and home.

Karsten became our sailing mentor. Through this generous, young single-hander, I believe we became 'adequate' sailors. His boat was also a ketch, two masts and a sailing rig similar to ours (twin foresails, main and mizzen). Although we were already a long way from the early days when, with only small exaggeration, we didn't know which 'bit of string' to pull, we matched our sail configuration to his, across the Gulf of Carpentaria, all the way to Darwin. We might never be skilled enough to turn heads in the Solent, but more and more often thereafter we got it right and our heavy steel duck responded. Running with the incoming tide, we threaded through the outlying islands and into Darwin Bay at eight knots and holding – speed freaks! From that time on, during quieter times at sea, we would practise, checking our performance against wind speed: four knots for twelve of wind, eight knots for twenty of wind. Hitting the optimum, to use a nautical term, put us in a 'buoyant' mood. 'Always remember,' said Karsten, 'when in doubt, let it out.' So we would haul up the mainsail, swing out the boom, then with an eye on the speed log, draw in the sail, inch by inch, until, as with an engine, we would hit the 'sweet spot' where *Imago* would settle into her smooth serpentine movement through the water. Clamp the wheel, feel her running free.

Spending time in one small area of a huge continent fails to provide a 'feel' for the culture or atmosphere. Darwin felt transient and inconsistent, as if the inhabitants were temporary and waiting for direction or a kindly turn of fate. A rugged frontier town, it had low wooden buildings, a pub on every corner, and a hubbub of languages from all over the world. Every day a group of aboriginal people sat on the grass opposite one of the municipal buildings, drinking cans of beer, smoking roll-up cigarettes, and glaring myopically at passers-by.

We were not allowed to disembark until customs officers had made a thorough search of all provisions, every locker. They even unscrewed the plates of steel on top of the fuel and water tanks. Any meat-based product was confiscated: tins of spam, ham, and chicken, although we did manage to negotiate about our stock of Kilner jars, having explained that they were only opened at sea. Vegetables and fruit were collected in bags for incineration. The officers were very courteous, but very strict. We carried Dudley ashore in a wire cage to be examined for any obvious signs of vermin or disease before they would release him with a warning to keep him aboard. Any infringement would be a death sentence for him. We gave our solemn promise that his paws would never touch Australian soil.

A day spent in the museum offered a more rounded picture of Australia and how rapidly it has evolved since convicts from Britain arrived there in 1788. Indians in America, Inuit in Canada, aboriginals in Australia, forest peoples in Brazil, all crushed by the blood-soaked clash of civilisations and the power of the gun. The energy inspired by conquest and religious fundamentalism is breath-taking: temples, monasteries, seats of government, and innovative architecture. The skylines of Manhattan and New York. The Sydney Opera house. Big bold statements of superiority and human enterprise. Inevitable therefore, that those who lived in harmony with their surroundings would suffer the consequences, that their values would be denigrated and scorned rather than integrated.

The museum exhibits did much to redress the past and restore a mutual respect between the victors and the vanquished. Aboriginal art may be difficult to decipher (dots and swirls), but the colours are striking. They reminded us of dreams and the way bright sunlight is distorted into a kaleidoscope when we squint our eyelids against the glare of its light.

A preserved saltwater crocodile lay stretched out on the floor, an exhibit as compelling as any of the pre-historic monsters, in the British Natural History Museum. Eighteen feet long, too wide in the body to sit astride or step over, with fearsome rows of teeth lining its gaping jaws. A disturbing reminder of the fellow sailor who had only, recently, suffered such a horrifying death.

Although we always appreciated more sophisticated facilities and the chance to reconnect with a life of modest luxuries: longer showers, book swaps, fresh food, we now wish we had spent more time in the enchanting islands of Indonesia, but it was getting close to the change of weather that marks the Monsoon. Even before we reached Singapore conditions had already deteriorated and wind on the nose brought in regular thundery squalls. We almost got used to them as they rarely exceeded twenty-five knots and were usually spent within an hour, though a tender boat might struggle. They approach very quickly, with winds careening right around the compass like miniature cyclones. Despite the discomfort and having learned from other sailors that it was a worthwhile detour, we stopped over at Ashmore Reef which is an Australian conservation area. Despite the claim of being a nature reserve, the wardens dash around the anchorage in high powered inflatables, churning up the reefs and the delicate sand dwellers. We were granted permission to walk around the tiny atoll amongst several hundred nesting terns, each protecting five square inches of ground and one egg.

Since being shown a perfectly preserved Nautilus shell that a cruising boat had netted from the sea, we had scanned the area in the hope of finding one as a keepsake. Much is made of 'Golden Cowries' (a pair were presented as fitting gifts to our own Royal Family), but I would gladly have swapped them for a Nautilus. The atoll was littered with their remnants that had been broken on the reef, but although that one 'perfect shell' never came our way, we did manage to find a few sun-bleached specimens to cut in half and marvel at their construction. They were the inventors of Scuba Diving, employing intricate chambers within the shell to hold or expel air and achieve neutral buoyancy. It introduced us to a new round of 'cockpit talk' during which we tried to list the inventions of nature that mankind has copied: glue, poison, camouflage, darts, and decoys. The most extraordinary, in what would become a long list, was a spider's web with zig-zag stitching!

A thirty-knot squall prevented us from snorkelling the reef, as did warnings about the world's largest, most diverse, sea-snake population. Nevertheless it was a magical place to stop at, even for a couple of days, just to watch those hundreds of acrobatic birds twisting and wheeling below a pale blue sky, constantly chattering away and fussing about as they returned to their nests.

Many cruising sailors are amateur cartographers who venture into small sheltered anchorages in out of the way places. They sell the information, in pamphlet form, to help fund their travels. With our copy of *Charlie's Charts*, it was possible for us to 'island hop' our way to Bali.

***

Depending on which areas of the brain are compromised and to what extent, any recovery is achievable beyond that of a so-called 'vegetative state' is impossible to predict. Many cases have been documented where comatose patients, even those with 'locked in' syndrome have defied their prognosis in some significant way. One of the most distressing consequences of brain trauma can be a drastic change in personality. A strong, capable person may become childlike. An amiable, kindly, and sociable person can suddenly change into someone who is cranky, disagreeable, and socially inept. What a mystery that is. How disturbing to imagine that a personality might be shaped as much by neurons as through learning and experience. The nature/nurture dichotomy remains open to debate and a long way still, from either scientific or mystical conclusions.

For the first few years, Ken was the personality I knew as intimately as his facial features. Although he was slow to engage, he responded fluently to questions about his early life, building his boat, and yarns about his cruising adventures. Names and places would always be hard to recall, but jobs and places he had lived, seemed easy to remember.

But there are no guidelines, no maps to chart a course, nothing but that which would reveal itself over time. There are no predictable steps to anticipate when a mind is mending. Skills regained may appear and disappear several times before becoming stable.

In all of the fourteen years that have now passed, there was only one disability that threatened our resolve to always manage Ken's care at home. For eighteen months he developed uncontrollable diarrhoea. It wasn't just a normal daily movement. It happened several times over twenty-four hours but mostly at night. I slept in the same room so always knew. Twice, sometimes three times a night he would need to be washed and changed. Our carers would leave out bowl, cloths, soap, and towels to make things easier for us. Once again, as with waking to suction his potentially choking mucus, it wore me down. Even as I worked, the bleak prospect of institutional care loomed large... he would be left until morning, by which time the faeces would have dried. He would then have to be scrubbed clean ... painful ... pitiless ... sore skin ... bedsores.

How many carers feel the same reluctance, for fear of what the truth may mean? Was this another consequence of brain damage? Had Ken lost muscular control over this basic function? Would his spectacular progress now be undermined by such a socially alienating disability?

Fear had clouded my judgement. We need not have struggled for so long in the belief that the cause was a consequence of Ken's stroke. When I finally spoke to our G.P., he referred Ken to gastro-enteric clinic. A colonoscopy revealed age-related diverticula, a condition that might be relieved by a change in diet. At the follow-up appointment, a rectal examination revealed that Ken had normal muscular control, which suggested that mal-absorption could explain his symptoms. The consultant prescribed an oral medication, taken as a drink twice a day to firm up his stools. The affect was immediate and permanent. Two months later, I was enthusiastically thanking the consultant for an intervention that had changed both our lives. He was visibly moved by our gratitude. 'It's what we hope for too,' he said.

There would still be the occasional 'accident', but from that time onwards it was never at night. By incorporating 'toileting times' at lunchtime and just before our carer came to prepare him for bed, his faecal incontinence became a manageable part of our daily routine. 'Better in the toilet than on the bed,' Ken would say. I felt chastened. He had known and it had troubled him too.

CHAPTER 32

A TEASPOON OF RICE – A CAREFULLY GIFTED FLOWER

Passage through the Java Sea proved to be a long, pleasantly languid journey alongside the Northern seaboard of Indonesia. Early each morning small one-man fishing boats with a single triangular patchwork sail, emerged from rocky promontories like bats from a cave. Our own second-hand sails looked race-worthy in comparison. Every third day or so we would consult a *Charlie's Chart* sketch map and anchor overnight. The landmarks might be a 'large, black rock lying ten metres off-shore,' or 'gnarled tree roots sprouting from rocks halfway up a cliff.'

Had we been travelling in convoy, we might have looked for a settlement where we could engage with the inhabitants, but most of the country is strictly Muslim. As 'infidels', we could never be sure about how we might be received. Dotted amongst this huge archipelago are islands so small and disparate that it is hard to imagine that they are regulated by central government, let alone amenable to outsiders.

Bali. Was there a song about it? Was it the setting for a film? We had reached an island that had similar connotations as do Hawaii, Tahiti, and Polynesia, in being a truly romantic destination.

Almost everyone is a woodcarver. Even the smallest shack has its own mound of wood shavings lying close by. Half-finished cockerels, giraffes, cats, masks, and reptiles lie scattered around in every shade and density of wood there is. Having met up with several other cruisers for 'cockpit talk', five of us hired a rental car, (six dollars each for the day) to explore the history of the island and its violent geological past. We were taken to a huge volcanic crater. A still-active blowhole formed a perfectly round hole in the centre, looking like an eye, molten magma boiling inside it like a bright red pupil.

Balinese are master carvers. We visited a large workshop where apprentices were hard at work, often under the tutelage of Chinese Masters who had long influenced such work on the island. Although we admired the rural examples that were offered as tourist souvenirs, it is the 'specimen' piece that best demonstrates a marvellous skill that has evolved over centuries. Creations to make you gasp in admiration. Many stood more than a metre high, every centimetre intricately worked. It was the depth of the carving that made each piece so unique and special: a bug clasping the edge of a leaf, a small tunnel might lead to the head of a mouse, coils of a snake winding through the sculpture, from front to back. Intimate studies of meticulously observed birds, preening, singing, and about to take wing. Each exhibit had taken months to execute and command a price of several hundred dollars.

Many aspects of the Hindu religion make a deeply spiritual impact. It can make other religious observances appear superficial. In every home, bank, small business, wayside shrine, and even on a small, rocky outcrop in the hills, a daily offering is made. A teaspoon of rice, a single chilli, a piece of fruit, or a small, handwoven palm leaf basket, containing a carefully arranged flower. It seemed to us that every aspect of daily living is celebrated in art form. However modest the home, the canoe, the paddle, and the person, each is painted in bright complimentary colours and patterns. Even the food is presented and displayed as art. We had not encountered a society so artistic and religious. We felt that the Balinese people had gifted us with an understanding of the connection between the two.

We joined a melee of tourists at a site of ancient temple ruins which were strictly supervised by rather begrudging monks. Visitors are issued with a body sling to wear, setting them apart from those who were there to worship their past. Tourists, though indulged, wore their scanty, 'holiday in the sun' clothes, unaware that it might cause offence. There is no intention to be disrespectful, except to say that it would, after all, be unseemly in their home country.

At the main tourist areas, the beachside promenades, street vendors were persistent to the point of irritation, but if you are prepared to stand and bargain, which is the only and expected way of doing trade, a mutually agreeable price, that is 'special for you' is soon agreed. To exclaim 'outrageous' at the first offer, to show that you know the game, begins a bargaining contest which both parties enjoy! Very quickly though, the one vendor becomes fifty and the noisy bustle exasperating.

Hinduism and Buddhism share a similar respect for other living beings. Despite the museum-quality carving that had so delighted us, the most rewarding excursion was to the bird park. Everything about it brought wonder and delight. Beautifully constructed aviaries, made from bamboo and sisal twine, each carefully thought out environment housed birds that were healthy and active. They were not only Indonesian birds, but exotics from the whole region. We saw our first Cassowary, its 'dowager' expression, its sturdy scaly legs with three toes pointing forward like a giant chicken. Staff moved slowly, almost deferentially, among the various environments. Food and water containers were immaculately clean. A vast lightweight net covered the tops of the rain forest trees. One could stand for hours, watching different birds flitting into view without causing them any alarm. Toucans sat unperturbed in the trees. Enchanting birds, over-endowed with such preposterous beaks yet perfectly adapted for their large fruit diet and ridiculously proud of it, judging by their posture. I had hoped to collect some unusual brightly coloured feathers, but cage cleaning was so meticulous that there was not a single feather to be gleaned. There was a reverence about the sanctuary that was almost religious in its appreciation of 'all creatures, great and small'.

Working our way through the rest of the Indonesian islands might have been a long and tedious haul for any cruisers in a hurry. Light winds interspersed with hard on the nose NW headwinds ricocheting from cliff sides forced us to motor-sail most of the way. But the scenery on both land and sea, the morning exodus of brightly painted fishing boats with their rice bag sails made slow feel right.

With thousands of square miles of shallow seas, supplies of fish, shrimp, and cuttlefish appear to be inexhaustible. A lot of the fish are as small as whitebait. At each coastal village, thirty metre strings of netting are set down on the sand to dry each huge catch. Most of it is exported to other Asian countries as well as to the main cities like Jakarta. These industrious, patient, people were generally curious and friendly, showing no signs of aggression or bad intentions, though in more strictly Muslim areas, a waved greeting was rarely returned.

Nevertheless, cruising through these little known, isolated parts of the world made us feel vulnerable, so we were relieved to find four other yachts sheltering in a large bay. We were British, Dutch, and American and soon agreed to continue our journey in convoy. At each planned anchorage, we usually came in within a couple of hours of each other. Knowing that we would probably chose different routes after reaching Jakarta, we all decided to visit one of the small outer islands, Karimunjawa. We could not be sure of a welcome, but there is something about small islands that makes cruising experiences more adventurous and memorable, and in this respect we were not disappointed.

The most indelible of sailing memories can be as inconsequential as a pet monkey, tethered to a post by a neck collar. But its tiny humanoid face, its despair, longing, and desperation, has never left our minds.

Another disturbing sight were the dozens of small shacks, supported on poles six to nine fathoms deep, often several miles from the mainland. Single room dwellings with fish nets set below them. Women and children sat huddled in the doorways. Perhaps the huts were temporary fishing bases for their menfolk, but it looked utterly desolate.

Most of our convoy crossed the narrow approaches to the Strait of Malacca towards Singapore in Malaysia. For the skipper of *Viskie*, one of the most anticipated highlights of his voyage was to sit in Hemingway's Bar. A garrulous retired English teacher and prodigious drinker, his boat was well-named. It may well have been his wife who persuaded him to set sail! A few years later, we read a wonderful account of his travels, for which an apt title would have been, *Bars of the World*. Having sailed well over a thousand miles since leaving Bali, we spent our time anchored off Sumatra, checking our equipment, servicing the engine, and repairing sails. The Straits have a reputation for fierce currents and whirlpools and is a busy shipping route.

Wherever cruising boats gather there is always a skipper or two who know the local hazards well enough to offer good advice. 'Follow the Swordfish boats.' These distinctive fishing boats needed the right conditions to spot their prey and ensure a strike. The slim, streamlined vessels looked very like their swordfish prey. A man with a harpoon sits astride a three-metre bowsprit while hand signalling to the helmsman when the fish is spotted. Using these weather windows of opportunity, we hoisted all sail and made haste for Port Klang on the South Coast of Malaysia, close to Kuala Lumpur.

A long inlet from the Straits led to an extraordinary water settlement of stilted shacks, separated by wooden pontoons. We had witnessed poverty: one-room dwellings and most others forms of deprivation, but nothing as shocking as what we now witnessed. The small spaces between each shack trapped a mouldering mass of debris. A toilet, dustbin, and refuse dump. Rats surfaced among the garbage. The stench was indescribable. For some reason, that defied our imagination it was a tourist attraction! A minibus would arrive to disgorge camera-toting visitors who would then photograph families through their open doors, nudging each other, holding their noses. Incomprehensible and utterly disgusting.

As the history of ocean sailing slowly encompassed the whole world, so grew the reputation of certain treacherous and forbidding areas where many ships had foundered. Even with today's knowledge of seasonal weather patterns and the precision of GPS, they continue to exact a toll and a fill a mind with trepidation. The Bay of Biscay, Cape Horn, Cape Agulhas, The Southern Ocean, The Red Sea, the passage from Australia to New Zealand, and the so-called Bermuda Triangle. For us, both Biscay and the Malacca Straits had posed no threat, but for our friends aboard *Deusa*, the very word 'Malacca' would forever be remembered.

Tara, their Jack Russell, was gifted by Robert to Rosemary as a puppy, only days before transiting the Panama Canal. Although she leaped into the sea at every anchorage, she had never lost her footing, even in the turbulent seas of the Pacific. She was the finest guard dog a convoy could have, the loudest barker, owner of two humans and a yacht. So proprietorial was she that she would see off a fish breaking the surface. Even the light slap of a curling wave against the hull would put her into 'bouncing on the spot' mode. Like Dudley, she brought companionship to the night watches and that wonderful communication that is as undeniable and as deeply rewarding as any human friendship.

How it was that she was lost overboard would never be known, but Robert and Rosemary knew within an hour that she was gone. I think we were closer to their feelings of loss and grief, because we could imagine how devastating it would be to lose Dudley, though we only heard about it later.

Tara was found by local fishermen, close to exhaustion but still swimming. They brought her ashore and took her to their village. Somehow word spread about finding a dog swimming in the sea, miles from land. Four days later a call on Channel 16 alerted the yachting community to this wondrous event. What an ecstatic, tearful, re-union it must have been. How extraordinary that Malaysian fishermen (normally indifferent to dogs) should have rescued her. Robert and Rosemary calculated that Tara must have been swimming for more than eight hours! It was such an unusual and heart-warming story that it was featured in a Malaysian Newspaper.

Tara would continue her life as a 'sea dog' for several more years before becoming a 'land-lubber' in both Mozambique and South Africa, along with her skipper and his wife. Her life was altogether one of wild excitement. Whether Zebra, antelope, flying fish or dolphin, they moved and must therefore be barked at and chased! Her end was fitting...elderly, one last chase...dying in the arms of her shipmates.

CHAPTER 33

NEARLY ROBBED, THEN REALLY ROBBED. A 'MERE' WOMAN SAVES THE DAY!

ADVENTURES ON THE INDIAN OCEAN.

We now seemed to be travelling from metropolis to metropolis, encountering little to distinguish one from another. The Pacific islands had bewitched us with their self-sufficient ways, their crafts and traditions, and their more careful rationing of resources. We realised that we might never again snorkel in warm turquoise shallows or gaze down on vibrant healthy coral, or swim with sharks.

The 200nm run from Penang to Phuket in Thailand proved uneventful in terms of weather, but we both spent our nights lying on the cockpit seats, partly to be sure of spotting small fishing boats that rarely show a light, but also because attacks on cruising boats have been recorded in these border areas. Quite what we would do if threatened by pirates, other than to arm ourselves with flares and two small fire extinguishers was thankfully not tested. Ken never asked why I kept our bag of potatoes under the companionway ladder (a spud in the face might be useful last resort).

At some time in the future, our adventures would all become memories. Images of people, landscapes, the wide encircling ocean, the smooth green slope of a majestic wave, and silence. A feast of memories. None would rely on either latitude or longitude or even the where and when. Sometimes they would come to mind only as colours: green and grey (noisy, gale force colours), bright, yellow based, blue, (radiating from a tranquil island bay), ghostly silver from a full moon, a forested landscape in every green there is, cliffs and mountains, weighty, majestic, imposing, declaring their endurance in a way that seems to put humanity firmly in its diminutive place. The emotions that belong to each image are also vividly remembered. They have ranged from paralysing fear to a tranquillity so overwhelming that it can make you cry. And above all, a sense of awe that could be religious.

If we were to fully appreciate such recollections in the future, the experiences themselves would have to lie waiting in the past, as do childhoods. For that to happen, our journey must have an ending. Like athletes, we had trained, sweated, and aspired, all for that defining race...win or lose, only needing to be certain that we have run our best.

Anywhere North East of the Suez Canal would feel like a homecoming.

The direct route from Phuket in Thailand to Aden is a long haul of over 3,000 miles, the equivalent of another Atlantic crossing. Our second-hand sails have taken us three quarters of the way around the world and it shows. Even when hauled amidships, they sag and billow in noisy, flapping furrows, wrinkled as are our own faces, from the burning glare of a tropical sun. Closer to home, we would buy a new mainsail. It would be crisp and white, the wind would slide across its face with barely a whisper.

Galle, lies at the South West corner of the island of Sri Lanka and would bisect our journey across the Indian Ocean. A useful place to rest or find shelter if we met harsh weather. Eleven days of sailing was longer than we had experienced since crossing the Pacific from Galapagos to the Marquesas. We had to prepare ourselves, as well as our small ship, for this final challenge.

'Chinky, chinky Chinese.'

'Dog-eating bastards.'

These and other, even cruder messages, blared out on channel 16! I'm doing the 2am-6am night watch. Any maritime hazards would be relayed on this emergency radio channel. It was an astounding breach of etiquette. Passing freighters were trading insults, tailored to suit the stern flag that identifies the country of origin. Presumably, their Captains were sleeping and the crew was having 'fun' in the radio room. More disturbingly, they were slurring their words which suggested they were also having a grog session! Mindful of tradition, I ignored the racial slurs as man-blagging, (heard at most football and cricket matches), but when it escalated into the most disgusting sexual slurs I'd ever heard, the latent suffragette in me erupted!

'I'm a single-handed woman sailor. You are disturbing my sleep with your vile talk. Change channel please.'

Surely this would invite a torrent of abuse. The radio crackled. I wasn't going to engage further, being quite satisfied to have supported the 'sisterhood' and said my piece, but the voice I now heard, spat on the behaviour far more eloquently than had I.

A deep, growling Scottish brogue. 'Well said, lassie, I'm master of the vessel on your starboard side, they're nay sailors ye are hearing. Good luck and fair sailing to ye.' And for a moment there I felt a wave of infidelity and had fallen in love!

Knowing that a final ordeal awaited us (there is never an optimum time to traverse the Red Sea), we decided to stay in the harbour at Galle to stock up, add more patches to the sails, service the engine, and to prepare for the longer run towards Aden. We were more than a mile off shore when the speedboat shot out of the harbour towards us. Guns, military uniforms, sunglasses, and Kalashnikov rifles! Scuba divers were deployed to swim beneath our hull. A checklist of questions. Every locker searched. Even the mattress swabs were dragged from the bunks. Later in the day, we set out with our passports and ship's papers to report our arrival. The harbour gates were flanked by sentry boxes manned by military personnel. A sense of unease crept over us.

The office contained a single, preposterously large desk, manned by a surly-looking official, wearing a western style suit and tie. Nothing in the room suggested a government department, such as national flag, photograph of the president, noticeboard, or file cabinet:

the usual accoutrements of officialdom. Only the fact that we were carrying extra cash, to spend on food stock, averted the shame of becoming 'persona non grata'. The atmosphere was too charged with menace to object to the extortionate sum of 300US dollars! Neither Ken's raised eyebrows nor my wince, altered the stony look on the face of 'the man with the stamp.' It was three times more than we had ever been charged for booking into a country. The cash went into a drawer and no receipt was given. We were waved away. Our timid acceptance of corruption may appear to condone the practice. It doesn't. It is simply a sensible compromise when visiting other countries. The only other option is to leave, though the fact of having already set foot on their soil may have legal implications. Corruption affects even the most sophisticated of societies and in every case it is an internal matter and definitely not one to be challenged by ocean sailors. Memories of a voyage around the world are so numerous and inspiring that something like an exorbitant booking-in fee would normally be too trivial to remember, but to be charged so much for two terrifying and sleepless nights can sharpen resentment somewhat!

It sounded like a crash of thunder. *Imago* shuddered. Dudley screeched in fear. Rolling out from our bunk, we scrambled into the cockpit. Ken naked, me with a hastily grabbed pillow preserving my chastity. No rain, bright stars above, calm water, no sign of a plane crash, an explosion, or even signs of agitation from any of the anchored boats! Three hours later. Another explosion. Closer still. Only then did we realise the implications of the search at sea, military personnel guarding the gates of a harbour... the country was at war! Sleeping below decks was impossible, and our steel hull acted like a drum to magnify the sound of what we presumed were stun grenades. They would not damage the anchored boats, but the noise and vibration was overwhelming. We sat in the cockpit, bleary-eyed, waiting for dawn and watching the soldiers in their dinghy, tossing the explosive munitions into the water.

Next day, we hastily stocked up with only enough perishables to last ten days and cancelled any plans to see elephants at work, a tea plantation, or some of the colourful and ornate temples we had heard about. In terms of cost, it was like paying for two nights at a posh hotel, only to be served a lousy breakfast! Ken spent the rest of the day servicing the engine. We would sleep in the cockpit and leave at dawn.

Despite the long passage from Sri Lanka to the Gulf of Aden, it was delightful sailing. A consistent fifteen knots of wind and a favourable current propelled us smoothly over the ocean at an average of five knots, both by day and by night. Perhaps for the last time, we gazed up at an unpolluted night sky, peering past the brightest stars to where the faintest stars filled the spaces with glittering dust, knowing that what we were seeing was one of the very reasons why we had chosen to build a boat and sail it around the world.

As the two land masses of Africa and Asia closed around us in the Gulf of Aden, the wind became more unpredictable. By the time we had closed to within a mile of the Yemeni Coast, it had dropped to zero. As *Imago* quietly swayed and bobbed in a gentle current, we decided to wait on the wind for an hour and enjoy a strong cup of coffee (a rare treat it is, when the mug can be filled to the brim and safely carried from galley to cockpit without spilling)!

A boy stood on the rocks at the shore line. Waving both arms high above his head, then more frantically in front of his face, calling at us to come in. We held up our palms before pointing ahead to indicate that we would be moving on. As the current swung us slowly past the coast, the boy began to run. He wore a loose shift which fluttered round his knees as he ran barefoot, over the rough rocks, begging us to follow.

What happened next was possibly the most potentially dangerous of all our encounters. It played out like one of those mystery dramas that suggest a number of possible endings. A small wooden powerboat shot out from an inlet towards us. Aboard were four young men and one who looked middle-aged. After tying up against our hull, they all stood up, as if to board us. The older man held out his hand. 'Papers. Passports.' Exercising a skipper's right, Ken motioned for only two to come aboard. Both men sat silently in the cockpit while Ken went below to find the paperwork. The older man scrutinised our passports page by page while the rest were scrutinising me! None of them caught my eye, but they were looking me up and down. I was never so glad to be wearing long cotton trousers and a bra under my top!

'Cigarettes, woman films.' I passed him the nearly full pack that was lying on the pedestal shelf.

'More.'

I shrugged. 'Long way to go…we need.'

At just that moment a puff of wind ruffled the mizzen. 'Here comes the wind, Ken, raise the mainsail.' As *Imago* picked up speed, both men quickly disembarked as their powerboat, now being towed alongside, rocked from side to side and began to ship water.

With their powerful outboard they could easily have caught up with us, but the throaty roar of our engine seemed to deter them. They hastily powered back to shore.

'Did you see what was in the bottom of their boat?' said Ken.

'No, what?

'Kalashnikov rifles!'

'Thanks, love,' added Ken. 'Well done, I don't know what would have happened if you hadn't said what you did. I sensed trouble but didn't want to alarm you. They weren't wearing a uniform so they had no right to board us at sea.'

'What on Earth did I say, Ken?'

'You...a woman...telling me to set the mainsail. They never heard the like of it.'

Heroine? Wonder-woman? Not only was Ken twice their size, but we also had a huge killer cat aboard... surely that was it?

***

The realism of war movies. Medical documentaries. Hospital-themed soap dramas. News stories about untrained citizens, witnesses to horror, saving a life by using a belt or tie as a tourniquet. The family of an epileptic, responding in a practiced and automatic way to

355

the fits: recovery position, check that the tongue is forward, make sure that nearby objects are removed to prevent injury, reassure the patient as they regain consciousness. Yet however competently the situation is managed, it is a sudden crisis and always shocking to witness.

Fortunately, Ken was still in bed when he had his first seizure in June 2014. He uttered a low moan. His eyes rolled. I called to him, but he was unresponsive. The rigor started as a tremble, soon his whole body was convulsing. By the time I had removed his dentures, his arms and legs were thrashing about so violently that his hospital bed was rocking wildly.

I know I called for an ambulance because it arrived within minutes but cannot remember either making the call, the journey in the ambulance, or even what treatment he was given by the paramedics.

This was a different kind of fear than I had ever encountered at sea. At those times, it was a fear that heightened perceptions rather than dulling them, a state of mind that allowed us to make logical decisions about what actions to take in order to survive. It was that innate mammalian 'fight or flight' mode that is fuelled by adrenalin.

The peculiar fugue state I felt now was perhaps the kind that 'roots you to the spot,' shields you from imagined consequences – even that of death. Emotional shock. The mind shuts down and refuses to accept what is happening... I thought Ken was going to die.

I'd said it so often: I must outlive Ken, he cannot end his days in a nursing home. It's the right way round for us. I have to see him through.

Now, faced with that very prospect...I couldn't face it.

By late evening Ken had regained consciousness and was able to recognise me. After three days in hospital to monitor his recovery, he came home. Soon, having both recovered so to speak, we were back to our daily schedule. 'That was a nasty cold you had, love.'

'Hmm, yes I didn't feel too good.'

CHAPTER 34

THE RED SEA:
WHERE WORLDS COLLIDE AND THE SUN IS THE COLOUR OF BLOOD

The might and power of a Southern Ocean gale is undoubtedly the sternest test for a cruising yacht and her crew, adding greatly to the reputation earned as a circumnavigator. Why then, should sailors who choose the tropical 'coconut milk' route fear a virtually land-locked sea that looks no more innocuous on a marine chart than a long placid lake? But fear it they do and for good reasons.

Whether travelling its length from NE or SE, the wind propels you to the middle then tries to spit you back from whence you came! In all directions the coastline is scoured by the shimmering heat, devoid of any vegetation that might soften the colour and shape of the landscape. Oil rigs, dense shipping, and bizarre luminescence. False horizons confuse the eye and sand particles fill the air. Unmarked reefs extend for a considerable distance from areas of coastline, and the relentless blistering heat vacuums the moisture from your body until you feel your limbs curling up, like the legs of a swatted fly. Lying to port and starboard are some of the poorest countries in the world, where poverty is life-limiting, yet for the most part simply endured with a dispassionate malaise. Our own frugal ways would last for the rest of our lives, not as a statement or in protest, but simply because enough is sufficient, but when confronted with the levels of destitution we now encountered, even frugal was a privileged life.

Soon after 'saving the day' with such a timely female indiscretion, Ken set a new course, to Djibouti, on the Eastern side of the gulf – a decision that served us well. Yemen, according to radio traffic, appeared to be on the verge of civil war, while in Aden, the hull of an American ship, *S.S. Cole*, had been holed by a mine while anchored in the harbour. Several sailors lost their lives. Ken promoted me to Admiral!

The customs officer sat behind his substantial, completely bare, desk. A large man, with a stiffly upright, square-shouldered pose of entitlement. A minion had ushered us into his presence. Since neither man spoke or met our eyes, we carefully placed our passports onto the desk. The big man stared at them as if we had dropped litter! No chairs – we stood before him, hands clasped in front – what a deferential posture that is!

Glasses first, left hand drawer, placed carefully and slowly onto the desk. Next came the ink pad – right hand drawer. Finally, the stamp, which he tip-toed over the ink. With a determined and unexpected jab, which made me jump, he thus accorded us permission to be guests in Djibouti. As we leaned forward to retrieve our passports, he coughed loudly, in a way that was meant to be noticed. From yet another drawer he produced an old-fashioned, breast-shaped bell and with a rather 'prissy' motion, pressed the nipple with his forefinger, at which the white robed minion re-appeared, picking up the passports before backing out of the office, bowing as he went, gesturing us to follow.

Despite such 'theatre', we played our sober, deferential part, perhaps sensing that such distinct social stratification and fawning compliance are still the cultural norms in many parts of the world. A lampooning sitcom such as 'Yes Minister' would, after all, have been unthinkable in Victorian England – not so long ago. Such pomposity is now satirised with gleeful transparency, but the 'big man' syndrome is no laughing matter if the consequences of rebellion are destitution, or even death. So, not funny at all (other than in the telling).

Most travellers feel uncomfortable when confronted by thin, ragged, hopeless people for whom there are few opportunities to learn, who must simply obey. Yet poverty is a relative term. In lush tropical environments, there are fruits and vegetables to harvest, fish to be caught, and the means to build shelter. But in this scoured region of the world, poverty is a stark and ugly reality for many thousands of people.

'Cockpit Talk' is a unique forum for debate and travel focuses the mind on such issues. Neither eloquent voices, many dedicated lives, nor even the wish and will of so-called 'ordinary people' has succeeded in alleviating the suffering of millions, or raised its lowly place on the international agenda. A cruising sailor can change a life by gifting a pair of second-hand spectacles – how many millions more are tossed into landfill sites? As one ex-accountant sailor put it, 'Billions are allocated by rich governments as "foreign aid" only to be siphoned off by corrupt rulers and their cohorts. There is little accountability about how the money is used, yet there are charities with dedicated volunteers who would use the money to improve infrastructure, build schools, medical facilities and provide basic housing.'

After our recent encounter with the Customs Officer and his passive underling, our own contribution to the debate was to suggest that the biggest obstacle for those whose need is greatest, is that they are still trapped in their ancient history of Pharaoh, Emperor, and Caliph. Until there was a popular revolution, the excesses of their rulers would remain as false symbols of their country's greatness. Like many great and wonderful edifices, the Pyramids of Giza are monuments to enslavement and 'disposable' lives.

Small wonder then, that every country in the world has its own palliative; opium, peyote, betel nut, Kif, Bhang, Kava, and alcohol. In the Arab world, it is Qat, a green foliage which is stuffed, hamster-like into a cheek until, over time, the skin is stretched so much that it becomes a permanent white lump like a facial tumour.

There is little about this part of the world that resembles western modernity. Sights, sounds, and odours blend together to create an exotic atmosphere that belonged to an ancient, yet still living, history. Small homes, like white boxes, nestle beneath towering cliffs, and minarets and towers rise up between them like fairy castles. The smell of newly baked bread, open air fires, camel dung, and sea brine perfume the heated air. The plaintive, operatic call to prayer floats across the desert, and lingers there before fading away. A beautiful sound.

Customs and tradition are strictly observed and difficult to negotiate, especially those that concern relationships between men and women. We were bound to transgress… and we did. I think that cruising sailors may have more sociable encounters by behaving like visitors rather than tourists and having therefore, an instinct for modesty of person and of dress. I certainly didn't want to inflame the passions of Qat-chewing men!

Nevertheless, we were as conspicuous as clowns at a funeral: chatting together, walking side-by-side, smiling, at both men and women as they passed. For a woman, my walk was too confident, my head held too high. When a German couple ran low on fuel off the coast of Saudi Arabia, the authorities allowed him ashore to fill his jerry cans but ordered to keep his wife below decks… 'she must not be seen.'

We dared not sail at night, except in the broader reaches. With merchant ships moving at twenty-five knots, any rig or engine problems might put us in serious jeopardy… as would stray ordinance…we could hear bombs exploding in the distance as Eritrea and Yemen descended into war.

Occasionally we followed a small group of cruising yachts into a Marsa, an opening in the reef, leading to small anchorages in the desert itself, where there was shelter from the waves if not from the wind. The monotonous landscape stretches out into the distance. Small sand storms rolled across the land like tumbleweed. From far away, a row of moving dots appeared as camels and donkeys are led over the dunes.

Romantic 'Lawrence of Arabia' depictions of nomadic Bedouin peoples wandering their traditional routes across the vast desert is now a somewhat dated perception. Although they still choose to set up camp rather than be confined in the cities, many of the groups are now relatively (sometimes exceptionally) wealthy. Tents are no longer draped with animal hides, they are more likely covered with canvas. Much of their wealth comes from breeding pedigree camels for the elite in Saudi Arabia. They have also recognised the benefits of tourism, encouraging visitors to visit their camps to experience what remains of the Bedouin culture: try on a beaded veil, smoke a bong, and have the women decorate you with henna tattoos. Both parties enjoy these temporary connections – because that is what they are, lucrative but temporary. Today's camel train will have a Jeep and small trucks following behind.

Having clawed our way up the Red Sea as far as Sudan, we decided to stop for a couple of weeks, partly to re-provision, mainly to rest and recuperate before the final push to the Suez Canal. We were no less tired than if we had crossed an ocean! For the previous 200 miles *Imago* had been the 'lead boat.' It was the rugged no-nonsense look of her we think. Every early morning Ken and I would gauge the wind strength before deciding whether to stay at anchor or venture out. On other boats close by, their crew would stand by the anchor winch awaiting our decision!

By setting out at dawn, we might cover forty miles by late afternoon. On other days, thirty-knot winds joined catabolic gusts sweeping down from mountain ridges and high dunes. Bowing our heads before the weight of twin demons: superheated air and lunging seas we would retire, defeated, and seek refuge in any anchorage where other boats were sheltering. Moving through the water at barely two knots was unrelenting misery and frustration – ten miles in five hours is an unacceptable ratio for any self-respecting vessel! Despite having sailed the world's largest oceans, our sailing skills remained basic. Everything about *Imago* was heavy: her construction, carrying capacity (fuel and water), her sails, too many spanners, and too many books. Neither of these last two culprits was negotiable! We watched enviously as smaller, lighter boats headed into and through the wind, nimbly enough to dodge the shipping. But *Imago* was more than a vehicle, she was our home and 'clutter' made her so.

Not since the earliest years of our sailing adventure had we felt such fatigue and anxiety. Ocean squalls and gales are generally short-lived and often followed by several days of languid, effortless sailing. We coined a rhythmical phrase… 'read-a-book-a-day-times.'

Fair exchange if ever there was! A turbulent, sleep-deprived, adrenalin-fuelled engagement (no, not a battle) with the weight of the wind, followed by a reward of such sublime peace, that when brought to mind, our very bodies sway with the memory.

At all times, Ken and I wore loose cotton pants, oversized T shirts, and wetted cloths around our necks. It was so darned (too mild an expletive) hot that I really didn't want to wear a bra, but although minimally endowed, as in small all over, a mere hint of a nipple would mark me as a fallen woman, a wanton, a harlot! So I suffered the constraint and the suffocating heat of a garment that doesn't waft.

However sensitive a traveller tries to be, with regard to tradition and cultural norms, it was impossible to even recognise, let alone conform to an alien culture that literally 'collides' with any other. The 'real life' contradictions suggested an almost Freudian repression of human nature. The local lads would row out from their fishing boats to the foreign yachts… 'give woman pictures…give us woman movies.' We didn't have 'Esquire' or 'tits galore' mags. We just hoped that the rather more muted 'lady pictures' in 'National Geographic' would not be looked at until we had left the anchorage!

CHAPTER 35

SUDAN:
A JOURNEY INTO THE PAST

One of the most rewarding reasons for travel is to experience cultural diversity. Anthropologists study the subject as a science, whereas a visitor may only be aware of its physical manifestations: of dress, rituals, utensils, dance, food, and dwellings. A curious traveller will find such variety fascinating, intriguing. A few will make comparisons with their own culture and miss the point entirely.

A social fabric is shaped by history, environment, social control, notions about death and an afterlife, the availability of food, and sexual mores. Unlike most animals (unless they undertake seasonal migration), humans have proved so adaptable that they are not confined to any specific niche on planet Earth and yet, despite their largely similar physical characteristics, each community constructs a distinct culture and value system.

Although the Arab culture has evolved in much the same way as any other, it proved difficult, sometimes in disturbing ways, to negotiate. Perhaps the forbidding landscape and the strictures of Islamic faith may account, in part, for what discomfort we felt, but it seemed to us a harsh culture – especially for women and donkeys. Women are an alluring temptation that must be strictly controlled and guarded against at all times. A donkey cannot be led, it must be goaded with a stick or fist. We saw a hugely obese lady astride one poor beast. Its donkey legs trembled with every step. Behind her, being led by a lead, was a strong, well fed, mule.

Had it not been for our experiences at Port Sudan, we might have been left with a somewhat jaundiced view of Arab culture. Impressions, we realised, are just that – formed in ignorance and without due reference to those who live within it. In cosmic time, it was only seconds ago in our own culture that bear-baiting and horrific forms of public execution were viewed as 'entertainment,' and when the strictures of religion resulted in witch trials and the brutality of the Inquisition.

Even as we set anchor, conspicuous (in being the only yacht) among merchant vessels, fishing smacks, and in-shore rowing boats, a young man paddled out to us in a small flat-bottomed punt, declared himself to be Matthew, and asked if he could be our 'agent.'

'Many agents...me the best.' We wondered how long and from where he had watched our approach in order to be first in the queue for his share of the booking in fees. But he was young, smart, and affable. We warmed to him. His deference was courteous rather than servile. Perhaps it was benevolence towards a couple old enough to be his parents but looking like grandparents. Passage through the Red Sea is an ageing experience!

Our faces and arms were burned well beyond 'salon tans' – more the colour of new house-bricks. My hair looked like parcel string. Ken fared better, a sun-roasted man appears rugged, 'interesting', whereas I looked like a favourite shopping bag!

Matthew was our protector and tourist guide. In many ways, despite his tender years, he was a teacher also. Resort operators may wish to note that a single friendly encounter can enhance the reputation of a venue more dramatically than any advertisement or gimmick.

He introduced us to AL-HAZIMI computer and fax service so that we could e-mail friends and family. Having not made contact since leaving Bali, it served to put many a mind to rest. This was the so-called 'modern age' – our loved ones couldn't understand why we couldn't communicate regularly – we couldn't help it! The owners of the business were delightful and eager to learn about Britain and our travels. A group of young male students gathered in the shop most days. We were soon welcomed into their midst, drinking strong coffee with them and debating a range of social and political issues. Sober discussions, no raised voices, and no dogma! Only a strong desire to improve their country's prospects at every level, despite the impending threat of civil war. Yet even here, among such enlightened and hospitable young people, there remained prohibitions that could not be breached under any circumstances. After one coffee too many, I asked if I could use their toilet. Consternation! Every head swivelled from side to side, arms fluttering in a semaphore of 'no's.

'I will have to go back to the boat, Ken. I'm busting to go'.

Having almost left the urge too late, I'd probably have to wee into the dinghy's baler, but go I must...and soon. After some frantic looking whispers, one of the students offered to escort me to the public toilet. A few corners away from the shop, my escort hid behind a street stall (selling water watermelons, would you believe!) and pointed to a long line of waiting women. A single corrugated iron cubicle stood at the front of the queue. A dense cloud of flies rose up into the air then landed each time the wooden door opened and shut. I couldn't look at the women. They couldn't look at me. In some way or another, I was about to defile their women-only, squalid, fly-blown, toilet. Just at the point when my humiliating intrusion could be made no worse than weeing where I stood, I entered the cubicle. A pot inside a pit, no toilet paper, flapping at my bottom to avoid carrying flies away in my knickers. An old, bent-over, scruffy little man (presumably judged immune to temptations of the flesh) entered the cubicle with a bowl of water with which to rinse my infidel urine from the rim of the pot. Humiliation. Defilement. Blame. And how do you even begin to make sense of it all?

When I was in my early teens, I once urinated in an alleyway, not realising that it led to the rear door of a police station! I can still remember the flush of embarrassment, but it was nothing like this wincing public humiliation. Perhaps I should have regarded myself as simply another woman in the queue, a solidarity with them, but whatever virtue was required for that, I couldn't find it and the shame of that was even more intense.

A few days later we gave the students our sailing date and explained that we needed to stock up in the market, but would join them once more before leaving.

'Tomorrow, come tomorrow.'

The following day we arrived with a tin of sweets, a packet of coffee, and a jar of home-made marmalade. Mohammed, the shop owner, presented us with a colourful laminated poster dated 25 March 1999. At the bottom of the poster (now a treasured possession) was the following message...

... "On this special occasion of your visit to Port Sudan we would like to present you this modest present as a sign of remembrance for the few beautiful days you spent with us. Bon Voyage. With best wishes."

It felt like being honoured with a Peace Prize. We all shook hands. I so wanted to hug them, but that would have been an even greater breach of etiquette. Even to have offered their hand to a woman was honour enough.

With Ken as my 'minder', we strolled around the open-air market. Having already discovered that Arab bread must be eaten on the day, before the weevils hatched, we concentrated on the fruit and vegetable stalls. Rice, lentils, and flour were sold from hessian sacks, but despite being temptingly cheap, they too would only end up as food for a thousand pet insects! Wherever you are in the world, markets are the throbbing epicentre of daily life. A place that teems with those who supply, those who shop, and those who meet friends for coffee. Daily re-enforcement of culture, norms, and expectations.

Far from being inconspicuous, women stand out starkly amid a sea of white robes, like a few black pawns, left over on the board after a one-sided game of chess. Arab men are remarkably tactile with each other, kissing foreheads or cheeks as they greet each other, hugging, and holding each other by the shoulders. A gender reversal of our British culture in which only best mates, military veterans, and footballers express their bonding in such a way. It struck us as more like young women meeting up for lunch or coffee and some 'gold-plated' gossip, or the young soldier parting from the woman he purports to love, yet longing to join the 'brotherhood' at war.

The meat stalls. We prefer not to think of chickens or beef cattle in their feathers or hair, clucking or mooing. Here in Sudan the reality of the thigh and the steak was full frontal: intestines, hearts, lungs, and kidneys draped from meat hooks. Nailed to the boarded front of stalls were whole cows' heads. Hair, glazed eyes, lolling tongues and all. I bought some nuts – an unconscious reaction I suppose to such an ethical confrontation. Occupying a conspicuous space at another stall was a DVD entitled 'Genocide'. Our level of tolerance was now exhausted. We were at least a couple of hundred years adrift here in terms of humanitarian concerns, however insincere they might be, however 'sanitised' to salve the public conscience. As they say, 'the truth hurts.' Earlier that morning Matthew had walked with us to a bank through which we had arranged a money transfer from the UK. Before we set sail, Ken's best mate had agreed to manage our account. He would also augment our 'shipwreck-fund' with money we had earned in Grand Cayman. It was an act of friendship that befitted his role as Ken's best man at our wedding.

A flatbed truck drew up in front of the bank as we approached. The driver and passenger got out the vehicle and made for the entrance of the bank, leaving their load of neatly packaged bundles of banknotes unattended! Where else in the world would that happen! Passers-by could clearly see a fortune parked at the roadside, yet after a quick glance, they walked on, unperturbed. Perhaps the punishment for theft is so severe that no amount of money could compensate for a lifetime of disability or even death. Islamic prohibitions are no less stringent than those of Victorian England when pickpockets were hanged or sent to Australia as slaves. A sobering encounter.

When Matthew said he knew of someone who would do our washing, I was overjoyed! Sailors can be rather grubby about housekeeping, especially as it involves using water. 'No undergarments,' he added. 'No,' I said. No, I thought, too! A woman doesn't want her 'undies' scrutinised. Somehow I couldn't imagine an Arab lady wearing panties decorated with flowers or lace edging. Bedding, pillow cases, trousers, T shirts, and even the small curtains covering the portholes were crammed into bin bags. All were returned next morning, clean, ironed, and folded. We happily paid him more than he asked for and gifted him a brand-new shirt, still in its wrapping and a music tape (a popular and welcome gift to have on board).

We wouldn't see Matthew again but will never forget him. Indeed, such encounters often come to mind these decades later, vividly connecting with what remains of our memories of the places where we met. It might only have been an eye-to-eye acknowledgement, a single kindly gesture, an inexplicable mutual liking, such as leads to friendship or would have done had we stayed.

It was only after we left Sudan and viewed the desert again that we realised what a profound affect such amicable experiences can have for a traveller. Our first impressions of the ocean had changed. Now it was the desert. Neither was the barren, featureless, colourless, forbidding image of our first impressions. Both have a subtle beauty that is sculpted by the wind and painted in a constantly changing palette of water colours.

CHAPTER 36

ADVENTURES AND MISADVENTURES IN THE LAND OF TUTANKHAMEN

With forty knots of wind swirling in from every angle and capricious waves slapping at our hull, we battled on towards Suez. Examples of the purist form of sailing were a rare sight. Only occasionally would a yacht break ranks, short tacking back and forth across the width of the waterway, perhaps to break the tedium of heading the wind. Most, like us, are doggedly motor-sailing, logging the miles as hopefully as marathon runners.

As novices still, the aptly named Foul Bay, Fury Shoal, and Gates of Hell were probably the greatest challenges we had faced, and despite having crossed three big oceans, the journey up the Red Sea proved relentless and debilitating.

Although we never doubted the robustness of *Imago* or our own physical stamina, there were moments when we felt that our minds were also on trial as we shouted at the wind.

Egypt. Gateway to Europe and the final legs of our voyage.

It was strange to think of Sudan and Egypt as part of the African Continent when the culture is so Arabic. Here, too, men predominate while women hide away, swathed in elaborate layers of cloth and colourful headscarves under which their luxuriant dark hair is confined. Hair that with occasional daring declares itself by the telling bulge of a wave or coil. And here too are the 'underclasses' wrapped in bundles of filthy rags and usually barefoot. The tea boys, the shoeshine lads, and the vendors with their small trays of laces, soaps, and five-a time cigarettes. After paying the dues to transit the canal and pre-booking the obligatory pilot for the two day passage a few days hence, we located a yachting crew that would keep an eye on Dudley while we joined other tourists to visit the Pyramids at Giza and the museum in Cairo.

Tombs. Usually they evoke a sense of reverence, remembrance. The dead lie still and inevitably one substitutes their body for yours, in the way that we gaze at a coffin during the funeral for someone we have known and imagine it will one day be ours. While every religion seeks to comfort us with the conditional promise of eternal life, for a Pharaoh the size of the tomb seems, rather literally, to represent a greater claim to salvation than that of mere subjects.

As architectural wonders, however, they deserve our admiration. At first sight they appear as a startling anomalies, standing alone and aloof, surrounded by desert. We wondered if we might sleep there, see their outline pinned against a twilight sky or bathed in gold as the sun rises. Ayers Rock, in Australia, Stonehenge, in

England, the Pyramids, in Egypt, each possessing an 'other-worldly' aura.

We felt the impact because we recognised it. Crossing oceans, gazing up at the night sky, and sailing towards the curvature of our planet were experiences that left us in a permanent state of awe. It is simply a comfortable acceptance of ignorance in which the only certainty we have (quantum physics included), is that the human mind is not yet equipped either to see or understand either our existence or our place in the universe.

So, did we object to seeing the more agile tourists climbing on the pyramids for photographs, eating their packed lunches on a ledge or playing 'tag' around their bases? It didn't really matter—to us or to them. Meanings are personal and sometimes best left private.

Being such an overworked joke and since the proposal was rejected, we doubted if the offer of 500 camels to become a 'wife' was genuine or even reflected the going rate! Still, it feels like a compliment and the lady in question taunted her husband. He responded with an 'eyes-to-heaven' look of patient resignation. 'Don't worry, Ken, not even 1000 camels would be enough, too much spitting and I wouldn't want to wash head wraps that are used to wipe noses.'

Egyptian men are flirtatious by nature, at every opportunity their hands will stray towards bosom or bottom. A fellow yachtswoman and her husband attested to this after an evening spent in their overcrowded cockpit with several local lads. That and the clamour for 'woman pictures' suggested a somewhat 'Freudian' state of sexual repression. 'Make that 2000 camels,' I said.

However, as we would learn to our cost, a joke that appears flippant may yet disguise a dangerous threat. Before visiting the museum, we decided to stroll around the perimeter of a large bustling market. Ken had paused to look at one of the stalls as I walked on.

Behold! An unaccompanied female!

A stallholder quickly left his goods and strode towards me. He held out his hand. Instinctively, expecting a brief handshake, I held out mine. He held on. He was still smiling, but differently. Then he was pulling me towards his stall. From the corners of my eyes I could sense several other venders, all male, moving towards us.

Suddenly, Ken appeared. All six feet two of him. A Viking figure, with a full beard. I think I called to him. In an instant, the men retreated to their stalls, as if a film had rewound. Now it was Ken's hand grasping mine. As soon as we were out of sight, I lifted the hand I knew and kissed it.

I plead guilty. My lack of probity, our ignorance of what was prohibited, failing to even observe, let alone interpret, the social conventions that in every country identify and personalise as distinctly as its flag. While some may only be a matter of custom and preference such as Haggis versus pie and mash, bar room etiquette, and wedding protocol, others are important social controls, especially where sexual mores are concerned. As visitors, it wasn't for us either to judge or make comparisons, but to learn as much as we could to avoid causing offence. Travel itself would be much less rewarding without all the ways in which human groups express themselves. National costume, foods, dwellings, and places of worship. We should have asked, sought guidance.

Nevertheless, it was impossible not to feel moments of disgust, particularly when our own society's hard-won moral victories were breached: child labour, dogs crushed into cages to be sold as food (Thailand), chickens, still alive, hanging from hooks, and geese tied together into huge feathered balls before being carried to market on a motorcycle. And women, millions of them, betrothed by order, mutilated by order, bartered, abused, and discarded as casually as commodities.

In truth, we couldn't find our way in such a strictured society and it just got worse.

Our hair was brittle dry and sun-bleached, and with split ends that looked more like feathers. So, when we happened on a barber's shop, the delicious luxury of a haircut proved just too tempting. I watched as Ken had his beard, eyebrows, nose and ear hairs trimmed. His head hair was cut in a rather traditional style, but at least it looked attended to. Finally, his face was swathed in hot towels and scented with pomade. I couldn't wait! And didn't properly register the momentary hesitation from the young men as I took Ken's place in the chair.

I emerged with a short back and sides and even endured the removal of middle-aged fuzz from under my nose with a twisted cotton thread (excruciating)! No hot scented towels for me!

'You look like a lad,' said Ken.

'And you look too old to be my father,' I retorted.

If there is ever a bright side to humiliation, the timing in this case proved to be extremely fortuitous. Indeed, had I not been mistaken for a 'lad', I could not have finished the strong, sweet coffee Ken ordered at an outdoor café. Still nervous, after the threat of being groped in the market, then shorn to the point where I resembled a young army recruit, I needed at least a strong coffee, better still, a stiff brandy and a hat!

Three grizzled old men and a pre-adolescent boy were the only customers. The café owner was surly, spilling our drinks when he dumped them on the table, and demanding payment there and then. A small black and white television, fixed above the doorway, flickered soundlessly. Grainy, blurred images, but unmistakeably it pictured a naked man about to 'do the deed' with a blonde coquettish paramour! 'Porn.' Hard porn at that...on public view... in front of two boys. Surely there was an on/off switch inside somewhere, in case a woman approached?

We settled for the single coffee (I needed several more by now) and left... to find a hat! Each to their own of course, but this closeted, predatory, proprietorial approach towards women spoke little about partnership and even less about love. Perhaps it needs another Cleopatra?

Yet what a legacy of riches was left to us all from such a glorious past. The museum in Cairo rivals any other in the world for its scale and artistic presentation. Vast marble and stone friezes stretch along the walls. Statues rear up from their plinths like giants, their form and texture smooth and lifelike, muscles and tendons faithfully sculpted. Utensils, amphora, and papyrus. Personal adornments fabricated in bronze or gold, inlaid with lapis lazuli, jade, and polished stones, Tutankhamen's death mask was displayed inside a large

379

rectangular plate glass case in a closely guarded room on the second floor, along with gilded jewellery of the rarest kind. A museum deserving of a much more dedicated tour than the cursory time we had to spare.

Ancient Egyptians, Ancient Greeks, the Roman Empire – and we look around these lands again and wonder what became of them.

***

23rd August 2014

Something was wrong. Ken's expression was vague, his skin pallid and clammy. 'It's probably a UTI infection,' said the paramedics. I stayed at the hospital until early evening. He was to be kept overnight for observation and intravenous antibiotic treatment. Our evening carer used her 'put-to-bed' time to check on him at the hospital.

I was putting together toiletries to take in next morning when the phone rang.

'Your husband is very poorly, Mrs Gogay. We think you should come to the hospital.'

The call went out among our 'sisterhood' of carers. Within minutes, one of them arrived to drive me to the hospital.

They all came. We were ushered into the nurse's changing room at the end of the ward. They all came – and were sitting around a table... crying. They knew. Ken had been eating a sandwich. Suddenly he let out a strange moaning sound as the seizures took hold...and died.

'There were at least ten staff at his bedside,' our carer said. 'They used both CPR and shock treatment to resuscitate him.'

They say people 'rock with grief.' They do.

Even when you know that death is imminent or even inevitable, there is never a 'right time.' A door on the future slams shut. Instead, below your feet, is an abyss – a gaping void.

A female doctor entered the room and saw us crying. Heard me saying, over and over, 'it hurts.'

'I have to ask you, Mrs Gogay, if it becomes necessary, do you want your husband resuscitated again?'

I'd worked in a pathology laboratory for six years, taken blood for analysis on ward rounds, and the implications were familiar; hypoxia, bed-bound, vegetative state, dumb, blind, tube feeding, possibly another tracheostomy. Set against his 'presence,' his eyes, his need of me, nothing other than his being alive could matter at that moment.

Perhaps the 'citizen' in me should have prevailed. The cost, the NHS resources. There was only one answer... 'If he will suffer, no. If it will just be about enhanced care, yes.'

'Can we see him?'

She nodded and left the room.

Unconscious still. The intubation tube still in place. Looking shockingly older but breathing on his own.

Six days later, Ken was discharged. Conscious, aware, and smiling in recognition. Although it soon became clear that he had suffered further neurological damage, the symptoms were mild. He would experience short bouts of confusion during which he would forget the day of the week, put on his bib at 1pm for dinner or offer up a course to steer! Small idiosyncrasies such as children have, as their minds roam between memory and anticipation.

But our daily routine was by now, so deeply ingrained in his mind that he was still able to participate and it proved easy to restore his attention with some small distraction or by responding to his own 'time frame' by joining it: '320 degrees it is, love, now it's time to do our exercises.'

Six months later our carers were making plans to celebrate his 80th Birthday on 21st of June 2016!

CHAPTER 37

THE GREY MUSEUM OF HORROR

Despite the well-buoyed route through the Suez Canal, an on-board pilot is obligatory. But to see a stranger at the wheel felt like a betrayal, a breach of trust in our beloved vessel. Ignoring the flapping 'go away' hand signals of our 'Fagin look-alike', one of us was always at his side.

Every note of *Imago's* engine is the voice of a familiar friend. Only we knew the ways of her, the balance of her. Several times our proxy skipper stopped at various way points to wave at his cronies (presumably these look out positions serve to monitor the cargo ships in transit). His knowledge of English was limited to just a few well-rehearsed words relating to 'Baksheesh.' 'They friends, you give Coca Cola, cigarettes, woman pictures?' Fortunately he also understood 'No!' Whereupon he petulantly revved up the engine, Ken or I would then ease back the throttle lever. It happened often enough to become quite comical – short meaningful conversations with an engine!

'Water,' he demanded. I went below and brought up a glass of water. He scowled. 'Wash hands, wash feet, Mecca.'

I apologised, despite his accusing tone, though wondered how long it would take to learn all the 'do's and 'do not's of this ancient, rigidly proscribed culture. After providing a suitable bowl for his ritual ablutions, I took the wheel. He turned towards Mecca with a look of horror on his face. A woman at the helm! Once again I felt like a suffragette!

We had aged. Was it only weeks ago that a fair wind had blown us into this placid-looking ribbon of water? It felt like months. But is there something about physical and mental trials that changes the way one experiences the world? As we entered the bay that leads into the Mediterranean Sea, we looked at each other with a newfound confidence and a mutual respect...little knowing that a future catastrophe would require no more of us than this journey up the Red Sea had asked of us. Holocaust survivors, soldiers, mountaineers, and lifeboat men, braver by far than we, but they too, knowing that to feel proud is sometimes more about personal satisfaction than a boast.

A cluster of small launches now gathered around *Imago*. One to take off our pilot, the rest insisting that we must take on a replacement to exit the bay. Ken knew it was yet another Baksheesh ploy. I shook my head (consternation). Ken shook his fist (sheepish hunching of shoulders). Up with the mainsail and twin foresails. With a courtesy and a bound, *Imago* surged towards the outer buoy and freedom with a female 'admiral' at the wheel!

Much of the discomfort and confusion we had experienced in these rigidly non-secular countries was caused by a feeling of personal shortcomings. It had been such a joy and privilege to experience different customs and beliefs, that any lurking prejudice, intolerance, or bigotry seemed unimaginable: in the sense that we felt that our travels, especially in the Pacific islands, had purged us of any such nonsense. Europe and England's historical religious wars had earned us individual freedoms and self-determination, and had enabled that most valuable freedom of all...that of free will and the opportunity, whatever one's status, first to dream and then to do, never minding how much or how far.

'Fortress' Israel extends well into the southern end of the Mediterranean Sea. No sooner had we wound our way between coastal and off-shore fishing boats, an Israeli naval cutter called out our boat name on channel 16 and ordered us to heave-to. A gun boat took up station nearby until we had given our particulars, then powered away to continue its surveillance of any approaching craft, large or small. Fighter aircraft burst out from over the horizon, emitting sonic booms as they passed overhead.

Finally we were given clearance to enter the Marina at Ashkelon. The contrast between this fledgling country and those we had so recently left behind was astounding and as welcome as an oasis. Running water, paved roads, greenness, well-stocked shops, open friendly faces, unisex shorts... bare arms! A young country full of young people, many of whom wear military uniform and carry guns. We knew that it was mandatory for both girls

385

and boys to serve as conscripts for at least two years. They appeared happy and willing to do so. Most of their grandparents had been murdered during the Holocaust.

For the world at large, the memory is still raw and vivid, perhaps in part because the horrors were not inflicted out of rage or battle fever, but as a cold, calculated, de-humanising genocide. The message from these young recruits was unequivocal... never, ever again – whatever the cost. A chilling but understandable declaration.

We always talked about what we saw.

'If someone killed you and then laughed,' said Ken. 'I would join you or avenge you.' A 'nuclear' statement if ever there was.

Along with the other yachts who had travelled north up the Red Sea, our first task was to hose off the sand from sails, decks and our hair, before ordering much more than we could eat at the nearest restaurant.

The Holocaust museum at Ashkelon, like so many other similar shrines in Israel, depicts the horror in such a visceral and potent way that anything one might have read or heard becomes bloodless and inadequate. The scale of it all, the inhumanity and the clinical detachment with which it was perpetrated. More horrific still is the fact that it continues: crucifixions during the Cypriot war, hideous machete killings in Africa, whole villages of men, women, and babies in Ruanda. Even slavery still earns its name. All at the behest of a God...so help us.

Whether by design or for symbolic reasons, stone steps led down into a grey cellar-like room of granite and slate-coloured stone. Stark shadows flickered about the walls like moving ghosts as daylight filtered through a grill set high in one corner of the ceiling. The effect was as dim as a nightlight in a child's bedroom. Long steel tubes pierced the walls, simulating the barrels of cannon. Photographs that had so shocked the world when the death camps were liberated, lined the walls. Faces of the allied soldiers mirroring the agony of the inmates. Living skulls, women's faces hardly distinguishable from the faces of the men.

You have to linger—to rush would be obscene.

Upstairs the light was bright, the mood defiant. Whatever the political rights or wrongs regarding the creation of a Jewish State, the solidarity and energy of its citizens invites respect and admiration. A million trees were planted. Irrigation channels turned the desert green. Everyone had a house to live in. Academics hoed the fields. For a people who had roamed Europe for some two thousand years, who never forgot the great biblical exodus, their suffering and alienation had ended, even though the cost was greater than any man should bear.

In another section of the museum, heroes of the Six Day War, when the combined Arab states attempted, yet again, to annihilate the Jewish people, were cited for extraordinary acts of bravery and self-sacrifice. Some of the accounts were scarcely believable.

Our friend Marian, indomitable single traveller and my colleague when we worked in the Cayman Islands, claimed her usual berth aboard *Imago* and hired a car to take us on the tourist trail: The Dead Sea, Jerusalem, and the Wailing Wall. At Bethlehem, Christians from all over the world gather in small excited groups to walk the 'Stations of the Cross.' For many it is the fulfilment of a lifetime ambition, similar to the Islamic Hajj to Mecca.

Clutching or wearing a cross, they trace Jesus's journey to Golgotha, stopping to buy souvenirs from strategically placed shops: a postcard, a crucifix, candles, rosaries, and even a splinter of wood from the 'original' cross.

Personally we thought that Jesus Himself might not have approved of either being a 'pop star' or a commodity.

Our friend is no longer with us. I never did tell her that the 'blessing' she received at the place of Christ's birth in Bethlehem was a sexual assault!

Unusually, we were the only tourists present at the time. The manger itself was rather uninspiring, a shallow depression in the floor, circled by stone blocks. A font containing 'Holy Water' stood close by. The curator, if that is who he was, emerged from an alcove. Scruffy robe, scruffy beard, only a little 'left' of elderly.

'Give you blessing lady,' he said to Marian. Dipping his fingers into the font, he 'christened' her forehead. 'Belly too'. He lifted Marian's T shirt and stroked more water over her mid-riff! The little devil then looked to me. I would have loved a picture of the look I gave him because it worked so well! He scuttled back to his hideaway. And just in case Marian had really been picked out for a 'special' blessing, I never told her.

Marian's son had volunteered at a Kibbutz during his idealistic twenties. Since he had spoken so enthusiastically during that period about the ideals of community enterprise and self- sufficiency, she was keen to visit and relay to him her impressions. Her son would later become a mountaineer – perhaps still searching.

The fledgling community was now a farming settlement with a sophisticated infrastructure of roads, houses, and shops. Although everyone we saw was busily engaged in one task or another, Marian, a brilliant 'people person', was soon talking about her son's experiences with a man who owned a farm on the high slopes above the settlement. He was on his way back there after shopping for fuel and supplies and seeing that we had a car, he invited us to visit his family.

The farm's main crop was tomato seed, most of which was exported. Acre upon acre of succulent fruits ready to be pulped in presses to release the seeds which were then dried on long racks – so precious were they that none could be handled for fear of fungal or bacterial contamination. The smell of the plants and the juice of squashed tomatoes perfumed the air like some exotic and expensive cologne.

Our host picked out a rifle from the back of a small truck. 'I'll show you the view,' he said. From the crest of a small hill we could see the West Bank in the distance and were struck immediately by the absence of trees or arable land. Our host expressed his feelings in a way that left no room at all for any discussion about Israel's incursions into Palestinian territory.

'They fire mortars at us. They are corrupt and lazy and jealous.'

The enmity between these peoples is as intractable as that between Republicans and Unionists in Ireland. Along with slavery, neither the famine nor the Holocaust will ever be forgiven or forgotten.

Here too, the heat was intense, adding weight to the wind and bellows to the furnace. The surfaces of rocks and pebbles shimmered in their own heat haze. Turning over rocks on isolated beaches always revealed tiny treasures: immature crabs and lobsters, anemones, a panic of darting little fish. Here in this crucible of heat we only found the occasional scorpion waiting on the cooler night time air. Among the profusion of rocks and fist-sized pebbles lay shards of pottery from some ancient dwelling or village. Several archaeological digs are being worked that suggest a post-nomadic era of villages and townships.

It was when we were picking up the fist-sized pebbles and wondering about their composition that we realised that these instruments of death lie so readily to hand that the practice of using them to stone someone to death was less a religious edict than a readily available, cost effective, means of execution. David was probably well practised with his sling shot when he slew Goliath.

Before making our sailing preparations to travel NE to Cyprus and Turkey, we wrote a newsletter to post to family and friends and collected the new mainsail which we had ordered on arrival in Israel. Oh, the whiteness of it, the crispiness of it! Set among the grey, saggy, second-hand sails we had started out with our rig now looked like half a job, like a house only half painted. Although it gave us an extra knot of speed, we didn't like it! So resistant to reefing and it never looked tidy when layered in its folds onto the boom. 'A bow tie pinned to a scruffy jumper' is what we called it.

A second batch of mail was waiting for us when we posted our own. Joined up writing on the envelopes, handwritten letters inside! While we had been travelling the world, the electronic age had arrived. Our fellow sailors were texting, twittering, tweeting, Facebooking, and queueing for e-mail cafés and ATMs. One of our letters was from our dear friend Bill who was delighted to have received a letter from us that had been 'posted' without a stamp at 'Post Office Bay' in Galapagos! It is a wonderful tradition. Visiting yachts leave a letter in a box on shore and wait for another yachtsman to retrieve the contents and carry it with them to send on. The cost of a stamp acts as payment for their own deliveries. Sooner or later the letters would arrive! A reliable and charming salute for those who sail the oceans. We chose Bill because he would take it to his mates at the pub. And tell them the story.

CHAPTER 38

'THE GOOD, THE BAD AND THE UGLY'

After booking in at Limassol in Cyprus, we sailed out to a small island lying some two miles distant where we might rest and adjust to a world which had gathered pace in our absence. The carefree, largely apolitical months of wandering among the tiny islands of the Pacific had slowed our minds to match the rhythms of nature. So we snorkelled, strolled along the deserted beach, turned over rocks, and gazed up at an unpolluted night sky once more – perhaps for the last time. We were nearing the end of our journey.

As if to confirm how imminent that was, a robin and a grey wagtail landed on the pontoon as we tied up in a marina near Marmaris in Turkey. They looked like rare exotic birds!

Turkey is a huge country with a long and fascinating history, stunning scenery, castles, strange geological formations, monuments, and ancient settlements. A destination where we would have enjoyed back-pack travel had we been younger. Tourism has now engulfed the coastal towns: speed boats and jet skis, Germans,

Scandinavians, Dutch, Italians, and more recently British. The Turkish Carpet seller was invariably an amiable, hospitable, garrulous, and insistent salesman. A connoisseur of the art of weaving would probably recognise the region in which they were crafted, but the difference between those costing a hundred pounds and those costing thousands was obvious even to the untrained eye. 'You look, you look.' A cup of tea or salted yoghourt thrust into your hand. Yet a rolled-up carpet is hardly something that can be packed into a suitcase or even accommodated on an average sized cruising boat. Perhaps they make arrangements to ship them out. We bought a rug. *Imago* has been craned out onto the hard for that most tedious aspect of boat maintenance, cleaning her bottom of weed and barnacles. Still, it was a working yard. The once familiar sounds of wood shaping and steelwork, of shot-blasting and welding reminded us of *Imago's* beginnings, from the day, twenty-two years before, when Ken laid down her keel. The hull of a Gulet, once a trading vessel, now a tourist boat, was taking shape nearby using ancient skills and craftsmanship.

The yard master was a woman! Young, competent and knowledgeable. Not only was her English impeccable, she also wore slacks and her hair was visible and fashionably coiled. She patrolled the yard every day to supervise the workforce and oversee the quality of work. She took a liking to Ken and I, often inviting us to have tea with her at the end of the working day. As a woman from a so-called developed country, I was deeply impressed by the fact that although British women were still struggling to acquire equal status, she had not made the mistake of parodying the masculine notion of how a 'boss' should behave. Rather than ordering people about or expecting subservient responses from her workers she was a facilitator: encouraging, fair and knowledgeable. The men listened and worked well, both to please her and to earn her approval.

If only she could have maintained her poise and self-confidence with the man she had fallen in love with. But she couldn't. Our hearts ached for her, but the traditional role of potential wife was a leap too far. He was surly, controlling, and undemonstrative towards her. Perhaps her attachment to us was due in part to our easy camaraderie and mutual respect, or the way I pretended to be wearing the epaulettes! When he asked if we would escort them both on a shake-down cruise in his newly acquired sailboat, he spoke only to Ken. Sensing the chauvinistic exclusion Ken referred him to me!

In a fair wind and with summer clouds meandering above like the daubs in a child's painting, our boats completed the fifty nautical mile run from Marmaris to Bodrum in daylight. Following close by their port side, we watched in dismay as a bright engaging young woman was bellowed at and ordered around deck as if she were a cabin boy sailing with Captain Bligh. Standing off until they had tied up to the wharf, we quickly turned about to find an anchorage. I looked back once. He was waving us in. She stood still, a small dejected figure beside him. Perhaps he wanted to thank us, but thoughts about their future together filled us with dismay.

After locating a pontoon berth in a small marina we ourselves began to think about the future. Nieces and nephews, their grandchildren, all grown into adulthood. Our friends entering their own dotage. Would we ever sell *Imago*? Would she cross oceans again? Was there somewhere waiting for us? If so, it will be small, with an open fire, comfortable chairs. A desk for me, a shed for Ken, and a very large table for hobbies and our Scrabble games. We would look out onto a rural landscape and claim a patch of our own to grow all that we needed. Chickens figured too (if you read on we will tell you why!) Recollections of our time in Turkey are blurred by grief, though we do recall how engaging and generous its people were.

Dudley was unwell. Normally he would wake up with a yawn from his favourite place on deck, usually a coil of rope. Then a full length stretch before sashaying along the side deck to the cockpit combing, followed by a hip-swishing 'Fosbury' flop into the cockpit. If we were not sitting at the saloon table, he would tip-toe down the companionway steps, but if he saw us, he would leap from the top step, landing like a sandbag onto the table, then onto my chest to 'suckle' on my neck! He seemed to have a 'marksman's eye' for avoiding mugs of tea and sandwiches! Over the next couple of days, his symptoms worsened. His litter tray was dry. We looked closely at the appropriately named 'poop deck.' Here and there just a few drops of urine but no faeces. The vet we located declared him to be constipated as well as having urine retention. He produced a human-sized catheter tube. Having worked both as a nurse and a path Lab technician, I knew it was preposterous and asked if he had a size more suited to a baby or a young child. After assuring us that he would locate one, he then insisted on a somewhat exorbitant fee up front. He would treat Dudley overnight. We could collect him next day.

We found him in a cage. The bloodied catheter the very same we had objected to. Dudley recognised us with his usual deep-throated rumble but was clearly distressed. 'Look,' said the vet, 'I fix.' He had squeezed a small pellet of faeces from Dudley's rectum. It was only later, as I was carrying Dudley home, that I remembered the stunned look of the receptionist when I bought a bag of 'Science Diet' food (recommended for weight loss) and saw her pull aside a curtain to watch us leave... She knew.

That night I stayed up in the cockpit with Dudley in my arms. Every movement caused him pain.

Next day we found another vet. 'Dehydration,' he declared. After injecting water subcutaneously, he too advised us to leave Dudley in his care overnight. It was the last time we would see him.

Anyone who has experienced the joy and privilege of bonding with an animal companion for all of its life will understand the grief and emptiness of our loss. They will also know that creatures shape our own personalities by being so authentically what they are and their place in the world. They don't strive to be a 'somebody,' their cruelty is not born of malice, and they have no need of explanation for their existence. Be they warthogs, toads, lions, or budgies they are beautiful in a way that we are not. A few years later, 'Tara-the terrier who sailed around the world,' also died. Rosemary and Robert too, were devastated. Tara's big little heart had failed while chasing away an intruding rodent one more time. Our friends had by then settled in South Africa, an environment in which Tara could fully express her nature. Dudley was denied his chance to roll in an English meadow, climb an oak tree, mark out a territory, or even die as he should have done... close by.

'They are not vets as we know them,' said a cruising couple who knew of our sadness. 'They only deal with horses, cattle, and goats, and you don't see many dogs or cats here.' It was true. For many Turks, dogs, along with pigs, are 'unclean.' A few days later the same couple told us of a cat sanctuary run by an 'eccentric' Englishwoman. They offered to take us in their car. However well-meaning, it didn't work for us or offer much comfort. Cats there were, perhaps a hundred of them. All colours, long haired, short haired, utterly fluffy ones, even a couple of Siamese. Well fed, stumps of wood to climb or scratch on, even a communal sand pit. We stroked a few and chatted with the enthusiastic lady who had 'rescued' them. But cats are territorial and walk alone. They spat and growled at each other or sulked in corners. But we did remember one marmalade cat that craved human company. She jumped up on my shoulder buried her face into my hair and stayed there while we wandered about. I had to prise her from me when we left. Our unopened bag of 'Science Diet' was gladly received, but we were still far removed from solace.

The town of Marmaris was a young person's holiday destination. Music blared out from every bar and café. Rowdy, barely clothed teenagers paraded, sauntered, and staggered between food kiosks and coffee shops. Young

Turkish lads would intercept them, carefully shaking the hands of their male counterparts so that they could ogle and flirt with the girls without risking confrontation. Deemed (we supposed) to be of trustworthy age, they would ask us to read out letters from 'girlfriends' they had met on holiday. 'Love of my life. Wait for me. Stay true and faithful until I see you again.'

'The boys leave the farms during the tourist season,' said one café owner. 'They all want a foreign girl. It makes their parents very angry but they still come.' He winked at us then said, 'We all forget don't we?' All three of us rolled our eyes to heaven!

Earthquake! A sound like a tipper lorry emptying a load of gravel, *Imago* rocking and snatching at her mooring lines. It was close to midnight and we were soundly asleep. A landslide? A tsunami? An explosion? We rushed out onto the wooden pontoon (scantily clad, as you are in a sultry climate) and promptly fell sprawling onto the decking which was undulating like a shaken carpet. Just as suddenly, all was stilled. We grabbed a couple of sheets and spent the rest of the night in the cockpit.

Next day we learned that the townspeople had camped out in the streets, which is what they always did in case their houses collapse. 'Just a small one,' they told us. Fortunately only one person was injured. In a state of panic he had jumped out of a second floor window. At 4.8 on the Richter scale, local people considered it to be a small quake! The most destructive have magnitudes between 5.5-8.6, each factor of one representing an approximate thirtyfold increment! Cataclysmic events such as those extinguish all human and animal life.

Claims them all, makes them puny. All of them. Earth holds sway: hurricanes, flood, volcanic eruptions, drought, and fire. And in such circumstances we have no more existential value than a woodlouse.

Once more we found ourselves negotiating an archipelago of islands on our way to Poros in Greece. The choice of route from the Aegean Sea into the Ionian is either to transit the Corinthian Canal or run South and round the mountainous southern peninsular. A Sirocco wind from the NW and the Meltemi wind from North Africa would blight either choice as did the now familiar bagatelle of currents between the islands. The Mediterranean Sea can be as capricious as any other, even during the summer months. The calm electric blue of holiday brochures is not the experience of most sailors. The excitement and enchantment of the Panama Canal and the recent ordeal of the Red Sea cancelled each other out. Although we stayed in Greece for several more weeks, we knew that we would eventually choose the southern 'less travelled' route.

Every one of our worldwide destinations and the many weeks we spent at sea generated a worthwhile yarn or two, but our time in Greece added greatly to our repertoire. Perhaps some of them didn't really qualify as yarns at all since they were not implausible, embellished or humorous, and certainly not suitable to after-dinner talk. We are mentioning them here for the first time only because of their impact.

Firstly, the puppies. We are in a marina. People would wander onto the tarmacked area that skirted a roadside by the moorings. We were sitting in the cockpit having a Mediterranean lunch of bread, tomatoes, cheese, and olives. A disturbance in the water. One splash. Two splashes. A small group of children had thrown two tiny puppies into the water! Grabbing the landing net, we rescued one of them. The other disappeared under the prow of a boat. The children gathered round us as we offered to return their sodden puppy. They stepped back.

'You buy,' they shouted. They had deliberately thrown the puppies into the water to elicit our sympathy! They cursed us as we turned away.

'Romany kids,' we were told. 'They do it all the time, especially if they think you are English. Being dog-lovers is part of your international reputation.'

A few days later a truck full of chickens stopped at a roadside café in the same area. Not just filled with chickens but stuffed full of them. Their heads stuck out from every blood-stained hole in the wire mesh that covered the sides of the truck. Destined for market, behaving as if they knew it. We could hardly complain... we eat chicken. But a whole lorry load of densely packed clucking and squeaking desperation was a chilling sight. The vehicle eventually moved away, leaving behind a couple of beer cans, cigarette stubs, and the detritus from two burger buns. A lone chicken flapped away from a rear wheel, barely a feather breadth from leaving a stain on the tarmac. With that comical mincing step of fledglings, it fluttered under the guard rail of *Imago* and onto the side deck, whereupon it hunched down, looking bewildered.

Our little pullet stayed on board for three days, pecking at mashed up sweetcorn, drinking from a mug of water, repairing her maternal deprivation by hoisting herself onto our laps, 'talking' into our ears and nibbling on them as she perched on our shoulders. Having so recently lost Dudley, she appeared like a gift and we loved her. She knew about seawater. Now and again she would peer down through the scuppers then back away. Bad things can happen when you 'nip out' for a loaf of bread! We returned to find her missing. If you love something, you genuinely don't care what others may think. We 'clucked and twittered' as we searched the pontoons, knowing that if she heard us she would find us.

Someone had taken her to roast or boil. Our future plans would now include caring for a few chickens for the whole of their allotted lifetime. So tiny, barely enough meat on her to make a sandwich. She lived on our boat. She was therefore stolen. A mean-spirited crime.

Greece, like Tenerife, had embarked on an orgy of building tourist facilities: empty, inaccessible marinas, tavernas, holiday homes, yachts for hire, and car rental. Something for everyone, all tastes catered to. Except that some 'tastes' are (as far as we know) aberrations not found in other mammals. Incest and prostitution however are worldwide human behaviours, perhaps best understood by reference to the animal world and its elaborate courtship rituals, its extraordinary evolved strategies to reproduce at almost any cost. The life cycle of a salmon attests to this overarching quest. Sex. The seller of goods, the dominant theme in art, literature, and fashion. Humans can never claim the moral high ground in most matters, but the suffering of one little girl in

Greece made us want to assume a totally different identity.

Perhaps she was four years old, though certainly no older than five. Had she not turned around, we would have presumed she was with an adult member of her family, walked on, smiled at her because of the international reputation about the closeness of Greek families. But she turned to face us. Bright red lipstick, blushed cheeks, false eyelashes, a halo of tousled 'Shirley Temple' locks. We sat on a low wall and watched her. As she searched the tourist crowd for unattached males, there was pleading and desperation in her eyes and gestures.

The 'give us a dollar' outstretched arm and open palm of begging was familiar and probably universal, but hers was with bent arm and curled fingers, offering her hand to be held. Then we saw the group of men, some fifty yards away, near where the road turned a corner, watching her every move. Dark glasses, smartly dressed in suits, looking as sinister as they surely were. Had we seen a policeman we would have reported a child that looked lost – which, in the saddest of ways, she probably was.

Still, matters of right or wrong, however starkly presented, can only be assimilated into a personal view of the world in which it is healthier for the mind to balance atrocity by seeking to understand rather than judge and to bring to mind the prevalence of generosity and compassion also encountered. It seems to us the only way to live is with hope and as the saying goes, 'you can only cultivate your own garden.'

The mountainous southern peninsular of Greece offered up some of the most spectacular and inspiring scenery of our travels. Sparsely populated, sheer cliffs jutted from the depths, guarding its isolation like the walls of an ancient fortress, the waves an attacking horde at the gates. The noise of their ceaseless bombardment echoed from every tiny inlet. The ripple effect of each boom and crash rocked *Imago* from scupper to scupper. A summer storm would make it a hazardous, even foolhardy passage. Remnants of shipwreck and the shattered bulk of a trawler could be seen embedded high up on the rocks. Each time we rounded one of the three headlands at this southern end of the Peloponnese, the wind met us head on, giving us a thorough wetting and a strenuous time adjusting the sails. But it was exhilarating sailing—we dared to think that fourteen years of experience might just have earned us the claim to be able seamen! A few weeks later we were to validate that claim with a journey in the most violent conditions of our time at sea!

The marina at Preveza on the eastern Ionian coast of Greece sits at the entrance of a large lagoon and was far enough from town to preserve us both from the hubbub of tourist night life and the dreaded 'Mediterranean tie-up' to town wharfs. Trying to moor *Imago* astern was like urging an unbroken colt to walk backwards. Our efforts were clumsy and inept. 'Bloody charterers' muttered one skipper who had watched us, hand on hip. Although it serves to pack in more yachts to the yard, it means losing every vestige of privacy. Our port and starboard neighbours and watchers on the wharf could see what we were having for dinner and seemed fascinated that we washed our smalls in a bucket!

The smooth waters of the lagoon offered a placid sailing experience for friends from England who could now afford to visit us. Though not yet urgent, the feeling that were heading home, suddenly became real as we hugged friends we had not seen for nearly fourteen years. Early spring. The air cool enough for us to walk along the edges of the lagoon, among the shrubs and early flowers. We came across an area where nets were spread across a large area of the shrub-land. The desiccated remains of a once brightly coloured finch hung like a rag from its folds. Further in, we identified a warbler by its slender beak, its feet stuck fast on a branch that had been painted with glue. Hapless beetles and ants lay embedded, heaped up near the corpse like a cairn.

Across the Mediterranean some 25,000,000 finches, warblers, pipits and wagtails are trapped in such ways to become a traditional delicacy called Ambelopoulia, though whether as pie or pâté we prefer not to know. That we should have 'dominion' over all the fishes, fowls and animals on the Earth was surely a biblical error in translation. We added Ambelopoulia to our personal list of culinary distaste which includes pâté de foie gras, shark fin soup, monkey, and caviar.

Having been denied 'cockpit talk' since leaving Turkey we were delighted to meet up with two other sailing couples, each of whom would become life-long friends. Linda and Peter lived on their self-built catamaran poetically named *Ghost of the Rockies*. Evenings in their cockpit soon developed into morning coffee, daytime excursions into town and 'Al fresco' lunches at various tavernas. 'Men only' and 'girl only' gossip serves as a most welcome respite for couples who live on cruising boats. As Linda put it, 'there is more to life than engine parts and distance run.' Like us, they had built their own boat and it was a sturdy comfortable vessel, but it was their incompatibility that made them so endearing. He, taciturn and politically ultra-conservative. She, of Irish descent but now a Canadian, a staunch republican and an ardent socialist. It was a triumph of a marriage! Peter was even conservative about sailing. He would call all the tackle on his boat by its proper name and call out 'Jybe' in eight knots of wind. She wanted to sail the Southern Ocean! They were wonderful company. Having owned a taverna for several years, they had a more rounded knowledge of Greek culture than that which we had experienced and of course there was (and always is) more to it than tourist manipulation, dead finches, and drowning puppies.

They introduced us to their favourite anchorages: Parga, Lefkada, and Cephalonia where we swam, watched the goat herds winding between gum trees and olive groves, and swapped stories beneath the dim glow of the anchor light, late into the night. Occasionally a bird twittered. Occasionally its call was answered.

Also living aboard their self-built boat with the patrician name *King Harold* was an Australian couple, John and Lynette Carter. John was born a mariner. The boat he built when he was seven years old sank at its launching, but he continued building them and sailing them until he had made a reliable ocean going craft. Lynette would sometimes crew for him, but by her own admission she was not an enthusiastic sailor so more often chose to fly out to meet him whenever he made it safely into some exotic port. Still, they had braved the Red Sea together, a remarkable example of wifely devotion. They called chickens 'chooks.' Animals were 'critters.' The British were 'pommes.' Lynette was the wittiest woman we had ever met. Her self-effacing humour was an amalgam of Joan Rivers, Pam Ayres, and Victoria Wood, all at once and from every angle. She was a stand up comedienne with a heart of gold.

9.11.2001. That day. That very day, when the hearts of some turned to stone and extinguished more than 3,000 lives in the name of a god. A day which changed the world as dramatically as had the assassination of President Kennedy, Hiroshima, and the two world wars.

Few of us had television, but the husband of another couple whose company we also enjoyed called us over to their boat to watch the drama unfold. The first of the Trade Centre towers had been breached by an aircraft. People could be seen hanging from windows or falling to their deaths amid fluttering clouds of paper. Flames and smoke billowed out from the upper storeys. It looked like the end of the world. When another plane smashed into the second tower, we thought the whole city was about to be erased. Microphones were picking up the screams of watching pedestrians and the headlong rush to escape.

Too close. Too real. What else? What next? It was beyond tears, beyond anger, and beyond comprehension. We watched in silence. A paralysing feeling of horror and disbelief and a deep sense of foreboding overwhelmed us all.

For several evenings thereafter, 'cockpit talk' centred on issues of religious dogma. The conversations were sober and undemonstrative, a fact worth remarking on since, along with politics it is generally a taboo subject which can lead to pedantic monologues and even unsightly quarrels. It just seemed so preposterous that any religion could condone the monstrous atrocities perpetrated throughout history on those who choose to differ.

Simply to be alive at all is such an unexpected gift and we die only to 'pass on the blissful baton' so to speak. To fear either speaks of dissatisfaction. Since we are not equipped to fully understand the workings of the universe, how is it possible to construct a heaven or hell, let alone a belief worth dying or killing for? Thoughts like these occupied our minds for many days until Ken said, 'I wonder if some of my atoms will become part of a frog's nostril in my next re-incarnation.'

'Sounds useful,' I replied. 'I favour becoming a wind-borne particle.' Simplistic as that sounds, it was just a way of expressing that everything we see and feel is an authentic and valuable part of existence.

As if to validate this 'no need to know' acceptance of all that is and all that happens, an abandoned kitten came into our lives to fill the empty space that had lingered aboard *Imago* since Dudley's death. I had taken a walk around the dock area. There was no particular reason for me to do so ... or was there?

No bigger than a cigarette packet, its four paws caked with thick tar, no sign of mother cat or siblings. We dissolved the tar with diesel, washed her tiny feet with soap and water, fed her warm milk using an icing bag and nozzle (back of the kitchen drawer and no idea why I brought it aboard!) We called her 'Pudley' and watched her grow into a fluffy, silver tabby.

CHAPTER 39

REFLECTIONS

We shall not live long enough to witness human colonisation of another planet in our solar system though we are certain it will happen, simply because it must. No doubt it will be viewed as a triumph. But as the politicians and generals leave behind 'battlefield earth' will they carry with them the malignant seeds of the urge to vanquish and subdue?

When Ken was felled, our dreams of self-sufficiency were dashed. Nevertheless we would strive to make our dependency fit with our childlike sense of awe and wonder. It was shocking to witness such a different world from the one we had left behind only fourteen years earlier.

What topsy-turvy, fretful, bustling, delusional, chaotic, indifferent ways there were to living a life in today's so-called modern world! And what beautiful, illustrating, hopeful elements jostle and nudge, albeit feebly, against our self-destructive natures. What exactly does it mean when wealth and celebrity confers such an insubstantial claim to status and prestige? Why had women become obsessed with augmenting their natural allure with disfiguring cosmetic surgery, pseudo-scientific age defying lotions and wonder drugs? Haven't we all seen a supposedly 'plain' man or woman become beautiful because of their bright and shiny personalities? And what is 'empowering' about a young woman with a tassel and two sequins taunting a young male and expecting him rather than her to control urges imprinted by nature?

In a remarkable book by Peter Prew, *The Human Reality*, human history is presented as a catalogue of atrocity and barbarity against all other living fauna and flora, including each other. We are in conflict with the natural world and our individual place in it has been subsumed. We are not free.

'According to the testimony of Hugh Brody, Colin Turnbull and other anthropologists, modern hunter – gatherers have regarded their wild environment as meaningful, friendly and sacred.'

Exactly what we had experienced by sailing the oceans in a small boat. Gazing up at the night sky, following the silver carpet laid out before us by a full moon, sensing the non-secular emotional truths that both diminished our self-hood and intensified our unique relationship with the world.

We are both genuinely elderly now. The clock is running faster. Our flat is part of a sheltered housing complex in which we are safe, warm, and comfortable. Our windows look out onto pine trees and gardens where squirrels play tag among the branches and birds pretend that they cannot be seen. A path leads to one of the loveliest of small parks. We 'know' every tree and touch a centuries old oak every time we pass it. As soon as the sun feels warm enough, I get out our mobility scooters once a week to watch the birds on the lake build their nests, hatch their chicks, until fluff becomes feathers and autumn brings the curtain down for another year.

Ken's carers are a 'sisterhood' of many years. They too have seen Ken breathe again, talk again, eat again, and walk again, and have helped me nurse him through every setback. They each possess the qualities that are truly feminine: caring, patient, and competent. We share a mutual respect, never miss an opportunity for affectionate banter, and Ken loves us all.

Such a brave, energetic, and determined man might well have found intimate care and dependency frustrating and irritating (as many do) but he is content, happy, and willing. A calm, matter-of-fact, engaging approach has enabled him to feel valued and as much a participant in our life together as when he was skipper of his vessel.

Our fascination for the exquisite ways in which animals and plants have found their niche in the world without despoiling or exploiting it remains a constant source of optimism and pleasure. Each passing spring is the way we count the years of our lives and the time when we buy caterpillars from a conservation group, watch them gorge and fatten, suspend themselves with glue, pupate and finally wriggle themselves free to emerge as an imago. And as if offering up a gift of gratitude, they then pollinate those flowers which provide them with nectar. Earthworms till the soil, trees produce an over-abundance of fruit to feed the many. The list is far longer than our memories, but all of nature is beautiful and useful.

We kept a vivarium for stick insects (sloth-slow eating machines) which eventually died of their own accord but were not replaced. Fascinating though they were, charismatic they are not! But frog spawn?! Now that is a breathtakingly awesome source of wonder…little commas dashing about the tank, growing legs and lungs as they develop into thumbnail-sized replicas of their kind. Ken knows that when I spread cling film over his bedside table it is to enjoy once more that shared awe about the world we have felt, both in faraway places and those close to home. It might be a huge orange bellied slug, a Jay's feather, a toad, or the desiccated carapace of a stag beetle.

Alas, we cannot home a chicken – a matter of abiding regret!

Despite the overwhelming evidence that mankind is rapidly approaching self-inflicted annihilation through military ambition, secular dogma, greed and corruption, we harbour a naïve hope. As Martin Luther said, we 'have a dream'.

Every man will have a home, even if it is made of palm leaves or bales of straw. All will have enough to eat. Women will be honoured for their role and allowed to control their own fertility. The provocative nonsense of 'nuclear deterrence' will be recognised as such. If only one country in the world would construct a non-competitive, corruption free formula that served need over want, the people would be free to express their potential as guardians rather than exploiters of this remarkable and beautiful planet.

Meanwhile, fear, slavery, child abuse, cruelty to animals, and a savage and relentless destruction of our habitat are very much alive and well. Technologically and physically we may be masters but in matters of spirituality and self-congratulation, we are a disgrace!

CHAPTER 40

A PERILOUS UNDERTAKING:
A WHALE WITH HER CALF
WELCOMES US HOME

Knowing the 'ways' of your vessel is a metaphor for friendship. You gladly accept both their foibles and their strengths, as they do yours. Shared interests often provide the starting point for human friendship, but it is the nuances that make it timeless and mutually rewarding. And as for people, so it is with boats.

Imago's stubbornness in coming about onto a new tack, her rolling gait in heavy seas were minor irritants when set against her ability to hold a course and ride between waves with the distain of a matriarch. Trusting her with our lives had made us confident, even adequate sailors. How much so would soon be made clear!

The man who was introduced to us was clearly distraught. He had engaged three young men to deliver his yacht to a marina near Trieste in Slovenia at the northern end of the Adriatic Sea. The lads had returned after only three days, having encountered bad weather and engine problems. He would lose his berth in the marina if a deadline wasn't met. The yacht was well appointed and Ken could find no fault with the engine.

'You have sailed around the world, please help me,' he implored us.

Helping fellow sailors is a maritime tradition. We could have offered him several lame excuses, but it did seem a good opportunity to test our skills on a production built boat with state of the art instrumentation. Ken was enthusiastic. I think I was rather concerned about the responsibility, but after he had checked all the boat's equipment we agreed to make the delivery.

Ahead would lie the most challenging conditions we had encountered in all of the 39,000 nautical miles we had logged!

We left in fairly lively conditions in which the light displacement yacht bounced and skipped over the short seas. The unfamiliar movement brought us close to sea-sickness for the very first time. It also introduced us to fast sailing. She too was a ketch and with all sails hoisted, she held six to seven knots with ease, heeling over on to her scuppers like a racing yacht. Crossing oceans at such an angle seemed preposterous, especially for the cook aboard. We would spend the next seven days living on unbuttered bread and hard-boiled eggs!

We paused at an anchorage in Italy near Brindisi to take on fuel and plot the rest of the journey. Yachts were piling into the anchorage with triple reefs in their mainsail, some bare-poled, others with roller reefing showing barely a quarter of the foresail. While we were re-fuelling a weather warning blared out from a VHF radio. A deep front was sweeping up the Adriatic with winds Force seven to eight. With a schedule of only five days for the last 400 mile run north, there were only a few hours in which to decide whether to abort or run with the wind. Had the wind been from the north, we would not have ventured out. Beating into a Force 8 headwind would be punishing and ultimately futile.

After charting several headlands and anchorages at which to take shelter, we weighed anchor in late afternoon, making course NE to avoid any coastal dangers. The wind had moderated into a steady Force 6. The seas were lively but with a single reef in the main and half of the genoa showing we made steady progress during the night, making good ninety miles on our course. So attuned were we to the sound and weight of the wind we had no need to monitor the anemometer.

By dusk on the second day, conditions began to deteriorate. Huge waves chased at our stern, swinging the boat from side to side as they passed under the keel. Some would catch us before we had slid into the trough, smashing into the stern with a booming crash that threatened to bury the bowsprit in fathoms of water. If it fractured, exposing such a large sail would place us in serious jeopardy. The boat would twist, as if trying to free itself from the grip of the water, leaving it at the mercy of a side-swiping wave that heeled her so far over that the dreaded ogre-green raced past the portholes. As the wind began to groan, a wave caught us on the beam, cascading into the cockpit and throwing us both to the floor. Ken scrambled below to find lifelines to shackle us to the pedestal.

Pitch black. So much spume in the air that any ship's lights would be invisible. Trapped at the wheel. Cold. Wet through. The wind now whistling and screaming.

And our whole world was condensed into a small circle of suspension – nothing outside of this cauldron of roiling water, darkness, and demonic screeching existed. Force 9 now, gusting storm Force 10. We are blind. We listen to the roar of the next wave rearing up behind, trying to tune into a change of note just before impact.

Were we afraid? I try to think back. I don't think we were. Rather it was a fatalistic acceptance of our predicament and a dogged determination to prevail. We wondered later, what does a soldier feels when he is ordered to engage the enemy? Does he, like us, refuse to contemplate death?

But we were not alone. A ship's siren, blasting out for three long seconds, silencing the wind. A strong beam of light bathed the cockpit. The small freighter lay less than 100 yds. off our starboard beam. A deckhand waved his arms. We waved back, trying not to make it look frantic.

Not alone. It filled us with an overwhelming sense of solidarity and hope. The ship might well have presumed that we were in difficulty and had taken the trouble to check us out. No doubt they must have been surprised to find a small craft out in such conditions.

The freighter itself was barely making headway. Despite her bulk, she was being tossed about like a toy in the hands of a petulant child. There were moments when she disappeared from view as monstrous waves swept over the superstructure from stem to stern. We wondered why her master had not stayed in port or

417

found shelter, though modern ships have highly sophisticated monitoring equipment so perhaps they knew the range of the storm and when it might abate.

Less than 100 miles from safety, daylight, respite. Daylight mattered most of all. A world that includes the sky brings with it a true sense of being alive. Starless, sightless nights feel overwhelmingly disconnected.

Ken went below, hoping to sleep for a couple of hours. I stayed, still shackled to the pedestal. It was more important for him to rest, he is stronger than I, better able to fix the gear and handle the sails.

Two hours before dawn the wind decreased to Force 6. After re-engaging the auto-pilot, I released the life-line and slumped down onto the cockpit floor, massaging the numbness from my legs and watched the waves discard their foaming tops and lengthen their stride.

Ken appeared through the companionway doors shaking his head in disbelief. On a barely undulating sea, the yacht skimmed lightly over the surface of the water, the land loomed ahead, ready to receive us, and the bright orb of the sun oscillated gently through the rigging.

Once the yacht was secured at her berth in the marina, we cleaned up the saloon, tied her sails neatly on the booms, and delivered a considerable amount of food to the boatyard office for distribution. While Ken replenished the engine oil, I gathered a bunch of wild flowers and placed them onto the saloon table. We left the boat looking like a charter vessel at the end of a peaceful day sail!

We called the owner. I spoke first, 'You have a very sound boat. She performed really well in Force 9 conditions.'

The owner was jubilant. 'They said you would get there.'

Ken then began a more technical de-briefing, explaining that he had carried out engine and instrument checks, but the skipper kept interrupting. 'I could kiss you both, this means the world to me.'

Although we were truly happy for him, the experience had shocked us deeply. Crossing oceans was no less hazardous but not imposing deadlines enabled us to ride out squalls and storms by lying a-hull, deploying stern ropes or adjusting our course, sometimes for days. Pushing up the Adriatic in storm force conditions had been foolhardy, regardless of the outcome.

Thoughts about the future now occupied our minds. Like many before us who have satisfied the urge to seek and explore, the urban environment felt contrived and constraining. The cynical power of corporations and an economy based on rampant consumerism was destroying both our humanity and the planet. The 'big wide world' of fiction is a myth. At the end of our journey, we know that it is small, vulnerable, and struggling. It's a 'they' world. They (scientists) will fix climate change, they (servants) will pick up our litter, 'they' are the enemy, and 'they' will save the wildlife, the trees, the reefs, the very oceans. There is no magic stop button and money adds not an inch to human stature or a place in the animal kingdom that could be considered noble. Our guardianship of planet Earth has been shameful.

Nature is self-regulating, always serving needs over wants. Its exquisitely adapted forms have occupied every niche in the landscape for far longer than human history. Not one of them has ceased to exist by their own claw, paw, or proboscis. Only mankind faces extinction by its own hand. Elephants, whales, and rhinoceros will soon be pictures from the past.

If we sound disillusioned it is only because we have witnessed first-hand 'garden earth' and love it so. Water will always be precious to us, we will probably die in the shoes we have worn for fifteen years, a plastic bag will never disgrace our home, charity shops will clothe us, we shall peel our own potatoes, and laugh at the 'new and improved' adverts. Especially those that promise age-defying allure and rejuvenation!

Having decided to travel back to England via the French Canals, we passed through the Messina Straights into the Tyrrhenian Sea before turning NE to pass between Corsica and Sardinia at the Straight of Bonifacio. As we turned East towards Sète in the Golfe du Lion, the wind dropped to zero and the surface of the sea lay flat and calm before us. We were motoring at barely tick-over speed. A large green shape drew along the starboard beam. Thinking at first that it was a submerged obstacle or wreck, we both leaned forward to dis-engage the auto-pilot, ready to alter course. Despite our forward motion, the shape was keeping station. A huge tail fin curved away from the green torpedo, with a leisurely flick, causing it to roll and reveal the sheltering calf. Measuring the whale against the length of *Imago*, we reckoned the mother to be twelve metres long and her calf a little over three metres. Immediately we killed the

420

engine before watching them slowly move ahead. A helicopter appeared overhead. As it circled the pair, a man stood upright in the doorway and gave us a thumbs up signal for switching off our engine.

The sea had offered up one more gift. A rare and sobering gift. We were deeply happy and grateful for it.

CHAPTER 41

HOME IS THE SAILOR

We could not have chosen anywhere better to wind down our travels than in the waterways of France. Mature trees lined both sides of the Canal Du Midi and between their trunks green and fertile land stretched away into the blue haze of late summer. Along the towpaths people walked their dogs, waved, and wished us 'Bon jour.' Long before English law would penalise dog owners who failed to pick up their pet's excrement, the walkers held the lead in one hand, scoop and bag in the other. And unlike British banksides and motorway verges, not even a sweet wrapper sullied the paths.

After arranging for our masts to be lowered into deck cradles at Sète, we negotiated the first lock and entered the wider section of the Canal Du Midi knowing, even then, that we would not raise them again even if we crossed the English Channel once more.

No fees, no restrictions! Indeed it was such a boat-friendly environment that many static boats and converted barges could have post delivered or collected from the nearest lock-keeper!

Six weeks after being neutered, Pudley came of age… and what a little madam she was. Fluttering her eyelashes at a group of beaus who called on her each evening, letting them take her on questionable twilight walks. There was Fluffy, Fat-Face, Ginger, and Tabby Handsome (the one she favoured…saw her kissing him), and a battle-scarred Mike Tyson sort. We felt like failed parents. Treats *Imago* like a hotel. Where did we go wrong? Then again, she was a beauty. Our little tar-footed, barely alive scrap of a kitten was entitled to all that felt good in her life. After dinner she would walk with us along the towpath until, deciding for us, she turned back for home.

We stayed at our bankside mooring, between Carcassonne and Beziers for several months, simply because no alternative seemed to offer more. Although we longed to reconnect with family and friends, finding a mooring in England would be difficult and expensive especially anywhere on the Thames.

The French are a proud polite people who fiercely protect their hard-won civil rights and who only think poorly of foreigners if they don't at least try to learn the basic courtesy words of their language. A yacht flies a stern flag that identifies the country of origin. Those aboard are therefore ambassadors and responsible for the impressions they leave behind them. Using a small basic French/English dictionary, we re-learned our rudimentary school day French. 'The cat sat on the mat' and 'close the door' once chanted in the schoolroom was rather irrelevant for casual social encounters, so we concentrated on please, thank you, how much? And an overload of oui and merci. The small grocery and butcher shops responded warmly to our excruciating accents. This small contribution towards entente cordial and esprit de corps felt like an international tour-de-force!

Kingfishers flashed to and fro along the banksides, mallards and swans promenaded with their broods, swifts and swallows soared above, and birdsong filled the air. Not a moment passed without some enchanting distraction.

To be wholly immersed in the present, the 'here and now' as it is called, is surely too rare to be properly described. Neither memories of the past nor thoughts of the future occupied our thoughts. The rhythm of our days matched that of the environment just as they had during full moon nights at sea.

A fellow boater introduced us to the weekly boot sale at Villeneuve. We rode back on a pair of second-hand bicycles on which to arrive there early in the morning to buy home-made preserves and augment our small wardrobe of tropical attire. I bought a frock!

We also bought a set of boules and much to the amusement of passing walkers who said we were playing it like the English game of bowls, practised on the towpath each evening before dinner. Pudley would sit Sphinx-like on a tree stump watching us. Moulles and French bread became our favourite meal. On the way to Villeneuve, we passed a lagoon that was home to a flock of pink flamingos: busy feeding on the pink shrimp that bred in the briny water and which gave them their beautiful rosy colour.

Christmas Day 2002 we ate a traditional dinner at the cockpit table. The starlings had already completed their spectacular aerial displays, dense as storm clouds above the town and were on their way to warmer climes despite the daytime temperature of 20C. If animals and birds could speak, they could interpret weather forecasts and seismic events far more accurately than we.

On May 4th 2003 Ken collapsed on deck. The third of our journeys had begun. We had built a boat together, sailed around the world for fifteen years together. It was this last journey that would make sense of it all as just another labour of love.